The Control of Resources

To my mother

PARTHA DASGUPTA

The Control of Resources

Basil Blackwell · Oxford

First published 1982
Basil Blackwell Publisher Limited
108 Cowley Road, Oxford OX1 4HB, England

British Library Cataloguing in Publication Data
Dasgupta, Partha
The control of resources.
1. Environmental policy 2. Human ecology
I. Title
333.7 HC79.E5

ISBN 0-631-12935-9
ISBN 0-631-13086-1 Pbk

Typesetting by Unicus Graphics Ltd, Horsham
Printed in Great Britain by The Camelot Press, Southampton

Contents

Preface

This monograph was written originally as a contribution to a project on environmental problems undertaken jointly by the United Nations Environment Programme (UNEP) and the United Nations Conference on Trade and Development (UNCTAD). The overall project was wide-ranging and addressed itself as well to a number of empirical themes. I was invited to contribute a paper on the conceptual issues that arise in the economics of environmental resources. Having recently co-authored a book on the economics of exhaustible resources I thought that such a paper would be reasonably easy to write; until that is, I persuaded myself (or rather, became persuaded by discussions with others) that environmental resources, as usually thought of, are not the sort of stuff on which Harold Hotelling wrote one of his seminal articles (The economics of exhaustible resources, *Journal of Political Economy*, 1931). It seemed to me that a central common characteristic of such resources is their regenerative capacity, and, therefore, that environmental-pollution problems ought to be thought about in much the same way as ought problems associated with the control of land, fisheries, aquifers and forests. What was not a difficult matter was recognizing this. The difficult part, at least for me, was to articulate the view in a way that I found persuasive. The article that I submitted to the project was as a result rather long, and Edward Dommen of UNCTAD, who had invited me to contribute to the project in the first instance, did me the exquisite courtesy of asking me to expand it into a monograph.

A difficulty in writing a book on this subject is that the existing literature is both varied and enormous. And in any case I wanted to pull together two strands of literature (viz. those on pollution, and resources like fisheries and aquifers), each of which for the most part has been going its own way. Much of this literature, however, is cast within an interpretation of welfare economics which is rather confining, and in my view misdirected. I have, therefore, undertaken a lengthy discussion of welfare issues here. It certainly exposes my own prejudices. No harm in that, especially if the reader finds my defence of them persuasive. There are in the main two sorts of books that can be written on the subject. One can write a mathematical work, concentrating on analytical matters, or one can write an applied, case-studies oriented sort of book which compiles a great deal of facts at the same time. Being impressionable, I like a bit of both and I have tried to write the monograph in a way which reflects this. (In fact there is a third kind of book, which concentrates on the grander issues without going much in either of the two directions, but I am not that impressionable.)

Some of the technical results reported in this work will be known to experts. But like other disciplines it is their interpretation which matters, and as noted above, the ones offered here differ considerably from those that are to be found usually. I take it that one of the tasks that an author should undertake in writing on a subject which has only recently been developed is to integrate it with the corpus of theory possessing a wider network. This is a good deal harder than I used to think it was when I was younger. But this has not prevented me from trying.

Given the context in which I was writing the book the sort of person I planned to reach is not one I usually write for. I imagined my reader to be a shrewd civil servant (possibly involved in resource management) who not only relishes analytical discussions but also thinks they are essential in outlining the contours of actual problems. I did not think that my reader necessarily knows the calculus; but I did assume that he has a young colleague who does and that they have occasion to discuss these problems. But being a teacher, I noticed as I was in the process of writing the book that the vision of the university student kept crowding in, and this final draft attempts to accommodate such a person's needs as well.

My greatest debt is to Edward Dommen and Jack Stone of UNCTAD and to Yusuf J. Ahmad of UNEP for having encouraged me at every stage of the project and for sharing with me their views on what they saw as the most pressing environmental issues, most especially in the international sphere. Reading some of the development planning literature one would be forgiven for thinking that environmental planning, even in the extended sense used here, is a rich nation's luxury. These gentlemen know better, and they encouraged me to write in a way that makes contact with this literature. For this I am most grateful.

The first draft of this book was discussed at an expert group meeting organized by UNEP in Paris in February 1980. I am grateful to the participants of this meeting for their comments, most especially Graciela Chichilnisky, Charles Cooper, Robert Dorfman, John Krutilla, Karl-Göran Mäler and Hirofumi Uzawa. The manuscript was also discussed at the Fourth Inter-Government Expert Group Meeting on Social Cost–Benefit Analysis of Environmental Protection Measures organized by UNEP in Istanbul in November 1981. I gained much from the comments of the participants, too numerous to mention individually.

In the process of writing this work I have accumulated any number of intellectual debts. But it would be shocking if I were not to record the help that I have received by way of discussions with Kenneth Arrow, Ezra Bennathan, Pablo Bifani, Charles Blackorby, Gardner Brown, Kanchan Chopra, Colin Clark, Andrew Cornford, Amiya Dasgupta, Carol Dasgupta, Uttam Dabholkar, David Donaldson, the late B. N. Ganguli, Geoffrey Heal, John Lane, Alan Marin, Ezra Mishan, Tapan Mitra, Swapna Mukhopadhyay, Philip Neher, Marion O'Brien, René Olivieri, Anthony Scott, Robert Solow and Henry Wan. The manuscript was completed during a most agreeable tenure as a Ford Visiting Professor at the Institute of Economic Growth, Delhi, during the autumn of 1981. The entire final draft was typed with remarkable speed and accuracy by Marion O'Brien at the London School of Economics, to whom I am most grateful.

Partha Dasgupta
London School of Economics

1 Preview

The view that the market prices of goods and services often differ considerably from their 'social values' has gained increasing acceptance in recent years. There are many reasons that can be advanced in favour of this view, and they have been discussed in several studies (e.g. Little and Mirrlees, 1969, 1974; Dasgupta, Marglin and Sen, 1972, hereafter referred to as UNIDO, 1972; and in a different context, Galbraith, 1974). There is now a substantial body of work directed at obtaining guidelines for public policy in general and criteria that reflect the social profitability of economic activity in particular.[1] One of the aims of this book is to fill a gap in the existing literature on development planning. The point is that for the most part this literature has shied away from an explicit treatment of the valuation of what may loosely be called 'environmental resources'. By this I do not simply mean the classical problem of the factory chimney polluting the atmosphere; I mean a great deal more, and I shall elaborate on them in what follows. Our starting point, however, is the observation that in many cases the malfunctioning of 'market forces' can be ascribed to the fact that for certain commodities markets simply do not exist. Sometimes they happen not to exist for accidental or historical reasons; sometimes there are logical reasons why they cannot exist; sometimes the nature of the physical and political situation keeps them from existing, or makes them function

[1] There are now several books and monographs on the social evaluation of investment projects. See for example Little and Mirrlees (1969, 1974); UNIDO (1972); Squire and Van der Tak (1975); Chervel and Le Gall (1978); UNIDO (1978); Helmers (1979).

wrongly if they do exist. We shall argue (see chapter 2) that environmental resources are particularly vulnerable to this problem.

The earth's atmosphere, which is in a continual state of diffusion, is a paradigm of such resources. When, for example, any one of us burns fossil fuels, then among other things the carbon dioxide (CO_2) content of the atmosphere is inevitably increased. So too is the content of the darkly coloured particulate products of combustion. These particulates absorb solar heat, whereas CO_2 produces a 'greenhouse' effect.[2] The net effect is that the combustion of fossil fuels tends to increase the mean global temperature. Granted that each of us can contribute only negligibly to this increase, but the combined effect of all, cumulatively over time, may not be negligible, and is currently feared not to be negligible. It is worth noting as well that none of us can restrict the CO_2 and particulates thus produced by our activities to our own 'air parcels' and, as is usually the case, one is not obliged to compensate others for the damages one inflicts on them (especially future generations) by such activities. Here, the earth's atmosphere is a *common property* resource for which private-property rights are difficult to define and enforce, so that there is an absence of markets for their transaction. The example suggests that its exploitation by one imposes costs on others that are not taken into account (see chapter 2). We shall see that environmental resources often are common-property resources.

Having noted this it is as well to emphasize at the outset that I shall *not* be arguing that wherever feasible common-property resources should cease to remain common property, that private-property rights should in such circumstances necessarily be encouraged. Market exchanges emanating from the establishment of private-property rights are but *one* form of social control over resources. They are by no means necessarily the most commendable mode of social control; even when attention is restricted to their *consequences*, e.g. the allocation of resources (see chapter 2,

[2] The concentration of CO_2 is more or less uniform up to about 100 km above the earth's surface. While CO_2 is relatively transparent to solar radiation it is a prime absorber of re-radiated energy from the earth's surface and helps to keep the surface temperature warm. This is the greenhouse effect.

section 2.3). But in any case, attention ought rarely to be restricted to this. What I *do* argue, however, is that in the absence of any cooperation among users of a common-property resource there are wastes, or losses. One of the tasks of environmental economics, therefore, is to identify what these losses are and who in fact bears them.

'Environmental problems' are often associated with resources that are regenerative but in danger of exhaustion from misuse. There is, of course, more to such problems than this characterization, and I shall elaborate on it in what follows. But for the moment it is as well to note that such a characterization is very much consistent with common parlance. Resources such as minerals and fossil fuels do not fall into this category, for they are not regenerative (except in geological time). The act of utilizing a unit of such a resource reduces the total stock by precisely that amount. There are no means by which the total stock can be increased. Improvement in technology (e.g. enabling one to drill offshore or engaging in recycling) can, of course, increase the quantity that can be used. But this is a different matter. Then again, discoveries of new deposits will increase the *known* available stock. This too is a different matter. Note as well that people usually do not regard the *depletion* of an exhaustible resource as an environmental issue, except in so far as the act of extraction and use in production has 'environmental effects'. Thus, to take two examples, the burning of fossil fuels increases the global mean temperature, and the smelting of ores is a common source of atmospheric pollution. The environmental issue, as usually understood, here pertains not to the fact that the world's supply of fossil fuels and minerals are being reduced, but rather to the fact that such activities have a deleterious effect on the earth's atmosphere.[3]

Durable commodities like buildings and automobiles are also not in this category of resources. Even if the entire stock of such

[3] Thus the environmental effects of exhaustible resource depletion are examples of the constructs that follow (see chapters 3, 4 and 8). These effects must obviously be taken into account in the extraction and pricing decisions of exhaustible resources. For a discussion of the social management of depletable resources see Dasgupta and Heal (1979, chapters 6 and 10).

a commodity were to be destroyed at one stroke at least a part of the original stock could, presumably, be replaced in time. To the extent that such durables require exhaustible resources in their production the possibility of replenishing them will, presumably, be circumscribed by the availability of these exhaustible resources. This again is a different matter.

We shall in the main be concerned with resources of a different kind. A good deal of our concern will be with those resources that are capable of regenerating themselves as long as the 'environment' in which they are nurtured remains favourable. Animal, bird and fish populations are typical examples. So is land, for the quality of arable and grazing land can be maintained by careful use. Overuse, however, will impoverish the soil and eventually produce a wasteland.[4]

Both water (be it a lake or an aquifer) and the earth's atmosphere generally undergo a naturally self-cleaning process as pollutants are deposited in them. But the effectiveness of such natural cleansing processes (i.e. the rate at which the pollution disappears) depends both on the nature of the pollutant and on the rate at which they are deposited. If the rates of deposit are unduly high over a period of time it may take a long while for the resource to regenerate itself.[5]

Underground reservoirs of fresh water display yet another characteristic. Often enough the issue is not one of depositing pollutants in them. Under normal circumstances aquifers are recharged by natural seepage and underground flows over the annual cycle, but if as a result of excessive extraction of fresh

[4] This often happens when peasants do not have the security of tenure; for in this case they have, quite rightly, little interest in the productivity of the soil in the distant future. Likewise, overgrazing and deforestation for firewood in common-property land (see chapter 2) can lead to desertification, as has for example, happened in the northern Sahel. We are now focusing attention on the excessive utilization of a piece of land. Downland soil erosion caused by deforestation in the uplands is a major problem today, but it is a somewhat different point.

[5] A good example of this is the discharge of degradable organic residuals into streams which, if carried to excess, results in the extinction of fish. This is due to the fact that bacteria in the water feeds on such residuals and in the process uses up the dissolved oxygen that is present in water.

water the groundwater table is allowed to fall to too low a level then, in the case of coastal aquifers, there can be salt-water intrusion resulting in the destruction of the basin (see e.g. Schmorak, 1967).[6]

Resources such as fish in their natural environment can normally survive as a species indefinitely so long as the stock is not depleted below a certain level by human encroachment. It will be seen in chapter 6 that if husbanded, a fishery can be exploited at a fixed rate more or less indefinitely, but excessive rates of catch, leading to the bio-mass falling below the species' threshold level, results in the permanent destruction of the stock. The social cost (e.g. in terms of the value of foregone catch) therefore rises dramatically when the stock falls slightly below the threshold value.

Each of the foregoing, quite patently, represents the kind of resources one has in mind when one reflects on environmental issues. Each also highlights a feature which did not appear in the characterization of environmental resources with which I began, that the stock of such a resource can, in the best of circumstances, never exceed a certain level. This last is of central importance, for it is a direct consequence of the earth being of finite size. To be sure, this upper bound can be large; so large in fact that for a long while one may not really be in a position to monitor the fact that the resource is being encroached upon. If the rate of utilization of such a resource has in the past never been very great the stock, for all intents and purposes, may be treated as unlimited. It could then be regarded as a free good; and it is most often so regarded. With the passage of time it can happen that a community's need for it rises and the stock is allowed to fall to low levels. Meanwhile it is still regarded as a free good. There is a presumption then that the resource, being free, is being exploited excessively. It is then that society becomes conscious of a 'problem' and wants to know what stock it ought, collectively, to aim at.

The earth's atmosphere is a good example of this. Its capacity to absorb pollution, while large, is clearly finite. Despite its limited

[6] Drilling costs increase as the water table drops. But this is a somewhat different issue – another possible source of intertemporal externality – and we shall discuss it in chapter 6.

carrying capacity it was thought reasonable to treat it as a free good until recently; for our capacity to pollute was even more limited. So much so that even 25 years ago atmospheric pollution was not a major item in any discussion of resource utilization.[7] Today it is a serious item on the agenda of public debate.

Another example is waste disposal into rivers, lakes and the seas. Until recently, the 'carrying capacity' of many such resource stocks could have been viewed as limitless; not so today. Moreover, for most societies such 'sinks' are much too costly to exploit effectively, for it requires a well-developed sewage system to carry wastes to them. For poor societies the option often is to rely on rain water, air and sunlight to degrade urban pollution. But in many cases they provide society with too slow a regenerative process for the need at hand. On occasion the quality (of the environment) falls to such a low level that it cannot provide society with its needs. This results in the outbreak of diseases, such as cholera and the plague. These days many call them 'crisis situations', in fact such situations have been with us always.

It is useful to recognize that the fact that environmental resources such as forests, the atmosphere and the seas, often have multiple competing uses merely accentuates the problem of malallocation associated with their use. Thus for example, forests quite apart from being a source of timber and pharmaceuticals provide joint products; e.g. a habitat for a rich genetic pool. In addition, they influence local and regional climate, preserve soil cover on site and, in the case of watershed forests, protect soil downstream from floods. Increased run-off of rain water due to deforestation helps strip soil away, depriving agriculture of nutrients and at the same time clogging water reservoirs and irrigation systems. The social value of a forest typically exceeds the value of the direct forest products, and on occasion exceeds it greatly. Likewise, the oceans are important for the production of food, and also for transport, mining, oil production and waste

[7] We are, of course, ignoring 'local' problems such as the air over London, and also 'extra-ordinary' problems, such as nuclear pollution, both of which were discussed before environmental problems became a major item of discussion. For a catalogue of pollution problems, see Freeman *et al.* (1973) and the encyclopaedic work of Ehrlich *et al.* (1977).

disposal. But unlike land it is difficult to partition the oceans for their different uses because, like the earth's atmosphere, they are in a constant state of diffusion. Oil spillage and waste disposal at one location will, over time, affect food production at a neighbouring site.

Related to this is the fact, greatly emphasized by ecologists in recent years, that the capacity of environmental resources such as the atmosphere and the seas to absorb pollutants is far less than one would suppose at first blush. Filter-feeding animals, such as oysters, can concentrate poisons to levels far higher than those in their surrounding environment. So too along food chains, where the concetration of toxics, such as DDT, tends to increase from one trophic level to another. Such systems act as what ecologists call *biological amplifiers*. Thus, the average content of pollutants in the seas, *on its own*, is no index of the damage that is caused by their presence.[8]

We have noted that environmental problems usually concern the intertemporal misallocation of regenerative natural resources. Such resources may be of direct use in consumption (fisheries), in production (plankton, which serve as food for fish species), or in both (drinking and irrigation water from underground basins). Often though, environmental problems are thought to arise as a consequence of the excessive production of pollution. It is usually most convenient when discussing the control of pollution to focus attention on the pollutants themselves, and this is precisely what I shall do in chapters 4 and 8. But conceptually it is useful to bear in mind (see chapter 8) that the emission of pollutants in effect means the *reduction* in the *quality* or the *size* (or both) of the stock of a regenerative resource; the resource being the sink into which the pollutants are being deposited. This is worth remember-

[8] Ehrlich *et al.* (1977), pp. 629–34, present a particularly lucid account of the phenomenon of biological amplification. They note, for example, that oysters have been found to possess up to 70 000 times the concentration of chlorinated hydrocarbon insecticides (e.g. DDT) that exist in their environment. This they explain by the fact that oysters capture food by constantly filtering the water they inhabit and that they live in the shallow coastal waters where pollution is usually the heaviest. They also provide a simple account of how it is that increased concentration of toxins are to be found higher up in food chains.

ing because it enables one to place pollution control in the more general context of utilizing regenerative resources. In particular, it enables us to recognize that there are many environmental problems whose origins have little to do with the production of pollution, as the term is usually understood. My approach is therefore broader here, and the formal models that follow will be capable of absorbing a wider class of interpretations than usual environmental models are capable of.

Pollutants can have an impact on welfare either as a stock or as a flow, or both. Persistent pollutants, such as detergents (e.g. ABS), pesticides (e.g. DDT) and industrial inputs (e.g. PCBs) have an effect both as a stock and as a flow. DDT as a flow is useful in agriculture as an input; as a stock it is hazardous for health. Likewise, the PCBs as a flow are useful, because they are an important ingredient in the production of plastics, paints and hydraulic fluids. About as non-degradable as DDT, they have damaging consequences as a stock in water. They appear to be fatal to the larger types of phytoplankton, which are microscopic plants. A decline in their numbers affects the food supply of zooplanktons, the slightly larger herbivorous animals that feed on the tiny plants. Zooplanktons, in turn, are normally consumed by tiny fish that are consumed by larger fish caught by fishermen. The PCBs as a stock affect a vital part of the marine food chain, and thereby indirectly affect the supply of food fish in any specific area. This dual feature is fairly typical of non-degradable pollutants. The stock is detrimental, either because of its direct effect on consumption, or because it has deleterious effects on production; while the flow is beneficial, either because it is useful in production, or because it is an unfortunate by-product of production which can be kept from inflicting damages only by the expenditure of resources. Pollutants of this sort are, as a stock, the conceptual opposite of resources such as fisheries.[9] (See chapter 5, section 5.4 and chapters 6 to 9.)

Stocks of persistent pollutants *may* display 'threshold' effects, rather like many regenerative resources. For example, the effect of small deposits of toxins may well be negligible and this may well be true over a range. Beyond this range the deleterious effects

[9] Keeler *et al.* (1972) and Mäler (1974) make fruitful use of this insight.

often rise rather rapidly as, for example, would appear to be the case with DDT concentration in human body fat (see chapters 4 and 8).

It is worth re-emphasizing that unlike computers and tractors, environmental resources usually affect welfare directly as *stocks*, not merely as *flows*. (An exception is noise pollution.) Fisheries and aquifers are useful not only for the harvest they provide: as a stock they are directly useful, since harvesting and extraction costs are low if stocks are large (see chapters 6 and 7). As we have seen, forests are beneficial not only for the timber they may supply: as a stock they prevent soil erosion and help maintain a genetic pool (see chapter 2, section 2.4, and chapters 9 and 10). Likewise air and water quality have direct welfare effects (it is, let us remember, the concentration of pollutants which is relevant here). Finally of course, there are stocks of natural resources that are valued for the amenities they directly provide (e.g. places of scenic beauty), and species that one feels ought to be preserved on moral or aesthetic grounds. The direct welfare effects of environmental resource stocks are in some cases relatively easy to evaluate, in others impossibly difficult. We shall have several occasions to analyse the implications of such 'stock effects' in this book.

These features are worth bearing in mind. They suggest strongly that in discussing environmental issues we ought to be thinking of regenerative natural resources and, what is equally important for our purpose here, that we can bring to bear resource allocation theory when debating such issues.

So far we have stressed the intertemporal nature of environmental problems. However, of at least equal importance is the fact that more often than not the environmental effects of various activities (e.g. the emission of different sorts of pollutants) are unknown. This is unavoidable particularly if the effects are cumulative over time. No doubt in many instances pilot studies can be conducted, but these also take time.

Uncertainty about the effects of different forms of pollution is one reason why debates on environmental issues are often so acrimonious. Divergence of opinion about the extent of the uncertainty is usually great even among experts. This is as true of the effect of, say, mercury deposits on marine life as it is of the effect of aerosol and high-altitude supersonic jets on the upper layers of the atmosphere. The Icelandic fishing dispute suggests that there is usually considerable uncertainty about the size of the existing stock being disputed, not to mention the uncertainty over the bio-mass at which a species is endangered. Then again, deep differences of opinion exist about the magnitude of the climatic changes that are likely to be generated by increases in CO_2 emission, or for example, the effect of persistent toxins such as DDT and the PCBs on marine life. But even if we were to ignore the divergence of opinion it is an inescapable feature of environmental issues that decisions are required to be taken in the face of significant uncertainties. As new products are introduced and as new technologies are relied upon to produce these products new effluents are emitted into the environment. Even as information is acquired about the effects of existing types of effluents there are always additional forms introduced, whose impact is uncertain.

To sum up: environmental discussions need to be conducted in the face of a clear recognition that, (a) these resources are often common property, (b) resolutions of environmental problems usually involve changes in the allocation of property rights, (c) resource use may well be irreversible (e.g. it may lead to their exhaustion when in fact this could have been avoided), (d) resource stocks often affect welfare directly, (e) the environmental impact of certain types of activity are cumulative and only become noticeable at some time in the future, and (f) the environmental consequences of economic activities are uncertain. It is no wonder that environmental problems are formidable to analyse, let alone solve.

I have emphasized these various features at the outset, partly because it is my intention to consider each of them in the chapters that follow; but partly also because I would hazard the guess that many concerned individuals think of environmental problems and their resolution almost exclusively in terms of points (a) and (b) above. If this is true it should not be surprising, for the traditional approach to the study of environmental problems has been an appeal to the theory of externalities.[10] I would not wish to claim

[10] The best treatments of the theory of externalities are in Arrow (1971a), Starrett and Zeckhauser (1971), Meade (1973), Baumol and Oates (1975) and Mäler (1974).

that the approach is unfruitful, but it is becoming increasingly evident that where matters concerning environmental resources are at issue, conventional remedies proposed for simple cases of market failure may be inadequate to achieve the outcome desired. Efforts to deal with these complex matters often require some form of centralized coordination and control. The reasons are clear enough. They are, to repeat, that the environmental impact of current production and consumption activities occur in the future; in some cases quite far away in the future; it is on occasion irreversible, and always uncertain. Therefore, in the absence of an adequate set of forward and risk markets recourse to a direct curtailment of certain types of consumption and limiting the use of some production processes, may be found necessary. (There are other reasons as well that are somewhat technical in nature. In some cases these reasons are due to point (c) above. I shall study them in chapter 3, 4 and 8.)

I emphasize this because in what follows I shall not be providing orders of magnitude. It is not my intention here to attempt to catalogue environmental problems, far less to do so in their order of increasing importance.[11] I take it that there are many communities for whom atmospheric pollution is not (yet) an issue, but for whom lack of an adequate sewage system is of paramount concern. I take it also that there must be communities for whom the reverse is the case. My aim in this book is to discuss a conceptual apparatus which is designed to articulate what one often means by an 'environmental problem', and then to discuss remedies. In the process of doing this we shall proceed by way of simple algebraic examples. The constructs that follow must be regarded as strict prototypes. They can be expanded in various directions to suit requirements and on occasion I shall indicate the manner in which this may be done. But for the main part the purpose of this book is, by an appeal to economic analysis, to develop a conceptual framework for addressing the kinds of problems environmentalists have recently laid stress upon.

In fact much has been written on the subject matter of this book: by environmentalists, political scientists, sociologists,

[11] *World Conservation Strategy*, prepared by the International Union for Conservation of Nature and Natural Resources, and its accompanying monograph by Allen (1980) present an attempt at identifying major environmental problems.

economists and lawyers, among others. There is also the irresistible temptation, when reflecting on environmental problems, to search for and identify the kinds of social ethos which deserve our allegiance. Much has been written on this as well (see e.g. Schumacher, 1973; Daly, 1973; and, at the sharper tradition of political economy, Galbraith, 1974, Part 5, and Lindblom, 1977, in his assessment of existing polyarchies). The transition from one mode of social organization to another is never an easy matter. We are here thinking of the social and psychological strains that inevitably accompany them. Much of this is still unknown terrain, even though people have thought about them, experienced them and have written about them. Every environmental problem has its unique features, and any reasonable discussion of it requires specialized discourse. On reflection it is, to take an example, perhaps not surprising that much of the debates undertaken at the United Nations Law of the Sea Conferences and over the oceanic enclosure movement has been dominated by lawyers and political experts. What I have outlined in this chapter and shall pursue in the rest of the book is the belief that there are nevertheless several pervasive elements in environmental problems. My aim is to draw them out and to see how one might think about them.

It must be granted that societies both precipitate and attempt to cope with environmental problems by means that vary from place to place and from time to time. Peasants are on occasion massacred and entire communities are forced to migrate. In a more benign climate votes are bought, officials are bribed, agency loyalties are maintained and lobbyists have their way. For the social critic and commentator, stopping short at this observation and even to document cases, as has admirably been done by many, is not enough. It is important as well to understand how resource problems ought to be resolved in the light of professed social goals. At the general level it is good not to be overwhelmed by the vested interests and administrative rigidities that inevitably would balk at the implementation of such resolutions. They vary enormously across regions and time. Furthermore, to take them always into account is to accept their presence. To be sure their presence will influence the choice of policy. But then the social critic needs a standard by which to judge what has been foregone.

2 Common Property, Externalities and the Distribution of Income

2.1 The problem of the commons: an introduction

> Picture a pasture open to all. It is to be expected that each herdsman will try to keep as many cattle as possible on the commons... As a rational being, each herdsman seeks to maximize his gain. Explicitly or implicitly, more or less consciously, he asks, 'What is the utility to me of adding one more animal to my herd?'... Adding together the component partial utilities, the rational herdsman concludes that the only sensible course for him to pursue is to add another animal to his herd. And another; and another... But this is the conclusion reached by each and every rational herdsman sharing a commons. Therein is the tragedy. Each man is locked into a system that compels him to increase his herd without limit – in a world that is limited. Ruin is the destination toward which all men rush, each pursuing his own best interest in a society that believes in the freedom of the commons. Freedom in the commons brings ruin to all.
>
> (Hardin, 1968, p. 1244)

It would be difficult to locate another passage of comparable length and fame containing as many errors as the one above. There is a germ of an idea, to be sure; one which has been appreciated for long, and which I noted in chapter 1: to wit, that a resource in finite supply is *likely* to be over used if available free of charge.[1]

[1] Good non-technical discussions are Gordon (1954); Scott (1955). However, it is possible to invent non-pathological examples where the bias is in the direction of *under* utilization of the free resource! On this see Buchanon and Karfoglis (1963).

But it would be wrong to suppose that each herdsman in Professor Hardin's example will add cattle without limit. Animals are not costless, even to the herdsmen who own them. And such private costs set limits on the number of animals each herdsman finds most profitable to introduce into the common pasture. But the point remains that in the absence of a binding mutual agreement each herdsman will typically ignore the cost he imposes on the others when introducing another animal into the common. One supposes then that the system will entertain too many animals in the pasture, in the sense that it would be in the herdsmen's collective interest to curtail the number of animals. However, an excessive number of cattle in the common does not necessarily mean that it will be ruined. For we cannot know without further information just *how* excessive the numbers will be. Whether or not the common will be ruined depends on a number of factors, an important one of which is the price of output (i.e. beef or milk) relative to the private cost of rearing cattle (see especially chapter 6). Freedom in the commons does not necessarily bring ruin to all; in fact it may ruin none. Moreover, we shall note that if the resource ceases to remain a common property *and* if rent is charged by the usurper for access to the resource, each of the users could well be worse off. The users may even become impoverished. The distributional consequences of an alteration in property rights always bear close scrutiny. What *is* implied by Professor Hardin's example is that each of the herdsmen could benefit if *they jointly* were to exercise some control over the common and if nobody were to enter the scene to collect rents for its use. The interesting question that arises then is why environmental resources are likely to be common property.

In chapter 1 I noted that in usual parlance environmental resources are those resources which are regenerative but potentially exhaustible. I noted as well that the sustained flow of services provided by them can never exceed some finite rate (for formalizations of this see chapters 6 to 9). A striking further characteristic that many environmental resources possess can be described by saying that they offer acute problems for defining and enforcing private rights to them. Thus, while property refers to rights, not all possible rights, especially private rights to many environmental resources, are possible pieces of property. This too was mentioned in chapter 1. The central implication of this feature is that in the absence of cooperation, actions not directly controlled by an agent – be the agent a firm, or an individual, or a well-defined group acting in concert – affect the set of outcomes that the agent can attain by the use of actions that the agent *does* in fact control. Such phenomena are called *externalities* in the economics literature and they have been much discussed. The definition offered above may appear overly abstruse; however, the examples that follow will clarify.

Consider first underground water basins. While it is easy enough to envisage different individuals in a community having titles to adjacent plots of *land*, owning titles to the water underground is an entirely different matter. (This problem occurs as well in the case of oil and natural gas if the rule of capture prevails.) One usually does not know precisely how much water lies below a given surface area of land, even when there is a reasonably sharp estimate of the total stock in the entire basin. Add to this the fact that nothing is easier for a farmer than to extract water from under his neighbour's plot without anyone being the wiser, and one can see why private-property rights on aquifers are difficult to define, let alone to enforce. One can of course define such rights by legislating that all water that lies under a given parcel of land belongs to the owner (or lessee) of the parcel. But this is not useful, since there is a tendency for water to migrate within the underground basin and thereby altering the extraction costs of neighbours, particularly so when pressure gradients are caused during the process of extraction. The source of the problem here lies in the uncertainty as to the original location of a given quantity of water extracted at a given location.

In the face of this problem most communities have fallen back on the 'riparian doctrine', under which each owner of a parcel of land is allowed to extract as much water as he desires without regard to its effects on the owners of neighbouring parcels. The doctrine therefore provides no protection to a well-owner from the lowering of the water table under his land caused by his neighbour's actions. This suggests at once that in the absence of any intervention (e.g. rationing at the well head through cooperation) the doctrine will encourage an excessive rate of overall water extraction, leading *possibly* to an eventual ruin of the basin.[2] This possibility is particularly telling if in fact it is in the community's long-term interest to keep the basin alive. But if the circumstances are such that this is a distinct possibility the question can be asked why the farmers do not see the impending destruction of the basin. The answer is that the farmers may know nothing about the natural rate of replenishment of the water basin and therefore may not know that the total annual rate of extraction exceeds this rate. In fact they may not know what the threshold level of ground-water stock is. Moreover, and this is particularly important, under the riparian doctrine no farmer on his own has much incentive to learn about the natural regeneration rate of the ground-water basin. Under the riparian doctrine, each farmer is much like the traditional 'free-rider' (see Musgrave, 1959). In chapter 6 I shall analyse the kinds of policy measures that would be desirable in the face of such a form of market failure.

Common-property marine fisheries suffer from this problem in an acute form. The point is that the oceans are not only a habitat for fish stocks, they are at the same time a sink into which pollutants are deposited. The problem is accentuated by the fact that much industrial effluent is discharged into coastal wetlands, such as the Wadden Sea and the Indus delta, which provide a nursery to many marine species. Moreover, the fact that the major pollutors are not the fishing industry suggests at once that marine fisheries suffer from the twin problems of excessive pollution and overfishing.

It is as well to remark that while each of these twin problems has acquired special notoriety in the case of international waters, they occur in acute form within national boundaries as well. The apparent destruction of fisheries in the freshwater steams in Fuji, Japan, by discharges from paper mills is a case in point. Overfishing off the coast of Kerala, India, and in the Gulf of Thailand, are others.

[2] For a formal demonstration of such a possibility, cast in the form of a differential game, see V. L. Smith (1968); Khalatbari (1977); Dasgupta and Heal (1979, chapter 5); Hartwick (1980). In chapter 6 I shall provide a formal intertemporal model to discuss this possibility.

While marine pollution has drawn considerable attention in the literature for quite some time, the problem of overfishing from the commons would appear to have entered public consciousness only recently. If this is so it may be because unlike certain types of pollution which are tangible and are relatively easy to monitor, overfishing is not. As we noted above in a somewhat different context, no individual fisherman has incentives on his own to acquire sufficient information about the ecological implications of common-property fisheries. Today it is thought that something like 25 of the world's major fisheries are seriously depleted. In chapter 7 I shall present a formal intertemporal model that will enable me to discuss what 'serious depletion' might mean. But it is as well to note here that as a stock gets depleted unit cost of catch typically rises, as fishermen have to travel farther afield or obtain less catch at every attempt.[3] It is in this manner that today's catch rates impose an *intertemporal externality* on the future, something which is not taken into account – or internalized, as economists are prone to saying – if there is no intervention or an agreement in a common-property fishery. This often has serious distributional consequences at certain locations. If harvesting costs continue to rise at a particular location, what once formed a part of a poor man's food intake at that location may no longer remain so.

The magnitude of the problem of overfishing patently varies from case to case. For marine fisheries with *free entry* the foregoing problem can arise via a seemingly convoluted process. In free waters, where *historical rights* to the traditional fishermen are not respected, it can happen that large firms enter with modern fishing vessels. For the short run unit harvesting costs are thereby dramatically reduced, thus exacerbating the tendency towards overfishing. Meanwhile, the traditional fishermen, unable to compete with such equipment, are left impoverished for want of any catch.[4] But in the long run, as a consequence of continual overfishing, harvest costs increase, despite – one should say, *because* of – the use of modern harvesting techniques. Nor can one even necessarily argue that the introduction of modern harvesting

[3] V. L. Smith (1968) calls this a *stock* externality.

[4] Kurien (1978) provides an account of this for fisheries off the seaboard of India.

techniques in the seas is at least partially blessed at the altar of intertemporal efficiency; for the market wage-rental ratio in many less-developed countries is thought to be too high.

It is an observation of the utmost banality that the choice of production techniques is influenced by the institutional environment within which it is undertaken. In marine fisheries the slaughter of non-target animals in the process of each catch is a commonplace. This phenomenon, which is increasingly being taken very seriously by fisheries' experts, exacerbates the overfishing problem. Admittedly, in the case of fisheries it will always prove difficult to monitor the extent to which non-target animals are killed by each unit at each catch. Nevertheless, it must also be granted that common property fisheries provide little incentives to individual fishing units to reduce, what are euphemistically called, 'incidental takes'.[5]

On occasion, where the fisheries are in international waters and the stock is depleted to low levels, the matter receives considerable publicity, as for example has been the case for some years with the blue whales. International fishing disputes in the North Atlantic, the Bay of Bengal and North-East Pacific would seem to provide other cases in point. At the widest international level the protracted Third United Nations Law of the Sea Conference has been prompted by a clear recognition of the problems presented by common property resources – in this case the open seas. It is, however, worth bearing in mind that over 99 per cent of marine fish production occurs in coastal waters. Rough estimates suggest that something like 240 million metric tons of fish are produced annually in coastal waters, and only about 1.6 million metric tons in the open oceans.[6] In other words the open oceans, something like 90 per cent of the oceanic area, is essentially a 'biological desert'. In view of this the recent move on the part of nations to extend their Exclusive Economic Zones to 200 nautical miles of territorial waters off the coast line will clearly have a major redistributional effect. For example, if strictly enforced, Japan's

[5] In 1976 the world catch of shrimps was about 1.3 million tonnes. It is estimated that at least 6.5 million tonnes of fish were destroyed in the process of this harvest; see Allen (1980).

[6] See Ehrlich *et al.* (1977, p. 353). The original source is Ryther (1969).

traditional fishing grounds would be reduced by about 45 per cent. Indeed, it is estimated that a universal extension would appropriate about 90 per cent of the world's current marine harvest to national control (see Cooper, 1977). About 15 nations stand to control over 40 per cent of the enclosed oceanic space, with the first 10 controlling some 30 per cent. But leaving aside the distributional consequences – as regards both income and the augmentation and transgression of rights – such a reallocation of property rights on its own will not resolve the problem of excessive pollution and overfishing in waters within the extended Exclusive Economic Zones. The management problem within these waters will be merely shifted from the international to the national scene. The problem may well be exacerbated by such a move on the part of nations. For, if past evidence is anything to go by, among the more successful attempts to protect fisheries that have been made are those in the open seas by international agreement; the record of purely national regulations of limited resources does not make for particularly pleasant reading (see for example McHugh, 1972; Holt, 1975; but for a defence of the enclosure movement on the oceans, see Eckert, 1979). An extension of the Exclusive Economic Zones is by no means a certain escape from this problem. I shall return to this issue in section 2.3.

2.2 The problem of the commons: a formalization

These points are well known. Nevertheless it is worth reiterating them here so as to provide a ready background for the formal models that follow. It is with the help of such formal models that it is possible to check one's intuition and to see what policy options there are for environmental problems. In this section I present a simple construction to capture the problem of the commons and see the precise sense in which the commons encourage excessive encroachment.

For ease of exposition I have kept the example simple and suppose there to be N identical users of a common-property resource. The example can accommodate many interpretations. Here I give it an international flavour and identify each user with a nation and suppose that each country discharges its effluent into coastal waters, thus damaging a common fishery. Effluents are, by hypothesis, a by-product of production, and to keep matters simple, we take it that the only way one may reduce emissions is by reducing output.[7] The model is timeless, so I do not distinguish between stocks and flows. In chapter 8 I shall develop inter-temporal considerations. Let y_i denote the output of country i, where $i = 1, \ldots, N$, and let P_i denote its emission, where $P_i = \alpha y_i$ and α, a positive constant, is the emission–output coefficient. Clearly we can then choose our units of measurement of pollution so as to set $\alpha = 1$ and therefore identify P_i with y_i. Let us do so. Social benefit (or surplus) – not deducting for pollution damages – that i enjoys when it produces y_i is assumed to be given by the fuction $B(y_i)$. Since this includes the cost of producing y_i, $B(y_i)$ will typically have a shape as drawn in figure 2.1.

Pollutants reduce catch from the fishery. When $\Sigma_{i=1}^{N} y_i$ is total output, the loss in foregone catch to *each* country due to this

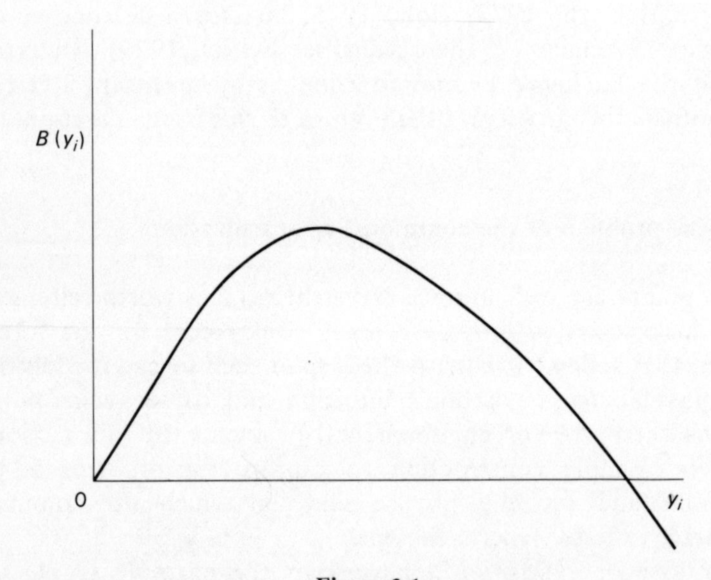

Figure 2.1

[7] In chapter 8 I shall formally take into account the fact that the emission–output ratio can be reduced by expenditure on pollution abatement schemes, etc.

pollution is assumed to be given by a damage function

$$D\left(\sum_{i=1}^{N} P_i\right) = D\left(\sum_{i=1}^{N} y_i\right),$$

whose shape is depicted in figure 2.2.[8]

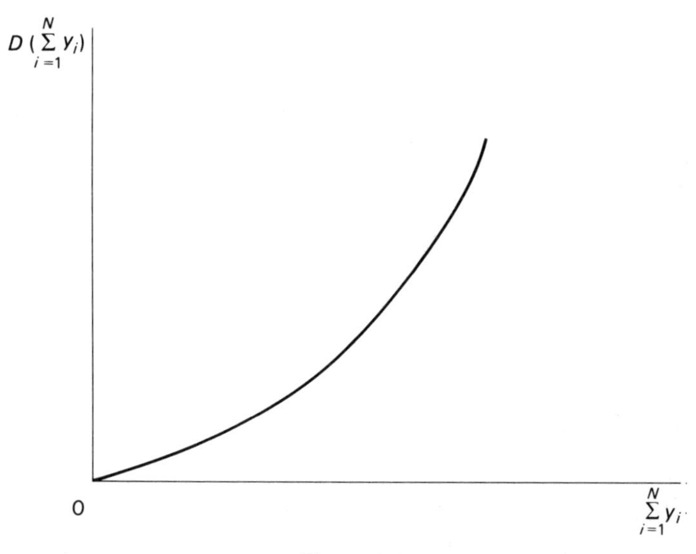

Figure 2.2

We first identify the *non-cooperative outcome*. Consider country i. Since the countries are by hypothesis identical we may as well suppose that i assumes that each of the other remaining countries will produce the same amount, say y. If this assumption were to prove correct its net social benefit – now including the loss from foregone catch – would read as:

$$B(y_i) - D(y_i + (N-1)y). \tag{2.1}$$

[8] Nothing essential is lost, for my purposes here, in assuming that marginal damage is continually increasing, as in figure 2.2; and much is gained by way of mathematical simplicity. However, if threshold effects are present then marginal damages are low at large emission levels. See chapters 4 and 8 for a discussion of this.

Country i is entitled only to select y_i. It regards the choice of output, y, by each of the others as given and maximizes *its* own net benefit. To find the maximum expression (2.1) must be differentiated with respect to y_i and set equal to zero (I ignore the possibility that zero output is best for i when each of the others chooses y). This yields *country* i*'s cost–benefit rule*:

$$\mathrm{d}B(y_i)/\mathrm{d}y_i = \mathrm{d}D(y_i + (N-1)\,y)/\mathrm{d}y_i. \tag{2.2}$$

Equation (2.2) is one equation in one unknown, y_i. Since the countries in this example are identical, if y_i is the optimal choice for i, and if this choice results in an *equilibrium*, it must be the case that $y_i = y$; that is, i's output equals each of the other country's output at the equilibrium. Thus, equation (2.2) can be written as:

$$\mathrm{d}B(y)/\mathrm{d}y = \mathrm{d}D(Y)/\mathrm{d}Y \tag{2.3}$$

where $Y = Ny$.

Since $Y = Ny$, we may conclude that equation (2.3) is one equation in one unknown, y. Let the solution be $\bar{y}$. It follows that total output at this non-cooperative equilibrium is $N\bar{y}$.[9] Following Tulkens (1974) we call such an outcome an *environmentally nationalistic equilibrium*. Now, equation (2.3) reflects the fact that this equilibrium is characterized by each country equating its marginal benefit from output (the left-hand side of equation (2.3)) to its marginal private loss from foregone catch (the right-hand side of equation (2.3)). We shall see presently that this is not an *optimal* outcome from the point of view of the countries taken collectively. There are policies under which every country is better off. We now proceed to calculate the optimal allocation for this example and see what binding agreements these countries will be advised to engage in. Since the countries are identical there are no momentous ethical issues to be contemplated. We look for a

[9] The outcome being described here, as the reader will recognize, is what is called a (non-cooperative) Nash equilibrium in game theory. For a good non-technical account of this, see Luce and Raiffa (1957). In recent years there have been attempts at quantifying transfrontier environmental damages. Estimates for the OECD countries suggest that they sum to over 1 billion US dollars annually (see OECD, 1974).

symmetric outcome in which the *sum* of the individual net benefit functions is maximized. Thus suppose these N countries undertake binding agreements to ensure that such a symmetric cooperative solution is implemented. If y is the output of the representative country then to obtain this solution y must be chosen so as to maximize

$$NB(y) - ND(Ny). \qquad (2.4)$$

Differentiating expression (2.4) with respect to y and equating this to zero yields the *international cost–benefit rule*,

$$dB(y)/dy = N\, dD(Y)/dY, \qquad (2.5)$$[10]

where $Y = Ny$.

This is precisely what one would have expected. The left-hand side is the increase in benefits to the representative country when its output is increased marginally. Output *per se* generates no externalities, but the associated emission does. The right-hand side is the *sum* of the marginal damages to each country. Thus equation (2.5) is precisely what one would have expected. It is an instance of the rule governing the optimal supply of public commodities (see Samuelson, 1954). Let y^* be the solution of equation (2.5). Then a comparison between equations (2.3) and (2.5) shows immediately that $\bar{y} > y^*$ and, therefore, that in the absence of binding agreements, the nations will pollute too much (see figure 2.3).[11] Each nation is better off at the cooperative solution y^* than at the environmentally nationalistic $\bar{y}$. However, in the absence of a binding agreement none will choose y^*. The example, while not identical to it, is reminiscent of the N-person version of the Prisoner's Dilemma game.[12]

[10] Again we suppose, to have an interesting problem, that the optimum emission rate is not zero.

[11] Note that pollution is a collective 'bad'. Thus the symmetric (non-cooperative) equilibrium sustains too much of it. One contrasts this with the insufficient supply of a collective 'good' as in Samuelson (1954, 1958).

[12] The Prisoners' Dilemma game has been discussed *ad nauseum* in the economics literature. A good treatment is in Luce and Raiffa (1957). The game assumes that each of N players has to choose between two strategies, x and y. Let U_i be the payoff function of player i. If $N = 2$ (the case most

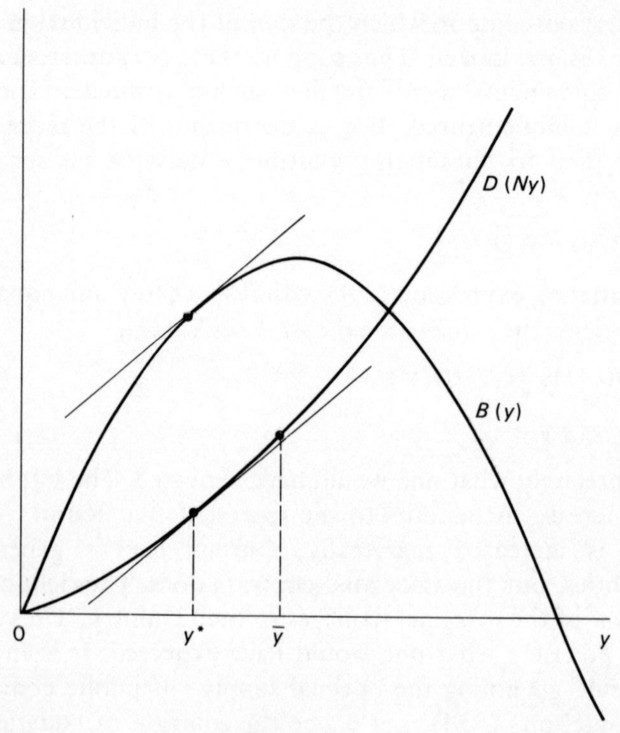

Figure 2.3

often discussed), suppose that $U_1(x, y) < U_1(y, y) < U_1(x, x) < U_1(y, x)$, and $U_2(y, x) < U_2(y, y) < U_2(x, x) < U_2(x, y)$. Then clearly in the absence of binding agreements each player finds y to be his dominant strategy: it is the strategy to choose no matter what the other does. But they would both be better off if they both chose x. This is the 'dilemma'. It is often thought that the supply of collective (or public) goods and bads suffers from a problem identical to this. It is not so. As we have seen, the essence of the Prisoners' Dilemma game lies not only in the fact that it possesses a unique non-cooperative equilibrium which is Pareto inefficient, but also in the fact that the equilibrium is sustained by dominant strategies. As equation (2.3) in the text makes clear, $\bar{y}$ is the best strategy for an individual country in our example if and *only if* the remaining nations emit a total quantity of effluent equal to $(N-1)\,\bar{y}$. That is, the environmentally nationalistic equilibrium is *not* a dominant strategy equilibrium.

2.3 Equity, efficiency and rights

There is a by now classical theorem in economics which says that under certain well-defined conditions an equilibrium outcome of the market mechanism is *efficient*. The notion of efficiency is in the sense of Pareto; that, there is no feasible alternative allocation which makes all agents better off. This theorem is so well known that it would be pointless to rehearse it here, except to emphasize the fact that the conditions include price-taking behaviour on the part of agents, and the existence of a market for each and every commodity in the economy – now and in the future and for every possible outcome of the world.[13] This last assumption is often termed the 'universality of markets' (see Arrow, 1971a). A glance at expression (2.1) tells us that missing markets abound in our example. It is this feature to which the *inefficiency* of the non-cooperative (or environmentally nationalistic) equilibrium, $\bar{y}$, may be traced. As expression (2.1) makes clear, one consequence of the fact that the coastal region is a common property, is that each country's output level contributes to each country's damages. Furthermore, it is because of an absence of private-property rights in the coastal area in the model we are considering that no international transactions can be undertaken in the exchange of such externalities; and indeed, they are not undertaken at an environmentally nationalistic equilibrium.[14]

Rights delineate the feasible sets of actions of agents. Alterations in the structure of rights usually involve an increase in the rights of some and a transgression of the rights of others. In what follows I shall study two alternative modes of social control of the

[13] Excellent accounts of this theorem can be obtained in Scitovsky (1951), Arrow (1971a) and Malinvaud (1972).

[14] If the common property in the example could be parcelled out equally among the N participants it would constitute a solution to the problem in terms of the *outcome* achieved, though of course *any* alteration in property rights involves the transgression of certain rights which can be defended in many cases, and not in many others. Even leaving this last aside the matter is deeply problematic if, as is always the case, the participants are not identical. The '200-mile' enclosure movement of the oceans, which is designed by coastal states to extend national sovereignty over what was originally international common property, is a pristine example.

common-property resource that I have been analysing, and I shall compare them solely in terms of their *consequences*, viz. the allocation of national benefits. But it should be recognized that each of these modes involves an alteration in rights, and in general this needs to be borne in mind when debating such issues. (For further discussions on this, see Dasgupta, 1980.)

It is clear that if *binding* agreements can be reached, the allocation obtained from equation (2.5) can be implemented by the imposition of *quota* restrictions on each country equal to y^*. This is often the way in which policies are implemented in the case of fisheries' catch. For pollution, the case being considered, such quotas are called *emission standards*, and often reliance is placed on the imposition of standards on offenders to control the level of pollution concentration (see chapter 8).

An alternative route, much discussed in the economics literature, is to impose an *emission tax* (or *emission charge*) on offenders. In the case of over-fishing from common-property fisheries the corresponding idea would be to impose a tax on each unit of catch (see chapter 6); and in the case of overgrazing, a tax on each animal. The effect is to reduce the offence, and the aim is to tax at such a rate that the resulting non-cooperative equilibrium outcome is optimal.

To illustrate this idea for the example at hand, suppose some central agency were to impose a tax rate T per unit of effluent discharged into the coastal waters and to pay each country a lump-sum subsidy of the amount S.[15] The idea is to set T equal to the marginal damage that any one country imposes on all others at the optimum. Call this tax rate T^*. Thus

$$T^* = (N-1)\,\mathrm{d}D(Y)/\mathrm{d}Y \quad \text{at } Y = Y^* = Ny^*.$$

Now consider the representative country, i. If each of the other countries chooses a level of pollution equal to y^*, its net benefit

[15] Which organization would actually administer the tax will depend on the example at hand. For the case we are discussing in the text, presumably it would be an agency within the regional commission of nations. For problems in the open oceans, it would presumably be an agency created under the auspices of the United Nations: something like the Deep Sea Authority. For reasoned discussions of alternative modes of controlling transfrontier pollution, see Scott (1973); OECD (1974); Walter (1975, chapter 7).

function is:

$$B(y_i) - D(y_i + (N-1)\, y^*) - T^* y_i + S. \qquad (2.6)$$

Country i chooses y_i with a view to maximizing this. Therefore it sets y_i at the level where

$$\mathrm{d}B(y_i)/\mathrm{d}y_i = \mathrm{d}D(y_i + (N-1)\, y^*)/\mathrm{d}y_i + T^*. \qquad (2.7)^{16}$$

Since by construction

$$T^* = (N-1)\, \mathrm{d}D(Y)/\mathrm{d}Y \quad \text{at } Y = Y^* = Ny^*,$$

a comparison of equations (2.5) and (2.7) tells us immediately that (2.7) has a unique solution for y_i, namely y^*! In other words, if T^* is imposed as an emission tax rate on all countries the resulting environmentally nationalistic equilibrium sustains the optimal production of pollutants.

Judged solely in terms of the final emission of effluent, standards and charges are identical as modes of implementation for this example. But their *distributional* effects are not identical, unless the tax revenue is returned to the N participants in equal amounts on a lump-sum basis; i.e. $NS = NT^*y^*$. This last is important to bear in mind. In the case of optimal *quotas* the participants retain the rent from the common-property resource. In the case of *taxes* they do not, unless the revenue is returned to them. Now, from the definition of y^*, we know that

$$B(y^*) - D(Ny^*) > B(\bar{y}) - D(N\bar{y}); \qquad (2.8)$$

that is, that each country is better off under the optimum quota than it is in the absence of any cooperation at the environmentally nationalistic equilibrium. The interesting thing though is that if instead taxes are imposed *and* if none of the revenue is returned to the participants (i.e. $S = 0$), then in general each country is worse off than it is at the unregulated environmentally nationalistic equilibrium. That is:

$$B(\bar{y}) - D(N\bar{y}) > B(y^*) - D(Ny^*) - T^*y^*. \qquad (2.9)^{17}$$

[16] To have an interesting problem we must suppose that $y_i = 0$ is not optimal for country i when each of the others chooses y^*.

[17] For a proof, see Dasgupta and Heal (1979, chapter 3). Weitzman (1976) provides a different framework for proving this point. Baumol and Oates (1975) give a simple account of this latter argument.

The point is that while in the unregulated case common property rents are to an extent dissipated through overuse, at least a part is captured by each country. On the other hand, if the optimal tax revenue is expropriated *in toto* by the central agency none of the countries retains any of the rents. Each country is worse off.

One's views of the distributional consequences of expropriated taxes on the use of what was once a common-property resource will plainly vary from case to case. On the one hand, a common-property resource is a common property, and a reliance on quotas does mean that society has given away the right to the resource users, a move which in some contexts may not be easy to defend. In an interesting article Christy (1977) has argued that one of the consequences of PL 94-265, the United States Fishery Management and Conservation Act (1976), which extends the US fishery conservation zone to 200 nautical miles from the US coastline, will be to grant domestic fishermen a gift of some 5 billion US dollars in capitalized value of fish resources. One expects that there will be a strong tendency, in the main, to grant licences only to domestic fishermen for the right to fish within Exclusive Economic Zones. There may well be an additional economic consequence, in that domestic fishermen may suffer from cost disadvantages compared to foreigners. On the other hand, a common property in question may be one from which an impoverished class of people have historically eked out an existence, and the distributional consequences of expropriated taxes on the use of this resource would be very difficult to defend. Now it is undoubtedly true that the allocation under the tax system offers a *potential* improvement on the unregulated case – in the sense that the tax expropriator can in principle compensate the common property users and make all better off in terms of income. However, this in itself is not a source of jubilation, since the compensations may not actually be paid.[18] And this brings us back to the

[18] It is this insensitivity to the distributional consequences of the oceanic enclosure movement which is the hallmark of the otherwise excellent documentation in Eckert (1979). Writing about the extent to which coastal states ought to have rights over their Exclusive Economic Zones, Professor Eckert says: 'The economic elements of this problem ... is to decide which individuals, firms, countries, other entities, or international authorities would

earlier points raised in this chapter. One of the great weaknesses of much of welfare economics has been its obsession with identifying 'distortions' and claiming in each case how awful it is to have them. The intellectual background for this obsession is yet another central theorem in economics, often called the Fundamental Theorem of Welfare Economics, which says that under certain precise conditions it is possible to sustain *any* efficient allocation by a suitable choice of lump-sum transfers (i.e. asset redistribution) and allowing competitive prices to prevail (see e.g. Scitovsky, 1951; Arrow, 1971a; Malinvaud, 1972). In particular, the economy in such a state is free of distortions. One problem (there are others) with using this theorem for policy purposes is the patent inability of governments to impose optimal lump-sum transfers. The correct question to ask them is this: what is the best set of 'distortions' to have if one must have them? Endowing private-property rights (if this is possible for the resource in question) on what was once a common-property resource (whether or not it is an international common) is not necessarily a move towards greater welfare.[19] One must look at the total

---

make "better" or "worse" allocations of ocean space among competing uses and users according to the criteria of avoiding *economic inefficiency*' (Eckert, 1979, p. 52; emphasis added). What is disturbing in the first instance is this straightjacketing of what constitutes an 'economic solution' to a problem (see chapters 3 and 5 below). In addition, it must be recognized that such an alteration in oceanic rights, and in particular the *manner* it is carried out, transgresses rights which must also be taken into account.

[19] Compare Marx's evaluation of the enclosure movement in sixteenth-century England:

> Communal property ... was a Teutonic institution which lived on under cover of feudalism. We have seen how the forcible usurpation of this, generally accompanied by the turning of arable into pasture land, begins at the end of the 15th and extends into the 16th century. But, at that time, the process was carried on by means of individual acts of violence against which legislation, for a hundred and fifty years, fought in vain.... The parliamentary form of the robbery is that of Acts for enclosures of Commons, in other words, decrees by which the landlords grant themselves the people's land as private property, decrees of expropriation of the people. (Marx, 1961, p. 724)

situation before judging the issue.[20]

The foregoing discussion on the intensity in use of common-property resources has been strictly game theoretic; that is, where rational agents are assumed to behave strategically in the light of their personal interests. In such an environment authoritarian modes of social control (whether via taxes or quotas) require the regulator to be able to monitor individual actions. This can be costly. In many circumstances, however, communities rely on preceptoral systems of social control, in which the need for monitoring actions is much less. Through education, exhortation and experiments with moral incentives, individuals are guided towards socially responsible actions even when these are not in their individual interest. In the past communities have often attempted to protect communal resources through persuasion; e.g. by an appeal to social conscience or via the development of social customs and codes of behaviour. This is still resorted to. When one refrains from depositing litter on the streets it is not necessarily because one is afraid of being caught. A strictly game theoretic analysis is nevertheless useful. It not only provides a descriptive framework for many situations, but is also often a guide to an understanding of the emergence of various forms of social control as circumstances change.[21]

[20] As we have noted earlier, the recent move on the part of nations to extend their Exclusive Economic Zones to 200 nautical miles off their coast-line is an instance of this. For attempts at estimating the redistributive effects of this move, see Anderson (1977); Bell (1978). For a vigorous defence of this enclosure movement on efficiency grounds, see Eckert (1979).

[21] See Demsetz (1967) and Alchian and Demsetz (1973) who somewhat single-mindedly observe only the emergence of *private* property rights as the mode of social control. For a survey of the 'property rights doctrine' see Furubotn and Pejovich (1972). Professor Eckert sees the UN Law of the Seas Conferences as stimulating an increase in the rate of oceanic enclosures, and he observes that: 'many who believed (and may still believe) that international procedures are the most effective mechanism for halting enclosures may be somewhat galled to learn that this mechanism actually promotes enclosures' (Eckert, 1979, p. 47). Just so; but the UN is what its members choose to make of it. There *is* something unseemly about the sight of mature nations making a scramble for oceanic resources, taking actions that vitiate the intent of conferences whose inauguration they were a party to in the first place.

2.4 Unidirectional externalities: An example of watersheds

My aim in this book is to attempt to clarify concepts, check certain beliefs by way of formal models, discuss policy measures, and above all, develop a unified underlying framework for analysing environmental problems. Although highly stylized, the symmetric version of the common-property problem which I have analysed in the previous two sections captures the essential features of many *reciprocal* environmental problems, occurring both at national and international levels. A great many environmental problems, however, are not nearly so reciprocal in character, and for analysing their central features this model simply will not do. In this section I present a prototype model of unidirectional externality and see what the main issues are.

Examples of unidirectional externalities abound. From the traditional example of the factory smoke damaging the neighbourhood laundry, to coastal developments damaging nearby wetlands, unidirectional externalities are at the heart of a great many environmental problems. At the international level, acid rains in Sweden containing sulphur carried by the wind from north-west Europe, most especially the United Kingdom, is an example that has attracted considerable attention.

Unidirectional externalities are just that: unidirectional – where a given agent (or a set of agents) imposes an externality on another (or others). Analytically this is all that distinguishes unidirectional externalities from the reciprocal externalities that are generated in situations involving the use of common property resources, where *each* agent imposes externalities on all others. However, it is not solely the *physical* circumstances in a given social situation involving unidirectional externalities that determine who is the inflictor of the externality and who is the recipient; that is, the direction of the externality. In fact it is a combination of the physical circumstances *and* the legal system – in particular the assigment of property rights – that determines this. Thus, for example, if a pulp and paper mill has the legal right to pollute a river, then it is the fishing industry which is harmed by the mill's exercise of this right. Indeed, that is why in common parlance one would talk in this case of the damages inflicted by the mill on the fisherman and why, in any negotiation under such property rights, the aim would be to find a mutually acceptable payment by the fishing industry to the mill for a reduction in pollution. In a classic article Coase (1960) argued the direction of the externality depends on property rights. For suppose instead that the fishing industry had the legal right to an unpolluted river. In this case, of course, it is the pulp and paper mill that is harmed by the fisherman's exercise of their right. Any negotiation between the parties under such property rights would be concerned with locating a mutually acceptable payment by the mill to the fishing industry for allowing the mill to pollute. Quite clearly, intermediate cases can also be considered.

The ecological literature, developed extensively in recent years, suggests that among the most pervasive examples of such uni-directional externalities are those that are found in processes that result in the degradation of arable land. Since in addition, inter-temporal considerations are of the essence in any analysis of soil degradation, we shall conduct our discussion of such externalities by way of a simple model of a watershed consisting of an area of forest cover and a region of lowlands.

In discussing land usage, environmentalists have, rightly, discussed changes in both the *extent* and *quality* of arable and grazing land. Thus, for example, land reclamation by means of drainage or by means of extensive irrigation schemes augments the amount of cultivable land. However, understandably perhaps, environmentalists have in recent years emphasized the extent to which prime agricultural land has been *withdrawn* for alternative use, such as urban centres and roadways.[22] It is important to emphasize that such withdrawal, even when it is prime agricultural land which is withdrawn, is *in itself* no cause for alarm. Like most other resources, land has alternative uses; and a case has to be made that the diversion of cultivable land to other uses, taking all costs and benefits into account, is socially damaging. In many instances it may well have been the right move to site urban centres on what

[22] Thus, for example, the 1979 OECD State of the Environment report estimates that during the decade of the 1960s more than 7 per cent of Japan's agricultural land was withdrawn from such use and that in Europe the proportion ranged from 1.5 per cent in Norway to about 4.5 per cent in the Netherlands. Environmentalists often find these sorts of statistics terrifying.

was previously prime agricultural land.[23] The environmental literature very often does not recognize this possibility. Since there are no pervasive externalities involved in the economic processes involving the withdrawal of land from agricultural use we ignore the issue of the extent of agricultural land and concentrate instead on its quality and the variables that affect it.

Soil 'degradation', which is synonymous with loss in soil fertility (or productivity), is a generic term. Environmentalists find it convenient to distinguish between, on the one hand, a reduction in soil nutrients and humus and, on the other, the erosion of soil (i.e. a loss of soil) by wind and water. To be sure, characteristics vary from place to place; but under 'normal' circumstances soil productivity, in both these senses, is regenerated under natural processes. Thus, for example, Ehrlich *et al.* (1977) remark that: 'The practical application of the detailed study of soils is to discover both the potential and the limitations of different soil types for the production of vegetation, and the procedures appropriate to using each type as a permanent or renewable resource rather than as a "mine" to be exhausted and abandoned' (Ehrlich *et al.*, 1977, p. 257). But in many locations the natural rate of regeneration is extremely slow and there may not be any means by which artificial augmentation can be made to take place. Thus, for example, the depletion of soil nutrients can quite obviously be countered by the use of fertilizers, but in the drylands a loss in top soil cannot be made good.[24] Moreover, under natural conditions of vegetation cover it may take anything between 100 to 500 years for the formation of 1 cm of top soil. Indeed, some experts fear that as much as one-third of the world's cropland will be destroyed in the next 20 years if current rates of land degradation continue (see United Nations, 1978). Soil erosion, leading to desertification, is therefore regarded as a major environmental problem today.[25]

[23] It is entirely possible, though, that in many instances urban developments have been made at wrong sites. As a political pressure group developers and contractors are often very powerful.

[24] In river valleys, on the other hand, the alluvial topsoil is augmented annually by silt brought by the river from the mountain slopes.

[25] The drylands, which include some of the most important rangelands and wheat-growing areas, are particularly vulnerable. For this reason the 1978

The causes of soil erosion are many, chief among which are overgrazing, deforestation (e.g. collection of firewood and slash-and-burn agricultural practices) and the clearance of steep slopes for cultivation. The phenomenon of overgrazing in common-property grasslands is captured in my formal model of section 2.2; consequently I ignore it here. A potent example of unidirectional externalities – our concern here – is provided instead by deforestation in a watershed affecting soil productivity of the lowlands.[26]

Watersheds are pretty self-contained ecological systems. That is why it is possible to have integrated watershed development projects. The most critical sector of a watershed is forest cover. The forest not only offers its direct yield to the rural population, it maintains ecological balance and water regime, prevents floods and droughts, wind and water erosion and sedimentation. The watershed lowlands are typically used for the production of staple food, and are usually flat plains of alluvial and heavy soil. (For a technical discussion of watersheds, see for example Gil, 1979.)

I am concerned with soil productivity of the lowlands. I denote the productivity level by Q, and write Q_t as the productivity at date t. I wish first to provide a broad category of factors that influence the rate at which productivity changes over time. To simplify the exposition I imagine precisely two sets of agents, one of which, the *farmers*, cultivate the lowlands and the other, the *foresters*, whose activities affect the productivity of the lowlands. We symbolize by A_t the totality of actions that the cultivators undertake on the soil at date t. A_t is typically a *vector* of actions, and it includes the various characteristics of the mode of agri-

---

United Nations Conference on Desertification laid special attention on this. It is thought that some 80 million people are immediately threatened by loss in productivity due to desertification. It is a problem faced by over 60 countries – countries in Africa's Sahelian and Sudanian zones, parts of North Africa, the Mediterranean and the Middle East being particularly vulnerable (see Allen, 1980, chapter 2). For country studies, see Bali and Kanwar (1977) and Das (1977).

[26] Other examples are discharges upstream affecting the quality of irrigation water downstream; and SO_2 emission in one region causing acid rains – and therefore an alteration in soil fertility – in another. Both these are known to occur at the international level as well, as is the example in the text.

culture practised by the cultivators. For example, A_t will include the characteristics and the quantities of fertilizers, herbicides and pesticides that are used at t, the quality of irrigation undertaken, etc. Next, we denote by E_t the set of actions that the foresters pursue at t. For our example, the most important component of E_t is the rate at which deforestation is undertaken. However, the rate of soil degradation in the lowlands is affected not so much by the *current* rate of deforestation as much as by the *state* of vegetation – i.e. soil cover – at the date in question. This state we denote by S_t. It is an index of the soil cover in the watershed forest. It is determined, among other things, by past values of E. That is, we suppose that the rate of change in soil cover is a function of the rate of deforestation. This function we write as $F(E)$ and so we have a dynamic condition:

$$dS_t/dt = F(E_t). \qquad (2.10)^{27}$$

If $t = 0$ is the date at which the problem is being analysed, clearly S_0 is a given number, having been determined by past values of E_t. S_0 is an *initial condition.*

We return to the productivity index of the lowlands. In particular, we recognize that soil management is shot through with uncertainty, in that a great deal of soil chemistry is only imperfectly understood. To capture this we let θ_t denote a random variable – a parameter whose value is unknown. It is most usual to suppose that θ_t is driven by a stochastic process whose underlying parameters are not known with certainty. We shall come back to this interpretation, but for the moment we should note that we may represent the evolution of land productivity Q_t by means of a function H, where

$$dQ_t/dt = H(A_t, Q_t, E_t, S_t, \theta_t) \qquad (2.11)$$

The soil productivity level at $t = 0$, Q_0, is presumably also an initial condition. Thus equation (2.11) says that the rate of change in soil productivity is a function of the current actions of the

[27] We are keeping things simple here by letting F be solely a function of E_t. In particular, we have assumed that F does not contain a random parameter. As the reader will notice subsequently, this is no loss of generality for the purpose at hand.

farmers and the foresters, A_t and E_t, the current productivity level Q_t, the current state of soil cover, S_t, and the random factor θ_t.[28]

Equations (2.10) and (2.11) represent the dynamics of the watershed in question. The *state variables* of the system are S_t and Q_t. The variables that can be controlled directly are A_t and E_t. Of these, A_t is chosen by the farmers and E_t by the foresters. The sample path of the random variable, θ_t, is 'chosen' by Mother Nature. By definition this 'choice' is not known in advance, and indeed, the two parties may hold different views regarding the parameters representing the underlying stochastic process driving θ_t. As I remarked in chapter 1, such differences of opinion lie at the heart of much controversy over the choice of environmental policy. It should also be clear that expenditure on research and development enables one to obtain information about the random variable. I shall discuss this latter issue at some length in chapter 4.

It will be noted that the ecological system described by equations (2.10) and (2.11) is a partially uncoupled one. For neither Q_t nor A_t enters the differential equation (2.10) representing the dynamics of the state of soil cover, while both E_t and S_t enter the differential equation (2.11) representing the dynamics of land productivity.[29] It is this asymmetry which reflects itself in the unidirectional nature of the externality we now proceed to study.

Let us suppose that the net benefits (or net profits) enjoyed by the cultivators at time t is determined by Q_t and A_t. Likewise suppose that the net benefits of the foresters at t are determined by S_t and E_t. But since *future* productivity, Q, is influenced by E_t, the flow of future benefits to the cultivators is a function not

[28] We shall not discuss possible functional forms of H. But we should mention that H will typically depend more crucially on S_t than on E_t, and that, as a first approximation, may even be independent of E_t. The so-called Universal Soil Loss Equation used by agriculturalists is related to equation (2.11). It relates annual soil loss per hectare to factors affecting it by means of the product relation: $A = RK(LS)\,CP$, where R is rainfall factor, K a soil factor, LS a length and slope factor, C a cropping factor and P a farming practice factor (see for example Gil, 1979, p. 34).

[29] It is in this sense that forests are the key sector of a watershed. It resembles basic sectors in multi-sector planning models (see for example Blitzer *et al.*, 1975).

only of what they do but also of what the foresters do. The reverse is not the case and it is in this sense that the externality that is generated is unidirectional. The point is that in the absence of any negotiations leading to binding agreements, future benefits to the cultivators are directly affected by present and future actions – here E_t – over which the cultivators have no control. Herein lies the externality. For presumably in choosing the time path of E_t the foresters take no cognizance of the effect of their action on the welfare of the cultivators.

The assignment of property rights, an issue we highlighted earlier, is relevant now. If the foresters have the legal right to deforest their land at any rate they choose, then it is the cultivators who are harmed by the foresters' exercise of this right. The presumption here is that in the absence of a binding agreement among the parties there will be greater deforestation than is socially desirable. Typically, the assignment of property rights takes this form. Then again, in many parts of the globe forest tracts under government jurisdiction are insufficiently monitored. 'Unauthorised' logging is a common occurrence. Furthermore, if forest lands are common property, then as we have already noted, downland farmers will be vulnerable to excessive deforestation. (There are ranges in the foothills of the Himalayas that are today devoid of trees.) It is for such reasons that in the environmental literature fear is expressed over excessive deforestation and the erosion of soil cover, rather than insufficient deforestation. However, it has been noted that if property rights take other forms matters are quite different. Suppose that the cultivators have well-defined rights against the flooding and siltation that would arise from deforestation. Then it is the foresters who are damaged by the cultivators' exercise of their rights, and in the absence of a binding agreement among the parties there may well be insufficient deforestation.

Often in such cases property rights are ill-defined and negotiations are costly. Moreover, the bargaining powers of the various parties are often uneven. It is for such reasons that it is argued by many that governments ought not only to supply public goods (such as soil and forest research), but ought also to engage in the coordination of the activities of the various parties. Integrated watershed development plans are an instance of this.

2.5 Resource exploitation and the distribution of income

The ownership pattern of natural resources affects the distribution of income and thereby the pattern of demand. This in turn influences the pace and direction of resource exploitation. To be sure the chain is a most complex one and is not wholly unidirectional; also the links vary greatly from case to case. Curiously enough, while this has not gone unnoticed in the recent environmental literature, not much has been done by way of analysing such influences in the context of specific resources.

Property is a system of authority established by government. It is a set of rights to control assets. I have noted earlier how the assignment of property rights affects the bargaining powers of parties and thereby the distribution of income and wealth. But reallocations of property rights can, and unhappily often do, occur by fraud, theft and on occasion violent robbery. The history of the reallocations of water rights in semi-arid regions, to take only one example, it littered with such battles.

Rights on natural resources often assume a somewhat nebulous form. As I noted in chapter 1, in certain cases it is the physical characteristics of the resource which are responsible for this. But by no means always. Custom can play its part and often the notion of *private* rights on certain types of resources may be alien to a community. Thus, for example, in the medieval manorial economy of England domestic animals were privately owned but grazing land was common property. For nomadic communities such as those in northern Sahel, grazing land in practice cannot but be common property. For them, as for forest-dwelling communities such as some of the Adivasis of India or the Indians of the Amazonian Basin, rights to a natural resource often are only *historical*. And historical rights, it would appear, are a prey to violation. Landlords and ranchers have been known to exercise such violence (by eviction and on occasion massacre of peasants); so have governments (as during slum clearance movements).

The conversion of agricultural and forest land into ranches in Latin America is a case that has attracted much attention in recent years (see for example Barraclough, 1977; Feder, 1977, 1979). Vast tracts of land that are at least a potential source of staple crops have been diverted to the rearing of cattle for beef exports that provide an input for fast-food chains. It is the deforestation of the Amazon Basin accompanying this territorial expansion which has attracted the attention of environmentalists. But ecological considerations apart, the phenomenon provides a good illustration of the influence of the (international) distribution of income on the pace and pattern of resource exploitation.

Now it might first be argued that if domestic consumption of high-grade protein is low, there is a case for engaging in projects that would increase the production of the source of such protein. The problem is that increased production does not mean that the population this production may originally have been aimed at gets it. In the case of beef-cattle production the problem has taken on an acute complexion because of the competing demand for beef products in rich nations. Private producers quite naturally seek the most (commercially) profitable outlet which, in this case, happens to be exports. So much so that over the past 15 years per capita consumption of beef would appear to have actually *fallen* in a number of these countries (see Feder, 1979). The phenomenon has generated much international debate particularly because private investment in the expansion of this specific agricultural business has been supported by domestic governments (in the form of tax concessions and the provision of infrastructure) and loans from international agencies. This massive expansion of beef-cattle production (total investment over the past 15 years amounting to over 10 billion US dollars according to some estimates) has presumably been at the expense of investment in the increased production of staple crops which continue to be imported in much of Central America. All this *in itself* does not imply that something is dreadfully wrong. For one might be inclined to argue that profits from these enterprises will be reinvested domestically in such a manner that *somehow* at *some* time benefits will filter to the rural poor. Unhappily there is nothing inevitable about such matters. For one thing large tracts of land (amounting to some 25 million hectares) have been sold to foreign firms. For another, individual holdings are large (in some instances ranches are over 1 million hectares in size). Repatriation of profits and a concentration of land ownership together suggest that the impoverishment of the rural poor may persist for a long while. The return from investment in beef-cattle production, when looked at from the point of view of the rural poor, would appear to be disastrously low.

3 Goals, Constraints and Accounting Prices

3.1 The use of accounting prices

A good way to conduct an *exercise* in planning is to agree on objectives, identify the constraints the organization is subject to, and then choose that option which is deemed best in the light of the objectives. In such a planning context the *shadow* (or *accounting*) price of a resource can under certain conditions be thought of as the increase in the maximum value of the planner's objective function if the organization were endowed with an extra unit of the resource (see appendix, section 3A.1). In this book I shall mostly think of the organization in question as an economy, and the planner's objectives as the *social* goals he is aiming to accommodate. The great merit in introducing shadow prices is that they often can be used by the planner to implement the optimum plan in a decentralized environment. I begin by illustrating this claim by an example very similar to the one introduced in section 2.2.

A particular type of effluent is a by-product of the production activity of a given industry. We assume that currently the industry is not charged for the environmental damage that is caused by the residuals (or wastes) that are discharged by it: i.e. the industry is free to pollute. To keep the example as simple as possible we continue to assume, as in section 3.3, that the emission–output ratio is unalterable and that wastes, once discharged, are prohibitively costly to neutralize.[1] Nevertheless, since the residuals are a by-product of production the industry can control the level of

[1] In chapter 8 both these assumptions will be relaxed in a model of pollution control.

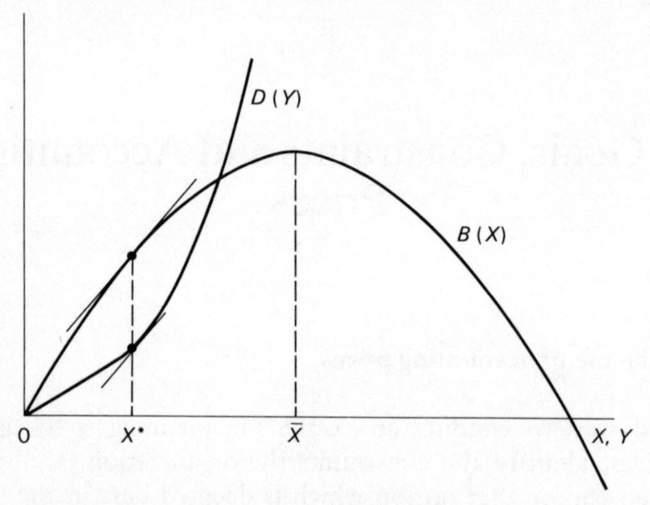

Figure 3.1

emission by a choice of output level. Let $B(X)$ be the industrial profit level when X is the quantity of waste emission;[2] $B(X)$ is drawn in figure 3.1. Since it is a profit function it may be taken that it declines at large output levels. The key assumption made, though, is that *marginal* net profit is a declining function of output. As figure 3.1 displays, $\bar{X}$ is the current level of emission, the point at which industry profit is maximized.

If Y is the level of waste *absorbed* by the environment from this industry, $D(Y)$ is the social damage caused. This too is drawn in figure 3.1, where it is assumed that $D(Y)$ increases with Y at an increasing rate. For simplicity of exposition we take it that the social objective function is $B(X)-D(Y)$ (see figure 3.2). We assume this simply because we are focusing on the damages caused by pollutants, and any further consideration will require of us to introduce additional notation. But in most cases industrial profits minus pollution damages will not be a good approximation for the measure of social benefits. When it is not one may introduce a further function, say $\Pi(X)$, to account for these additional considerations, and express social objectives by way of the function

[2] As in the model studied in section 2.2 we have so chosen the units that the emission–output ratio is unity, therefore, X denotes the industry output level as well.

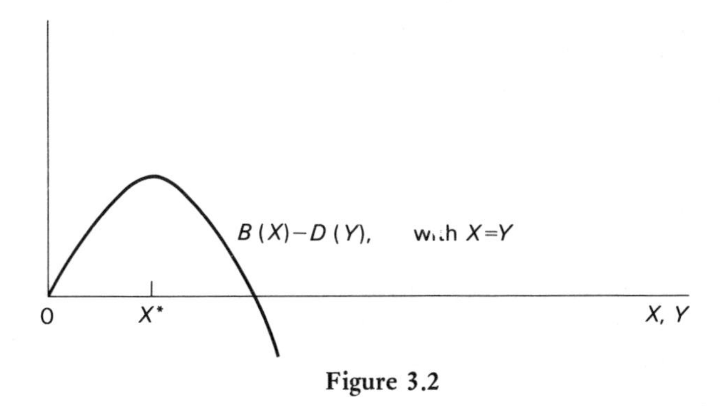

Figure 3.2

$B(X) + \Pi(X) - D(Y)$. For expositional ease we are assuming that $\Pi(X) = 0$.

Since X is the waste discharged and Y the amount absorbed it must, for our model, be the case that $X = Y$. Thus our prototype planning problem is to:

$$\left.\begin{array}{l}\text{choose } X,\ Y(\geqslant 0) \text{ so as to} \\ \text{maximize } B(X) - D(Y),\end{array}\right\} \qquad (3.1)$$
$$\text{subject to the constraint } X = Y.$$

In problem (3.1), the amount discharged, X, has been distinguished from the amount absorbed, Y, advisedly. The *constraint* in the planning exercise, that $X = Y$, yields the accounting price of pollutants, as we shall presently confirm (see also appendix).

The solution of problem (3.1) is trivial to find diagrammatically. In figure 3.1 I have denoted the *optimum* level of discharge as X^*, the unique solution of the social cost–benefit rule

$$B'(X) = D'(Y). \qquad (3.2)$$

As was noted in the common-property example in chapter 2, there are two routes that the planner can follow in order to ensure that X^* is the effluent level. One is the imposition of a quota. Since $B(X)$ is an increasing function of X in the interval $(0, X^*)$ – see figure 3.1 – the industry will choose X^* if this is the quota.

The other involves the use of an effluent tax (or charge). Let

$$t = B'(X^*) = D'(X^*)$$

be imposed as a unit tax on discharge. Thus the unit charge equals the level of marginal social damage at the optimum emission rate.

In the presence of such a tax the industry's profit function reads as $B(X) - tX$. It follows that profit, net of tax, is maximized at the point where

$$B'(X) = t. \tag{3.3}$$

The industry will patently choose X^*, the socially desired level.

The link between optimal taxes and accounting prices can be drawn out by this example. The optimum tax on a resource ought to be viewed as the difference between its shadow price and its 'market' price. In the absence of a tax the industry is free to pollute, and consequently pollutes too much ($X^* < \bar{X}$). The tax t is therefore the accounting price of the effluent. It is the gain in the maximum value of $B(X) - D(Y)$ if the constraint, $X = Y$, in the planning problem (3.1) is relaxed by a unit (see appendix).

Whether a government ought to try and use accounting prices or impose quantity controls (e.g. quotas) in implementing plans depends on a wide variety of matters. I have noted some of these matters in chapter 2, and in chapters 4 and 8 I will analyse yet others (see also chapter 3, appendix). Governments typically rely on a mixture of both, sometimes deliberately, but most often as a result of a series of *ad hoc* measures. There are production sectors (for example those experiencing pervasive economies of scale) where it would not do to rely exclusively on accounting prices. But this does not mean that accounting prices as a whole must be thrown overboard. In general plans can (and in practice should) be implemented by a judicious mixture of the two. (For further discussions on this, see Portes, 1971 and Weitzman, 1970.)

3.2 Multiple objectives and partial orderings

It is clear that the accounting price of a commodity or resource depends in general both on the social objectives and the constraints that are incorporated in the planning exercise. Indeed, in the example a knowledge of the optimum level X^* is a prerequisite for knowing what the accounting price is (since $t = D'(X^*)$). Now this is distinctly odd. What is the point of relying on accounting prices for implementing an optimal plan if one needs to know the optimum plan in order to calculate the accounting prices?[3] There are various answers to this, some of which I shall note in the following chapter when I come to discuss uncertainty. For my purposes here though the right question to ask is how *sensitive* accounting prices are likely to be to the specification of the planning exercise. It has in fact been argued that there are many circumstances where it is possible for the planner to estimate (albeit approximately) the accounting prices of goods and services in the absence of a precise knowledge of what the optimum plan looks like.[4] In such circumstances the role of accounting prices in implementing optimal plans acquires credence. However, what one must avoid in estimating shadow prices is the temptation towards excessive precision. Not only are the constraints a planning model is characterized by subject to grave uncertainties, social goals (or objectives) are usually wide-ranging and in many cases difficult (arguably impossible) to quantify. Take, for example, a sample of the many social objectives that are often espoused: national income per head must be increased; the degree of inequality in income and wealth (in the light of some summary measure, say) needs to be reduced; the level of unemployment ought to be lessened; the rate of inflation has to be pruned; the nation's resources must be conserved; the citizen's fundamental rights (suitably defined) must not be encroached upon; longevity of the population needs to be raised; the 'basic needs' of the citizens must be met within T years; and so on.

Some of these goals are, at least approximately, quantifiable, but not all. They are most often *non-basic*, in the sense that they are implied by a combination of some other goals (often only implicitly held) and contingent facts – e.g. in any discussion which attempts to establish the evils of high inflation rates. Moreover, they are usually *non-compulsive*, in that when in conflict *each* of the social goals is usually given some weight: no single

[3] For a vigorous critique of the use of accounting prices along these lines, see Rudra (1973).

[4] There is an enormous literature on this now. Little and Mirrlees (1969, 1974) and UNIDO (1972, 1978) present theoretical arguments and some applications. Little and Scott (1976) and Scott *et al.* (1976) contain a number of case studies in which accounting prices are estimated and then used to evaluate investment projects.

objective overrides all others.[5] In those cases where it is possible to quantify non-compulsive objectives by indices (e.g. net national income, the degree of inequality in income etc.) it behoves one to attempt to quantify the social weights that ought to be attached to them.[6] Such weights are designed to reflect the trade-off between social indices.[7] What goes by the name of *social cost–benefit analysis* is really an attempt to evaluate alternative options in terms of their contributions to each of the social goals. If the social weights are firmly specified the analyst is in effect in possession of a well-defined objective function – the weighted sum of the social indices.[8] In this case he can rank all options unambiguously. But it is only an analyst blessed with Calvinistic moral certainty who will work with precise weights. The problem though is that if they are not firmly specified not all options *can* be ranked. Option A may give a boost to index α and a kick to index β; but reverse for option B. In the absence of a precise specification of the social weight attached to α relative to β the planner (or social cost–benefit analyst) cannot necessarily rank A and B. However, just as cock-sureness is to be avoided, so is sheer witlessness. The fact that social weights are difficult to specify does not mean that the analyst cannot restrict himself to a range of values within which the weights may reasonably be thought to lie. But this implies that the planner can rank options only *partially*; that is, while some options can be ranked, not all can. In the world as we know it, he cannot surely be expected to do better than that.

[5] The terms 'basic' and 'non-basic'; 'compulsive' and 'non-compulsive' are used in Sen (1970) to classify *value judgements.*

[6] By our definition a *compulsive* goal is one which has an overriding weight over others. A lexicographic ranking of social goals would have this characteristic. No trade offs are allowed in such a case.

[7] See UNIDO (1972); Chenery *et al.* (1974). We shall discuss this further in chapter 5.

[8] These weights are not necessarily independent of the numerical values of the social indices. Thus, for a given level of income per head it may typically be judged that the weight attached to an increase in the degree of equality should be higher when the degree of inequality is 'high' than when it is 'low'. In the example considered in the previous section the social weight (relative to profits) attached to a *marginal* increase in wastes X is $-D'(X)$ (<0), and this by assumption increases with the quantity of waste.

To illustrate this suppose that the planner in our earlier example is loath to be specific about the social objective function, but thinks it most reasonable that it is of the form $B(X) - \gamma D(X)$, where γ is some number in the range $[\gamma_1, \gamma_2]$ with $\gamma_1 > 0$. What he does not wish to commit himself to is a precise value of γ within this range. Nor does he wish to appeal to the language of probability theory, because the issue here is not of not knowing facts precisely (e.g. not knowing the physiological effects of the effluent) but rather not being able to *evaluate* the social damage caused by the waste discharge.[9]

For each admissible value of γ, there is an optimum effluent level $X^*(\gamma)$ given by the cost-benefit rule.

$$B'(X) = \gamma D'(X). \tag{3.4}$$

From equation (3.4) we may conclude that $X^*(\gamma)$ is a decreasing function of γ - precisely what one would expect. In this situation the planner knows only that the optimum discharge level lies between $X^*(\gamma_2)$ and $X^*(\gamma_1)$ but cannot be more precise than that. Moreover, if $t(\gamma) \equiv D'(X^*(\gamma))$, then he knows that the accounting charge on the effluent lies in the range $[t(\gamma_1), t(\gamma_2)]$; nothing more.

The fact that the ranking is only partial does not, of course mean that an option will not be chosen (even the choice to do nothing is a choice); simply that the choice will not be defended on the ground that it is the best in the light of well-defined objectives. Indeed, it is difficult to see how we may expect a full explanation from the chooser under such circumstances; for the

[9] At an extreme is the valuation of life. Calabresi and Bobbitt (1978) present a compelling account of how societies not only avoid ranking options that have to do with who shall live (e.g. which patient gets the kidney machine) but also how they actually avoid consciously choosing among such options. Problems of a related (though different) nature arise when assessing the desirability of expenditures on reducing health hazards (e.g. from nuclear radiation). Black and Niehaus (1980) and Niehaus (1980), in their discussion of measures for increasing the safety of technologies that involve low-risk/high-damage consequences, suggest cost effectiveness as a guide to decision-making. This involves the estimation of expenditure which will save one 'equivalent death'. Though a grotesque thought, this no doubt forms part of the kinds of information one needs when deciding on such issues.

canons of rational choice do not dictate that choice must be based on a *complete* ranking of feasible options. They would seem to dictate though that there should be no discarded option which is ranked above the chosen one.[10] Herein lies the value of conducting social cost–benefit analysis even when options are only partially ordered. Such analyses facilitate choice. They also help expose the lip-service that is often paid by political leaderships to professed social objectives. In fact social critics and commentators inevitably conduct, albeit implicitly, some form of social cost–benefit analysis of options actually chosen by governments and compare them to those that have been discarded. How else is the critic to expose missed opportunities? The procedures for conducting social cost–benefit analysis that have been advocated in recent years have been designed with a view to formalizing the manner in which this may simply and consistently be done.

I have emphasized the difficulties that are often involved in the evaluation of the various impacts of different policies for good reason. Nothing can bring greater disrepute to applied welfare economic theory than over-stretching its use, claiming precision when it is not warranted. All but the simplest objective functions used in planning exercises are much too opaque, in that one cannot tell without a good deal of computations what are the implications of one functional form as compared to another. Maintaining flexibility in the formulation of planning models is therefore essential. It is useful to conduct sensitivity analysis; that is, varying the parameters characterizing the planning model and then calculating what their implications are.

The approach to social cost–benefit analysis being advocated here is vastly broader in scope than is usually to be found in the more technically oriented parts of the environmental literature. The aim of social cost–benefit analysis, as we understand it, is to assess the impact of policies in the light of the various social goals that are considered worthy of pursuit. Recognition that there are multiple objectives is of the first importance. This multiplicity arises, as we have already noted, not only because of the claims of different generations in the future, but also because the claims

[10] Buridan's ass, it will be recalled, violated this canon and thereby experienced an unfortunate consequence.

of contemporaries need to be treated differently (because, say, of income and asset differences), because of differing employment opportunities offered by different policies, and in the case of environmental issues because species may be thought worth preserving for their own sake; and so on. There is much that has been written, most especially in the literature on development planning, on how one might attempt to evaluate these impacts (see e.g. Little and Mirrlees, 1974 and UNIDO, 1972). These matters will be discussed in chapter 5. When we talk of social benefits or social costs (or damages) associated with a policy I shall take it that they reflect its impact on an aggregate of multiple objectives, recognizing all the while that a planner will rarely ever have a single aggregate at his disposal, so that ultimately choice will of necessity be based on an incomplete ranking of options. It cannot be emphasized strongly enough that the approach advocated here is *not* based on some version of consumers' (or producers') 'willingness-to-pay' or some variant of 'compensation tests' (see chapters 4 and 5).

3.3 Objectives and constraints

Pollution damages are often difficult to evaluate. But not always. For example, the corrosion of metals by exposure to sulphur dioxide (SO_2) can be evaluated in terms of maintenance and replacement costs; the eutrophication of lakes by loss in fish stocks, and so on. To be sure, there may be considerable uncertainty about the effects of SO_2 on buildings and plants, and likewise for losses in fish stocks. But that is a different matter. However, as I have remarked earlier, deep conceptual and moral difficulties arise in the *evaluation* of the human health effects of environmental pollution. Quite understandably one is loath to represent these effects by explicit damage functions.

One approach which seemingly enables one to avoid having to think of damage functions is to set *environmental standards* which society is to maintain. In chapter 8 we shall note that legislators often follow this route (see the formulations (8.8) and (8.9) in chapter 8). In the context of our previous example this route may be described as follows: it is recognized that in the absence of any intervention the industry will pollute at the level $\bar{X}$. This is clearly excessive. Now introduce a legislation that sets an upper bound on the pollution level, say $\tilde{X}$ ($<\bar{X}$). The legislators know that the industry will choose X with a view to maximizing $B(X)$ subject to the constraint $X \leqslant \tilde{X}$. From figure 3.1 it is clear that it will choose $\tilde{X}$.

It should be recognized at once that there is a difference between standards acting as *constraints* in a planning model (as is the case above) and standards (or quotas) acting as a regulatory device for *implementing* an optimal plan (as was the case discussed in the previous section when we distinguished pollution charges from pollution quotas). Standards as constraints (e.g. water quality or ambient air standards) in a planning model reflect social objectives – the standard in question being a level of pollution which, it is felt, it would be intolerable to exceed. Standards as a regulatory device (i.e. emission or effluent standards) are, on the other hand, not the goals themselves. They are an instrument for attaining social goals.

It should also be recognized that standards as constraints are formally identical to a very special form of social damage functions; one which imputes no damages for emissions (or concentrations) below the level specified and a sharp increase in damages at that level.[11] Indeed, the imposition of such constraints is often justified on the grounds that environmental damages take this form when threshold effects are important (see chapter 8). However, standards as constraints *can* have another rationale, namely as a compulsive social goal – an articulation of the view that beyond a certain level of pollution society must not entertain any tradeoff. Such a position could be derived from, say, some rights-based doctrine. Using torture as an analogy it has, for example, been argued by Sen (1982) that future generations may have a *right* to a 'clean' environment, a right which has nothing to

[11] Here I am not distinguishing between emission and concentration levels because I am abstracting from time, and so cannot distinguish between flows and stocks. Since in most cases it is the concentration level which affects welfare, standards are often imposed on them. Emission standards are also imposed, but their rationale would appear to be based on instrumental grounds; see chapter 8.

do with their *welfare* claims. For our purposes here the point is not so much whether this is a compelling argument; merely that if rights to a 'clean' environment (suitably defined) are *inviolable*, then the imposition of constraints on emission and concentration levels is the way to articulate such rights.[12]

Now it can be argued that there is no point in distinguishing between objectives and constraints. The theory of optimum control assures us that, provided certain technical conditions are satisfied, every constraint in a planning problem has an associated shadow (or accounting) price – the price of violating the constraint (see Theorem 1, appendix). Therefore, so the argument goes, one may as well drop the constraint and add the cost of violating the constraint directly to the objective function in the planning model. The solution will be the same. To illustrate this, note that in the example studied earlier there is an accounting price associated with the constraint $X \leqslant \tilde{X}$, say μ. Then instead of imposing the constraint on the industry by way of an environmental standard one could impose an emission tax rate μ on the industry. In this case the industry will maximize $B(X) - \mu X$ and will find that $\tilde{X}$ is its optimal choice. But while in terms of the *outcome* achieved these two procedures are identical, their interpretations are quite different. It would be wrong to claim that $B(X) - \mu X$ is the social objective function. One needs only to look at the contours of the function $B(X) - \mu X$ and compare them to the contours of $B(X)$ in the region $X \leqslant \tilde{X}$ to see that the interpretations are quite different.

3.4 Social cost-benefit analysis as an iteration

In the previous two sections we have discussed various modes for implementing an optimal plan. We now come to the question of locating an optimal plan and consider the role of social cost-benefit analysis as a tactical device designed to assess the worthwhileness of *moves* on the part of the economy in question.[13] The economy may, to begin with, be far away from the optimum.

[12] Nozick (1974) contains an excellent discussion of rights as constraints.

[13] See UNIDO (1972, Part III); Dasgupta (1978); Hammond (1980); Blitzer *et al.* (1981); Dreze (1981).

In particular, the planner may not know what the optimal plan is. In this situation a feasible policy is contemplated. The question is whether the policy is worth undertaking in the light of the social objectives. The method invoked for assessing the worthwhileness of the policy is social cost–benefit analysis, and the hope is that a sequence of worthwhile moves will lead the economy nearer the optimum and in the limit to the optimum. In what follows I illustrate this conception, as well as its limitations, by the first example studied in this chapter.

Consider once again figures 3.1 and 3.2. For simplicity of exposition suppose that the industry is in the public sector. Suppose now that the industry currently pollutes at the level $\bar{X}$ $(= \bar{Y})$. We may now view a marginal project in this industry as a small change in the level of pollution ΔX $(= \Delta Y)$ associated with a corresponding change in its production activity. It is as though the project consists of an 'input', ΔY, and an 'output' ΔX, with $\Delta X = \Delta Y$. If $\Delta X > 0$ the project consists of an increase in production; the reverse if $\Delta X < 0$. Since marginal net social benefit is $B'(X) - D'(Y)$, the social value of the project is approximately,

$$B'(X)\,\Delta X - D'(Y)\,\Delta Y \qquad \left.\begin{array}{r}(\text{with } X = Y \text{ and}\\ \Delta X = \Delta Y)\end{array}\right\} \tag{3.5}$$

and the cost–benefit analyst is concerned with its sign: that is, accept a project if expression (3.5) is positive and reject it if it is negative. From figure 3.1 it is immediate that $B'(\bar{X}) - D'(\bar{X}) < 0$; thus, accept only if the 'project' consists of a contraction. But a glance at figure 3.2 tells us also that the cost–benefit rule obtained from expression (3.5), if pursued, will ensure that projects characterized by $\Delta X < 0$ will get chosen so long as $X > X^*$.[14]

The reverse argument comes into play if, by chance, the economy initiates at a pollution level less than X^*. At any $X < X^*$

[14] It may immediately be objected to that often enough immediate reduction in concentration levels cannot be attained because of irreversibilities. In this case the irreversibilities must be included in the planning model – the fact that the amelioration of the environment takes time. In chapters 8 and 10 these features will be included. Their inclusion will not affect the argument being offered in the text.

expression (3.5) is positive if and only if $\Delta X > 0$, but

$$B'(X^*) - D'(X^*) = 0.$$

Thus, expression (3.5) is nil at $X = X^*$. No further project ought therefore to be undertaken once the economy is at X^*.

The procedure outlined above for conducting cost–benefit analysis is what is often called the 'gradient process' (or the 'hill climbing' method) for reaching the optimum. The terminology is obvious for our example. The net benefit function, $B(X) - D(X)$, is single-peaked. The criterion obtained from expression (3.5) ensures that moves in accordance with it has the economy climbing up the hill.[15]

I have noted the relationship between the approaches to social cost–benefit analysis outlined in this section and in section 3.1. In fact there is a close relationship between the accounting prices in them as well. Earlier it was observed that one way to achieve the optimal pollution level X^* $(= Y^*)$ is to impose an accounting charge on the industry and let the industry choose the level of pollution. In equation (3.3) this charge was seen to equal $B'(X^*)$, which in turn equals $D'(Y^*)$: that is, at the optimum a marginal project $(\Delta X, \Delta Y)$ is valued at the pair of accounting prices $(B'(X^*), -D'(Y^*))$. What expression (3.5) says is that for the example at hand this accounting price rule is not restricted to the optimum. It says that one ought to estimate the rate and direction of maximum increase in social welfare – the *gradient* of the (net) social benefit function – wherever the economy happens to be at, and one ought to use the gradient as the set of accounting prices at that point for evaluating marginal projects.[16] Thus, at any arbitrary state of the economy (X, Y) in our example the gradient of social welfare is the pair $(B'(X), -D'(Y))$. In expression (3.5) it is this which is used as the pair of accounting prices for the project $(\Delta X, \Delta Y)$.

[15] For an excellent account of planning procedures, see Heal (1973, chapters 3–9). The original articles on the subject have been reprinted in Arrow and Hurwicz (1977).

[16] The gradient of a function, $W(X_1, \ldots, X_n)$ is the vector of its partial derivatives $(\partial W/\partial X_1, \ldots, \partial W/\partial X_n)$.

3.5 Non-convexities and their implications

We now come to a limitation of the arguments offered in the previous section, a matter of considerable importance for environmental pollution management. As figure 3.2 displays, the net benefit function, $B(X)-D(X)$, I have assumed so far, is single-peaked. Formally, I have assumed that $B(X)-D(X)$ is a (strictly) *concave* function.[17] In particular, we have assumed that the planning problem embodied in (3.1) is a 'concave programme' (see appendix, and for further details see Heal, 1973). It is this assumption which is often not justifiable when environmental problems are considered. In what follows this will be encountered on several occasions. In section 3.6 I shall present a simple model of pollution for which the net benefit function has multiple peaks. What I shall do in the remainder of this section is to look at the implications of this.

Suppose then that $B(X)-D(X)$ is multiple-peaked, as in figure 3.3. There are two *locally* optimal levels of pollution, X_1^* and X_2^*. The *global* optimum is, of course, at X_1^*; and $X_2^* > X_1^*$. Now suppose the economy starts at the level $\bar{X}$, where $\bar{X} > X_2^*$. It is then immediate that a sequence of marginal moves, in accordance with the sign of expression (3.5) will lead the economy in the limit to X_2^*. Once the economy reaches X_2^* no further *marginal* move will look appetizing, and the economy will get stuck at X_2^*. But the economy suffers from excessive pollution even at X_2^*. Marginal cost-benefit analysis will not allow the planner to recognize this fact though. Indeed, as figure 3.3 demonstrates, so long as $X > \hat{X}$ the economy will move towards X_2^*.[18]

[17] A function, $N(X)$, is said to be *concave* (resp. *convex*) if the chord joining any two points on the function nowhere lies *above* (resp. *below*) the function. It is *strictly* concave if the chord lies entirely below the function. Thus, if $N(X)$ is concave the *set* of points on or below the function is convex. (A *set* is convex if the chord joining any two points in the set lies entirely within the set.) If $N(X)$ is a twice differentiable function, then $N(X)$ is a concave (strictly concave) function if $N''(X) \leqslant 0$ (<0) for all X. We shall appeal to this property in the chapters that follow.

[18] Notice that the *set* of points on or below the net benefit function in figure 3.3 is *not* convex (for a definition of convex sets, see footnote 17) and it is this which is the point of concern. This explains the title of the present section.

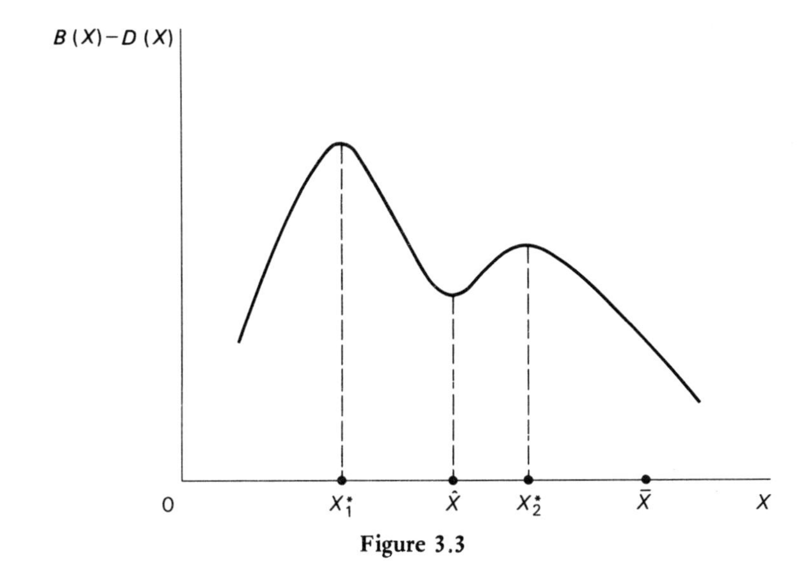

Figure 3.3

This example draws attention to a serious limitation of *marginal* social cost-benefit analysis. What is presumably required in such circumstances is *global* cost-benefit analysis – an exploration of the features of an economy far removed from its current state. This is precisely where intersectoral planning models can be of help. Such models consciously aim to incorporate interactions between sectors, a potential source of the non-convexities we have been discussing. This is illustrated below.

3.6 External diseconomies and non-convexities[19]

Consider a firm located upstream, whose production activity generates an effluent as a by-product. The effluent is deposited in the river whose water is an input in the production activity of a firm downstream. The downstream firm makes a profit maximizing production decision for each level of effluent, X, in the river. In figures 3.4 and 3.5 we denote this maximum profit

[19] The prevalence of non-convexities in environmental problems was noted in a seminal work by Starrett (1972). Much of the discussion that follows is based on this and Starrett and Zeckhauser (1971). For further details, see Baumol and Oates (1975).

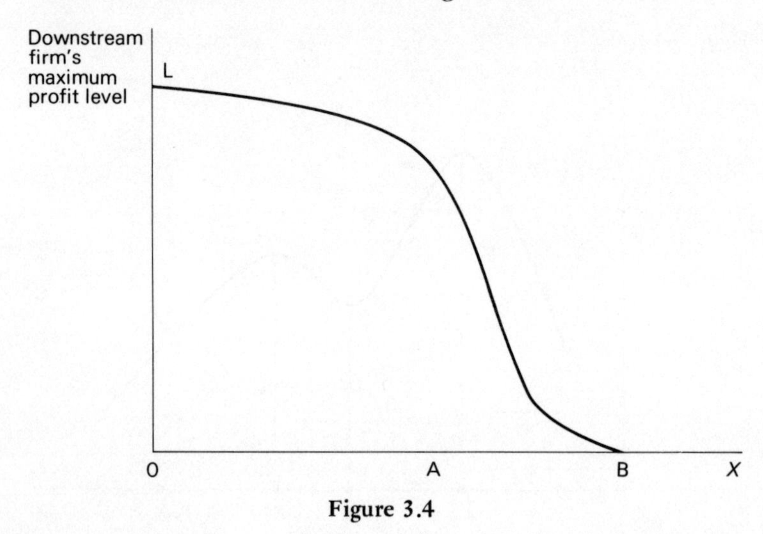

Figure 3.4

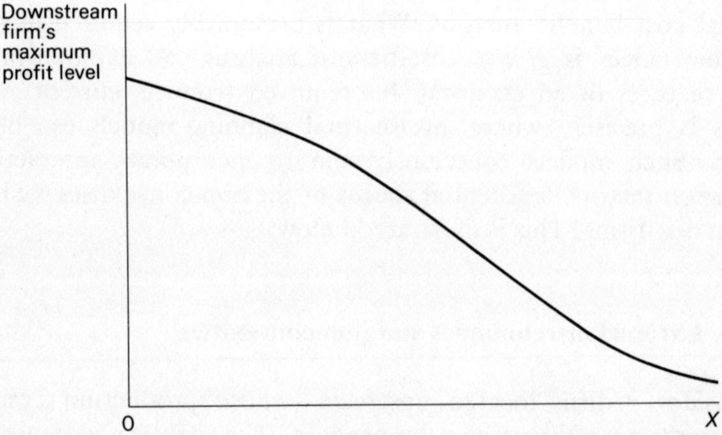

Figure 3.5

level as a function of X. Since the effluent damages the production possibilities for the recipient firm, this function must be downward sloping. It must also be bounded below, since the downstream firm has the option of closing down production activity and incurring only fixed costs. It follows that the maximum profit function cannot be concave over the entire X-axis (see figures 3.3 and 3.4). The diagrams depict two broad classes of cases. Figure 3.3 displays the case where the non-concavity of the profit function is 'sharp', with maximum profit falling dramatically in the neighbourhood of the level A, and becoming zero soon thereafter. The case depicted in figure 3.4 is one in which the non-concavity is 'smooth', with maximum profit tailing off gradually as the level of effluent emission X increases. In what follows I shall, for expositional ease, consider the case where the non-concavity of the profit function of the downstream firm is 'sharp'. In this case (see figure 3.3), the maximum profit function is the curve LB. It will be noted that the marginal loss in profit due to increased pollution (i.e. negative of the slope of the curve LB) increases with the level of pollution until about the level A after which it falls rapidly to zero at B and it remains at zero thereafter. In figure 3.6 the marginal loss in profit as a function of X has been drawn as the curve CDEBX.

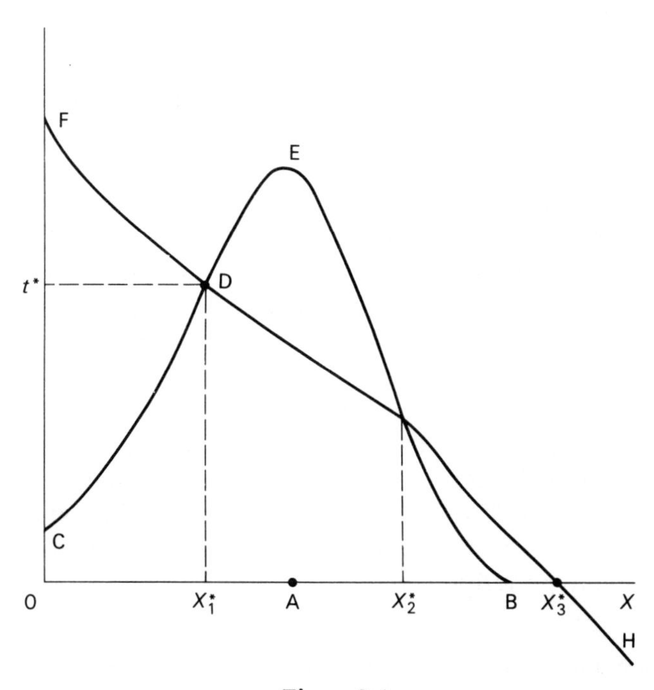

Figure 3.6

Turn now to the firm upstream. As in my original example (see figure 3.1) I assume that the *marginal* gain in profit enjoyed by it is a declining function of X. In figure 3.6 this curve is depicted as FDH. Marginal profit is zero at X_3^*, a point at which the firm downstream, unprotected by any rights, would choose not to operate.

Suppose, for expositional ease, that the market prices of commodities excepting for the effluent reflect correctly social opportunity costs; that is, that their market prices equal their shadow prices. We suppose next that the socially optimum level of effluent is the amount at which the combined profits of the two firms is maximum. In other words, by considering the two firms jointly we are 'internalizing' the externality that the firm upstream imposes on the firm downstream.

Begin by noting that at any local maximum or at any local minimum of the joint profit function, the marginal gain in profit to the firm upstream equals the marginal loss in profit to the firm downstream (this is true if we ignore the $X = 0$ point). But as figure 3.6 shows, there are three points, X_1^*, X_2^*, X_3^* at which this last is so. Of these, X_1^* and X_3^* sustain local maxima and X_2^* sustains a local minimum, as figure 3.7 demonstrates.[20] But the point to note is that each of these three levels of pollution is a potential tax equilibrium. For example, if the regulator tells the firm downstream that the pollution level will be X_1^* and asks it to announce its marginal loss in profit at this point then provided it answers truthfully it will quote a figure of t^* (see figure 3.6). (In chapter 4, appendix, tax schemes are studied that will ensure that firms *will* be truthful.) If the government now sets an effluent tax at the marginal rate t^* the firm upstream will pollute precisely at the level X_1^*, since at X_1^* its marginal gain in profits is t^*. Likewise, X_2^* and X_3^* are also potential tax equilibria. Let us verify that X_3^* is one. By hypothesis the firm downstream does not operate at X_3^*. Thus marginal losses to it are nil at this point, and so is the tax rate equal to zero. The upstream firm therefore will pollute at the level X_3^* since this is its profit maximizing level of pollution in the absence of any pollution taxes.

[20] Figure 3.6 has been constructed from figure 3.5 in the usual textbook manner.

Whether the regulator should choose X_1^* or X_3^* depends on whether the total area under the curve FDH between the points X_1^* and X_3^* (i.e. the downstream firm's loss in profits in having pollution increase from X_1^* to X_3^*) is greater or less than the total area under the curve CEBX between the same two points (i.e. the upstream firm's gain in being allowed to pollute more). In figure 3.7 we have depicted the situation where X_1^* is the global optimum. This would be so in those circumstances where pollution abatement costs for the firm upstream are small relative to the damage its pollutants cause to the downstream firm's production possibilities. But we can easily imagine a situation where (relative to other costs and the damage pollutants cause to the downstream firm), pollution abatement is overly costly. In this case X_3^* would be the global optimum and the downstream firm ought to cease production. But the point to reiterate is this: we noted in the previous section that if, as in this example, the social net benefit function is multiple-peaked, marginal social cost–benefit analysis cannot guarantee that the global optimum will be found. Marginal social cost–benefit analysis will lead the economy to X_1^* or X_3^* depending

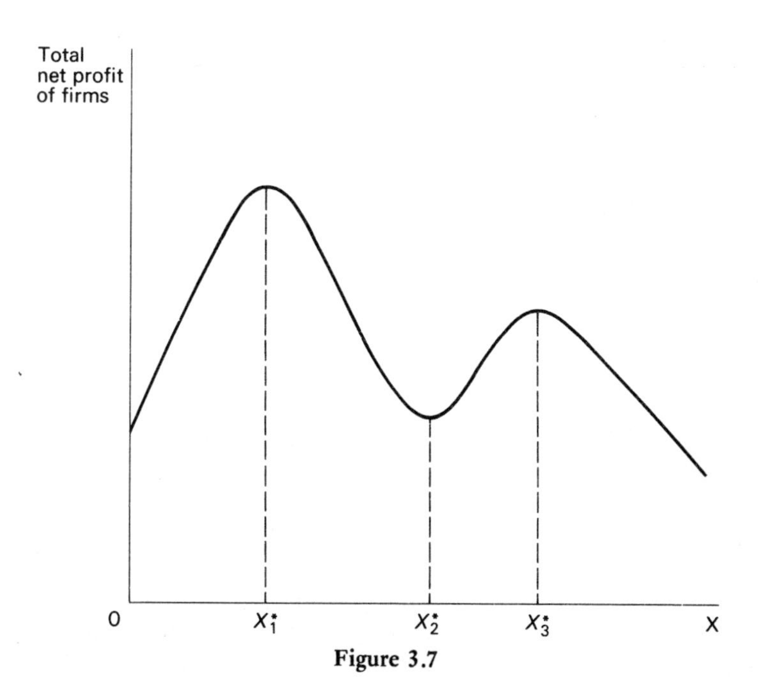

Figure 3.7

on whether the regulator finds the level of pollution initially at a level less than or greater than X_2^* (figure 3.7).

3.7 The role of systems analysis

The institutional framework in which environmental resources are controlled varies greatly from place to place and from time to time. But environmental resources *are* resources. No extra logic is required for their analysis. As with other sorts of resources, whether or not it is reasonable in any particular case to assume that decisions bearing on the case have serious implications on the rest of the economy is matter of shrewd judgment. If the energy sector looms large today in most economic debates it is because decisions within it are understood to have wide repercussions on the workings of the rest of the economy. But policies implemented on a single aquifer or a fishery may well not have such repercussions. Which features of the economic and political environment one may safely take as given (i.e. exogenous to the planning problem in question) and which features one may not in the formulation of a planning problem is a rather delicate issue. In the field of resource control there is a temptation to emphasize such repercussions, primarily because the resources in question may be critical in an ecosystem. Thus, it would be patently wrong to evaluate decisions regarding a watershed forest without considering their effects on downland farming.[21] It is desirable therefore to study the watershed as an integrated system. Nevertheless, it is obvious in advance that one must avoid the temptation of thinking that everything affects everything else. Even in the biological sciences – disciplines that are currently regarded in great favour as a model that economics ought to follow – this temptation is avoided, because everything does *not* affect everything else. Moreover it is of central importance to approximate, to ignore effects that are negligible. For example, it may be reasonable to think that decisions on an integrated watershed will not greatly affect the rates at which future benefits ought to be

[21] As a matter of *fact* the downland peasants may well be ignored in the calculation if they are not politically significant. In such a situation the discussion in the text is equally pertinent for the social critic.

discounted (see chapter 5). In this book I will for the most part approximate and measure social welfare in units of an index of per capita aggregate consumption (see chapter 5). In the procedure for this aggregation the prices that ought to be used must obviously take existing externalities into account. If investment in productive capital is at a social premium one requires an accounting price of investment (see UNIDO, 1972, chapter 14). I shall suppose this accounting price to be independent of decisions bearing on the resources under study. What one usually calls 'social product' is the sum of aggregate consumption and aggregate investment weighted by its accounting price. But this does not take into account income distributional issues which ought to be reflected in the measurement of social product. This involves taking per capita aggregate consumption as the benchmark and attaching weights to the consumption (or income) levels of different groups, capturing the idea that higher levels of consumption (or income) ought to be awarded lower weights. (Of course if the rich invest more in productive capital this feature is captured via the premium on investment.) In addition social overhead capital and amenities are directly valuable as stocks. We arrive at an approximate measure of social product when these corrections are added. In the constructs that follow social benefits and costs associated with policies are evaluated in terms of this index of social product. To be sure, it would be inappropriate to suppose that such policies will not affect distributional weights or the marginal social value of amenities. In what follows we shall not therefore suppose this. (For further discussion of this, and in particular the problem of valuing resource and capital stocks when these stocks yield direct benefits and costs, see chapter 5, section 5.3.)

In the chapters that follow I shall wish to focus attention on the resources under study. Therefore I will not elaborate on methods for estimating the accounting prices of other goods and services, such as bulldozers, unskilled labour, and so on. (For details of how such accounting prices may be estimated, see UNIDO, 1972 and Little and Mirrlees, 1974.) I will be much concerned with the *conceptual* issues arising in the 'estimation' of social benefit and cost functions associated with the control of environmental resources. In particular I will discuss at length how to make *use* of such functions once they are given and what their implications are. It is in fact in the estimation of these functions that what goes by the name of 'systems analysis' is of help. The model analysed in the previous section is an elementary example of it.[22] Then again, if we wish to assess the social cost incurred by a legislation on air quality it is imperative to use an inter-industry model, since we would presumably wish to know how the resulting cost increases in polluting industries affect prices in industries buying their goods. (An example of an inter-industry study containing pollution control possibilities is Leontief *et al.*, 1977.) Likewise it may be the case that in estimating the damage function $D(Y)$ in problem (3.1) some fairly elaborate system had to be analysed. But since there are no general *economic* insights to be had from studying complex systems in the abstract, I avoid doing it.[23] In short it needs emphasis that appearances to the contrary, the constructs that I will be analysing are *not* strictly 'partial equilibrium' ones. Whatever non-negligible effects there are will be taken to have been caught in the social benefit and cost functions that I will be working with.

[22] Nijkamp (1980) provides useful examples of what are the preoccupations of systems analysts.

[23] I am concerned with conceptual issues and not with conducting case-studies. Depending on the actual problem at hand it may well be necessary to study a complex system directly, as for example in Spofford *et al.* (1976). William Nordhaus' work on the global carbon dioxide problem, which I report on in chapter 8, was based on an elaborate 'linear programming' model.

Appendix

3A.1 The Kuhn–Tucker theorem[24]

Let R^n $(n \geqslant 1)$ denote the n-dimensional Euclidean space. A typical element of R^n we write as $\underline{X}$. A non-empty subset K of R^n is said to be *convex* if for any pair of points $\underline{X}_1$ and $\underline{X}_2$ in K any weighted average (with non-negative weights) of $\underline{X}_1$ and $\underline{X}_2$ also belongs to K. Formally, this can be stated as: for all $\underline{X}_1, \underline{X}_2 \epsilon K$ and for all $\alpha \epsilon (0, 1)$, $\alpha \underline{X}_1 + (1-\alpha)\underline{X}_2 \epsilon K$. A real valued function, W, defined on K is *concave* (*strictly concave*) if for any pair of points $\underline{X}_1$, $\underline{X}_2 \epsilon K$ and any number $\alpha \epsilon (0, 1)$,

$$W(\alpha \underline{X}_1 + (1-\alpha)\underline{X}_2) \geqslant (>) \alpha W(\underline{X}_1) + (1-\alpha) W(\underline{X}_2).$$

Let $W, G_1, \ldots, G_m$ be real valued functions defined on R^n. We may express a prototype planning problem as:

$$\left.\begin{array}{l} \text{choose } \underline{X} \text{ so as to} \\ \text{maximize } W(\underline{X}) \text{ subject to the } m \text{ constraints} \\ G_1(\underline{X}) \geqslant 0, G_2(\underline{X}) \geqslant 0, \ldots, G_m(\underline{X}) \geqslant 0. \end{array}\right\} \qquad (3A.1)$$

(Note that one of the m constraints could be of the form $\underline{X} \geqslant \underline{0}$, as in problem (3.1).)

The following classic theorem is due to Kuhn and Tucker:

Theorem 1

Suppose $W, G_1, \ldots, G_m$ are all concave functions and suppose that there exists an $\underline{X}^0$ such that $G_i(\underline{X}^0) > \underline{0}$ for $i = 1, \ldots, m$. Then $\underline{X}^*$ is an optimum – i.e. a solution of problem (3A.1) – if and only if there exist m numbers $p_1^*, \ldots, p_m^*$ such that:

$$p_i^* \geqslant 0 \text{ and } p_i^* G_i(\underline{X}^*) = 0 \qquad \text{for } i = 1, \ldots, m, \qquad (3A.2)$$

and

$$W(\underline{X}^*) + \sum_{i=1}^{m} p_i^* G_i(\underline{X}^*) \geqslant W(\underline{X}) + \sum_{i=1}^{m} p_i^* G_i(\underline{X}) \qquad \text{for all } \underline{X}. \quad (3A.3)$$

[24] I shall define only those mathematical expressions that will be used in this book, and state only that result which underlies some of the arguments. This appendix is merely to remind the reader of some definitions and formal results which are in the background of the analysis in the text. Readers not familiar with this material should read a detailed account. A good discussion is in Heal (1973, Appendix). For a rigorous account of programming theory, see Arrow and Hurwicz (1977). Heal (1982) contains a generalization of Theorem 1 below.

The expression $L(\underline{p},\underline{X}) \equiv W(\underline{X}) + \Sigma_{i=1}^{m} p_i G_i(\underline{X})$ is known as the Lagrangean of problem (3A.1) and what the theorem says is that $(\underline{X}^*, p_1^*, \ldots, p_m^*)$ is a 'saddle-point' of the Lagrangean. The m non-negative numbers $p_1^*, \ldots, p_m^*$ are called Lagrange multipliers in mathematics and shadow (or accounting) prices in economics. Note that condition (3A.2) says that if, for any i, $G_i(\underline{X}^*) > 0$, then $p_i^* = 0$; and if $p_i^* > 0$ then $G_i(\underline{X}^*) = 0$: in short, for each $i = 1, \ldots, m$ $\underline{X}^*$ maximizes $-p_i^* G_i(\underline{X})$ subject to the constraint $G_i(\underline{X}) \geqslant 0$.

To see why these Lagrange multipliers may be given the interpretation of prices notice that condition (3A.3) says that $\underline{X}^*$ is the solution of the following problem:

$$\left.\begin{array}{l} \text{choose } \underline{X} \text{ so as to} \\ \text{maximize } W(\underline{X}) + \sum_{i=1}^{m} p_i^* G_i(\underline{X}) \end{array}\right\} \qquad (3A.4)$$

The objective function in problem (3A.4) is the Langrangean of problem (3A.1). It is as though the planner imposes a 'cost', p_i^*, for breaking the constraint $G_i(\underline{X}) \geqslant 0$, so as to prevent himself from doing so.

If W, $G_1, \ldots, G_m$, in addition to being concave, are all continuously differentiable functions, then in order to locate $\underline{X}^*$ we may differentiate the expression in (3A.4) partially with respect to each of the components of $\underline{X}$ and set each of these derivatives equal to zero. That is:

$$\partial W(\underline{X})/\partial X_j + \sum_{i=1}^{m} p_i^* \, \partial G_i(\underline{X})/\partial X_j = 0, \qquad \text{for } j = 1, \ldots, n, \qquad (3A.5)$$

where $\underline{X} = (X_1, \ldots, X_n)$. Equations (3A.5) are n first-order conditions and, under the conditions specified by the Kuhn–Tucker theorem they are sufficient conditions as well. It is an easy enough matter to prove that if these m accounting prices are *unique*, p_i^* is the rate of increase in the value of $W(\underline{X}^*)$ if the ith constraint $G_i(\underline{X}) \geqslant 0$ is relaxed marginally; i.e. we have $G_i(\underline{X}) \geqslant -\epsilon$, for ϵ a small positive number.

The above summary and observations explain several of the claims in the text. I now apply the Kuhn-Tucker theorem briefly to two of the examples in the text.

3A.2 Examples

I wish to use the Kuhn–Tucker theorem to problem (3.1). Notice first that the constraint $X = Y$ can be written as the intersection of two inequality constraints $X \geqslant Y$ and $Y \geqslant X$. Thus, we may re-write (3.1) as:

$$\left.\begin{array}{l}\text{choose } X, Y\ (\geqslant 0) \text{ so as to} \\ \text{maximize } B(X) - D(Y) \\ \text{subject to the constraints } X \geqslant Y \text{ and } Y \geqslant X.\end{array}\right\} \qquad (3A.6)$$

By hypothesis $B(X) - D(Y)$ is a (strictly) concave function (see figure 3.2). The remaining assumptions of the theorem are satisfied by problem (3A.6). It follows that X^* and Y^* constitute a solution of problem (3A.6) if and only if there exist non-negative accounting prices p_1^* and p_2^*, and p_3^* and p_4^* such that X^* and Y^* maximize the Lagrangean:

$$B(X) - D(Y) + p_1^*(X - Y) + p_2^*(Y - X) + p_3^*X + p_4^*Y. \qquad (3A.7)$$

To have an interesting problem we suppose, as in the text, that $X^*(= Y^*) > 0$. From (3A.2) we therefore know that $p_3^* = p_4^* = 0$. Thus we differentiate (3A.7) partially with respect to X and Y in turn and set these derivatives equal to zero to obtain the first-order condition as

$$\left.\begin{array}{l} B'(X) = p_2^* - p_1^* \quad \text{and} \\ D'(Y) = p_2^* - p_1^* \end{array}\right\}. \qquad (3A.8)$$

From equation (3A.8) it follows that $B'(X) = D'(Y)$ at the optimum, which is equation (3.2) in the text. $(p_2^* - p_1^*)$ is the optimal effluent charge; i.e. $t = p_2^* - p_1^*$ in equation (3.3).

Finally, suppose instead of problem (3A.6) the planner is asked to maximize $B(X)$ subject to the constraint $X \leqslant \tilde{X} (< \bar{X})$, as in section 3.3. Again, by the Kuhn–Tucker theorem, if X^* is the solution to the problem then there exists an accounting price $\mu\ (\geqslant 0)$ such that $(\tilde{X} - X^*)\,\mu = 0$, and X^* maximizes the Lagrangean $B(X) + \mu(\tilde{X} - X)$. In fact, $\mu = B'(\tilde{X})$. This confirms the claims made in section 3.3.

3A.3 Non-concave functions

The hypothesis that $W, G_1, \ldots, G_m$ in the Kuhn–Tucker theorem are all concave functions plays an important role. It is easily checked that if G_i is concave then the set of $\underline{X}$s for which $G_i(\underline{X}) \geqslant 0$ is *convex*, a key feature in the theorem. Since I have argued in the text that resource management problems are often *not* concave programming problems (i.e. often do not satisfy the conditions of the Kuhn–Tucker theorem) we have to be careful in its use. I first give examples where the Kuhn–Tucker technique will not work; that is, where one cannot use accounting prices for implementing an optimum plan.

$$\left.\begin{array}{ll}(1) & \text{Maximize } X^2 \\ & \text{subject to the constraints } X \geqslant 0 \text{ and } 1 - X \geqslant 0.\end{array}\right\}$$

Clearly the problem has a solution; namely $X = 1$. The constraint sets are convex. But the objective function is not concave. This is the source of the difficulty, because the 'Lagrangean' of this problem, $X^2 + p_1 X + p_2 (1 - X)$ has no maximum in X (when X is unconstrained) no matter what p_1 and p_2 are.

$$\left.\begin{array}{ll}(2) & \text{Maximize } 2X + Y \\ & \text{subject to } X \geqslant 0,\ Y \geqslant 0 \text{ and } 4 - (X + 1)(Y + 1) \geqslant 0.\end{array}\right\}$$

This too has a solution, namely $X = 3$ and $Y = 0$. The objective function is concave but the constraint sets are not convex. This is the source of the difficulty, because the 'Lagrangean' of this problem, $2X + Y + p_1(4 - (X + 1)(Y + 1)) + p_2 X + p_3 Y$, has no maximum in X and Y (when unconstrained) for any $p_1, p_2, p_3 \geqslant 0$ (consider both X and Y to be large and negative).

If problem (3A.1) is not a concave programming problem we have to make do with the following, less attractive theorem.

Theorem 2

If there exist $\underline{X}^*$ and $p_1^*, \ldots, p_m^*$ such that

(i) for all $\underline{X}$,

$$W(\underline{X}^*) + \sum_{i=1}^{m} p_i^* G_i(\underline{X}^*) \geqslant W(\underline{X}) + \sum_{i=1}^{m} p_i^* G_i(\underline{X})$$

and

(ii) $p_i^* \geqslant 0$ and $p_i^* G_i(\underline{X}^*) = 0 \quad$ for $i = 1, \ldots, m$;

then $\underline{X}^*$ is a solution of the planning problem (3A.1).

Proof: We wish to locate m real numbers, $p_1^*, \ldots, p_m^*$ so that the vector $\underline{X}^*$ maximizes

$$W(\underline{X}) + \sum_{i=1}^{m} p_i^* G_i(\underline{X}) \quad \text{over all } \underline{X}, \tag{3A.9}$$

and so that it also maximizes

$$-p_i^* G_i(\underline{X}) \text{ subject to } G_i(\underline{X}) \geqslant 0 \qquad \text{for } i = 1, \ldots, m. \tag{3A.10}$$

If we are able to do this then we have maximized the *sum* of the expression in (3A.9) and the m expressions in (3A.10) subject to the m constraints $G_i(\underline{X}) \geqslant 0$. But the sum is $W(\underline{X})$. Thus we will have solved the problem.

Now notice that $\underline{X}^*$ solves the m maximization problems in (3A.10) if and only if

$$p_i^* \geqslant 0 \text{ and } p_i^* G_i(\underline{X}^*) = 0. \tag{3A.11}$$

But (3A.9) and (3A.11) are precisely conditions (i) and (ii) in the theorem.

Notice that Theorem 2 does not hypothesize that $W, G_1, \ldots, G_m$ are all concave functions. It says that *if* we can find $\underline{X}^*, p_1^*, \ldots, p_m^*$ which satisfy conditions (i) and (ii) above (i.e. if $\underline{X}^*, p_1^*, \ldots, p_m^*$ is a saddle-point of the Lagrangean of problem (3A.1)), then $\underline{X}^*$ is the optimum and the problem is solved. (The two examples noted in this section demonstrate that even when a planning problem has a solution, $\underline{X}^*$, there may not exist m numbers $p_1^*, \ldots, p_m^*$ satisfying conditions (i) and (ii) of Theorem 2.) As the discussions of sections 3.5 and 3.6 suggest, it is Theorem 2 which is more pertinent for solving environmental management problems, and it is a generalization of this theorem (which I do not present here) which will be appealed to in chapter 8.

4 Environmental Control under Uncertainty

4.1 Decision criteria under uncertainty

A great deal of discussion on environmental issues proceeds as though the consequences of actions are perfectly predictable. It is not uncommon, for example, to read an economic analysis of a fishery which contains no explicit mention of the fact that its growth function is only imperfectly known, or that there is possible disagreement about the size of the existing stock. This is often a necessary simplification. Stochastic models can rapidly become unmanageable, and an appeal to a computer in such cases often results only in the announcement of some numbers, with no accompanying insight about why the numbers have come out the way they have.

It should be recognized that the fact that an analysis contains no explicit mention of uncertainty does not necessarily mean that the analyst has pretended that there is no uncertainty. It could be that some kinds of averages of the various possibilities have implicitly been used in the discussion. The language of probabilities is the natural one to use in dealing with uncertainty, even although in the case of environmental problems the probabilities will often be *subjective* ones.[1] However, being subjective estimates, even

[1] For our purposes here I shall regard a probability distribution over various possibilities to be an *objective* one if there have been so many instances in the past that the probabilities can be estimated from the frequency distribution without too much difficulty (e.g. rainfall at a particular location). We use the term *subjective* probabilities for all others. The terms 'risk' and 'uncertainty' are often used to distinguish between these two cases. In what follows I shall use them interchangeably. For a good elementary account of statistical decision theory see Raiffa (1968).

experts disagree – often sharply – about the probable environmental effects of economic activities. Indeed, if there is a hallmark of environmental debates it is probably this.[2] But the fact that such probabilities are subjective is not an argument for not using the language of probabilities. Just as there is no single person whose estimates must always be relied upon, not every person's estimates of these probabilities are worth taking into account. For every new phenomenon there is some related phenomenon about which information is already available. Such evidence, in conjunction with pilot studies allow one to narrow down the family of distributions that might be used. As is invariably the case more information becomes available with the passage of time, so that the family is narrowed even further. The discussion in chapter 3, section 3.4, is relevant here. The best that can be achieved under such circumstances is to offer a range of policies that are optimal under the family of distributions. The social ranking of options will typically be only a partial ordering.

It is customary in welfare economics to encourage the government to accept the tastes *and* beliefs of individuals and then aggregate them in a suitable way. The fundamental theorem of welfare economics, referred to in chapter 2, is addressed to this kind of political environment. To be sure, it is recognized that it is desirable to make public various expert opinions and to enable individuals to base their beliefs on better information. The public provision of certain kinds of information, as we noted above, is one such implication. Nevertheless, the approach is to aggregate the *ex ante* 'preferences' of individuals, that is, preferences that incorporate individuals' tastes as well as their beliefs about various possibilities. Not surprisingly, a welfare optimum based on such an aggregation is called an *ex ante optimum*. Now, it may be asked why a government is required to respect individual *beliefs* about future possibilities in the same way as their 'tastes'. Tastes may be

[2] Aumann (1976) has shown that if two Bayesians hold the same prior beliefs about the occurrence of possible events and if their posterior beliefs about an event are common knowledge then these posteriors must be equal. To explain why environmentalists disagree one must therefore suppose either that they did not hold common priors or that their posterior beliefs are not common knowledge. There is a third possibility, of course, which is that they are not Bayesians!

refined or vulgar; nevertheless it may be held that a person's tastes must be respected. But beliefs can be *wrong*, and it is hard to see why it is undemocratic to disregard a person's beliefs if in fact they are wrong. It can no doubt be argued that we all have the right to take decisions on the basis of our own beliefs and to ignore evidence if it is psychologically convenient for us to do so (e.g. the hazards of smoking), and indeed that we have the right to make mistakes. But even if we accept this it is hard to see why a government ought to base *its* decisions on mistaken beliefs.

An alternative, therefore, is for the government to aggregate individual preferences over allocations at each state of nature – that is, their *ex post* preferences – and then aggregate these by the use of probability weights based on public information. A welfare optimum based on such an aggregation procedure is called an *ex post optimum* (also on occasion an Allais optimum; see Malinvaud, 1972).[3] This alternative therefore conveniently separates a person's *ex post* preferences from his beliefs and has the government respect the former but not necessarily the latter.

These foregoing arguments, and some further considerations that I shall develop in section 4.4, suggest that in many cases (most especially where public health is at issue) environmental protection is rather like a *merit good*, and so there is a case for the government to base its policies on only the most informed opinions.[4]

In what follows I shall, for expositional ease, assume that the government follows statistical decision theory and ranks options on the basis of their *expected net social benefits*. Now, even casual thinking on environmental problems alerts one to the fact that they sometimes involve a small chance of large-scale damage to society (or some large group) as a whole. However, these are precisely the kinds of problem statistical decision theory finds awkward to handle. It is possible to cast doubt on the plausibility of the 'expected utility hypothesis' in the case of risks that are

[3] In the *ex ante* case the government conducts an aggregation exercise only once, and in the *ex post* case twice. It is only in some restricted circumstances that *ex ante* and *ex post* optima are identical. See Broome (1981) and Hammond (1981a, 1981b) for deep explorations of these issues.

[4] 'The satisfaction of merit wants, by its very nature, involves interference with consumer preferences' (Musgrave, 1959, p. 13).

characterized both by 'low' probability and 'high' damage. On the other hand it cannot be claimed that there is anything as systematic and persuasive that can replace it. Seemingly appealing decision criteria, like 'maxi-min', display seriously unsatisfactory features when scrutinized.[5] 'Maxi-min' appears appealing precisely because it focuses uncompromisingly on the worst outcome associated with options, and in the field of environmental resources the worst may well be simply disastrous. Equally obviously, this feature of 'maxi-min' is its great weakness. A compromise, often resorted to, is to retain 'maxi-min's' distinguishing feature for worst outcomes by imposing constraints in the planning exercise by way of standards so that options that have the slightest chance of violating them are immediately ruled out – but otherwise to rank options by expected net social benefits. Likewise, really bad outcomes – even those with low probability – will be avoided by the expected social benefit criterion if the net benefit function is very steep at these points (see section 4.6 below).

4.2 Dependent versus independent uncertainties

It is convenient to distinguish between risks that are correlated across persons and those that are not. An increase in the emissions from automobiles in a region increases the chance that individuals will suffer from bronchial disorders. But to a reasonable approximation individuals face independent risks here depending on such personal factors as age and state of health. In contrast, the possible effects of massive deforestation on the global climate are jointly faced by all. Such risks are perfectly correlated, and the most extreme of these generate apocalyptic visions.

Environmental risks that are borne by individuals more or less independently of one another are somewhat easier to handle analytically, for one can appeal directly to the traditional theory of externalities. Moreover, economic theory tells us something

[5] The maxi-min criterion ranks options solely on the basis of their worst possible outcomes, no matter how low the probabilities of their occurrence (so long as they are positive) and no matter what the other possible outcomes are. A good account of different decision criteria under uncertainty is in Luce and Raiffa (1957).

about the relation between the ideal price of insurance against such risks and the risks themselves (see Malinvaud, 1972). It will be convenient first to draw out the distinction formally and see why it is the dependent case that usually generates the most acrimonious of debates, and ask whether one should expect this to be the case. We do this by means of a simple example. It will also clarify several other points that we have raised earlier.

Consider a group of N identical individuals. The representative person's valuation of his own income, we assume, can be represented by a function $U(Y)$, where Y is his income and where $U(Y)$ is an increasing and strictly concave function, as in figure 4.1; that is, $U'(Y) > 0$ and $U''(Y) < 0$. Strict concavity of $U(Y)$ means that he prefers a sure income to a lottery whose expected (or mean) outcome equals this sure income. Suppose that each person faces one of two possibilities: no damage, in which case his income level is $\bar{Y}$, or a damage, which is equivalent to an income loss L so that net income is $(\bar{Y} - L)$. If P is the concentration of pollutants, let $\pi(P)$ be the probability that the damage occurs. We naturally assume that $\pi'(P) > 0$.

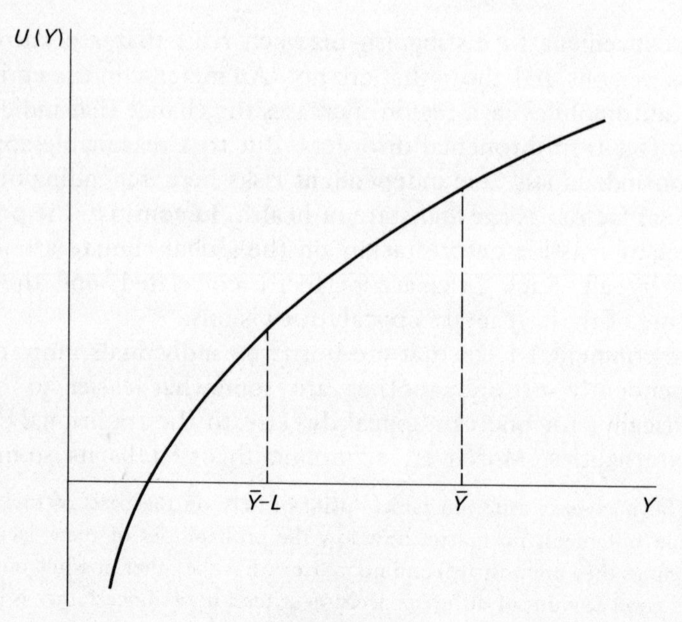

Figure 4.1

Consider first the case where individual risks are all independent of one another. If N is large then the fraction of people who will suffer the damage is pretty close to $\pi(P)$. In this case individuals can mutually insure themselves against the risk perfectly. If a person pays a premium of $\pi(P)\,L$ (his expected loss in income) and is guaranteed a net insurance payment of $(1-\pi(P))\,L$ in case of loss, he is guaranteed an income amounting to $\bar{Y}-\pi(P)\,L$ in either event. He is perfectly insured. The fact that N is large and that the risks are independent mean that such an insurance policy for each person is viable. Now suppose that we measure social benefits by the expected sum of the individual valuation functions. Then, under perfect insurance, expected social benefits is $E(B(P))_I$, where

$$E(B(P))_I = NU(\bar{Y}-\pi(P)\,L). \tag{4.1}$$

Suppose next that some activity increases the concentration level by a small amount, say, ΔP. Then the social damage caused by this can, on using equation (4.1), be expressed as

$$-\Delta E(B(P))_I \simeq N\pi'(P)\,LU'(\bar{Y}-\pi(P)\,L)\,\Delta P. \tag{4.2}$$

We come now to the other extreme case, where the risks are perfectly and positively correlated. In this case either *all* suffer the damage (with probability $\pi(P)$) or *none* suffers (the probability of this by definition $(1-\pi(P))$). In this case individuals cannot mutually insure themselves.[6] If P is the concentration level the expected social benefits, which we denote by $E(B(P))_D$, is

$$E(B(P))_D = N(1-\pi(P))\,U(\bar{Y}) + N\pi(P)\,U(\bar{Y}-L). \tag{4.3}$$

Suppose once again that some activity increases the concentration level by a small amount ΔP. On differentiating equation (4.3) with respect to P it is simple to check that the social damage caused in this case is:

$$-\Delta E(B(P))_D \simeq N\pi'(P)(U(\bar{Y})-U(\bar{Y}-L))\,\Delta P. \tag{4.4}$$

[6] They may of course be able to insure themselves with some outside agency as, for example, would be the case with flood relief if financed through benefit taxation. We are considering the case where this is not possible.

Now notice that because $U''(Y) < 0$, $E(B(P))_I > E(B(P))_D$. This is precisely what one would expect since individuals are fully insured in the first case and not at all when the risks are fully correlated. But in estimating the social damage due to an *increase* in pollution one must compare the *declines* in expected social benefits - not the expected social benefits themselves. As regards this the matter is ambiguous, because without knowing what $\pi(P)$ is one cannot tell how $\Delta E(B(P))_I$ compares with $\Delta E(B(P))_D$. If $\pi(P)$ is 'small' (the chance that any given individual will suffer the loss is small), then $-\Delta E(B(P))_D > -\Delta E(B(P))_I$ and so an increase in 'collective risk' is the case to fear. Not so if $\pi(P)$ is nearly unity. In this case the social damage due to a marginal increase in pollution is greater when the risk is *not* collective - in the sense that the risks are independent.

While absurdly simple, the foregoing analysis suggests that there is no obvious reason why we ought to fear an increase in collective risks more than non-collective ones.[7] It also shows that it makes great sense to fear them more if $\pi(P)$ is small and the loss is 'large' - i.e. $U(\bar{Y}) - U(\bar{Y} - L)$ is large. But this is the case of a small collective risk of a mammoth social loss - precisely the kind of example over which people express their greatest anxieties.

4.3 Environmental research

One way to reduce risks to to spread them by choosing one's actions appropriately. Indeed, a good part of the early literature on the economics of uncertainty was concerned with exploring circumstances in which diversification pays, and with analysing the related question of how mutual insurance schemes enable a society to achieve this diversification.

A second way to reduce risks is to obtain further information on the uncertain areas. Pilot studies designed to investigate the environmental effects of pollutants (e.g. their effects on fisheries)

[7] I am using the terms 'collective' and 'non-collective' to describe the fully dependent and independent cases. In either case pollution is a public 'bad', in the sense of influencing everyone's chance of loss. Niehaus (1980) makes the observation that beyond a point the occupational and public risk of producing safety equipment exceeds the reduction of an existing risk.

and research designed toward discovering cheaper pollution abatement technologies are examples. This is not the place to discuss at length the strong *a priori* reasons for supposing that a market economy is unlikely to sustain the right amount of expenditure in obtaining such information and directing it along the right route (on this see for example Arrow, 1971b; Dasgupta and Heal, 1979). But it ought to be evident that 'knowledge' (or 'information') has the attributes of a public good. Thus there is a presumption that to the extent the producer of additional information cannot enforce property rights on the product there is a tendency towards insufficient production in a market economy. At the same time, however, there is a force operating in the opposite direction. Since knowledge is like a common pool (i.e. a common property resource), it is likely to be excessively *used* in a market economy.[8] The discussions in chapter 2 suggest therefore that knowledge, as an int:qIL6I :e good, ought perhaps to be subsidized in its production, and taxed in its use. Both these are on occasion observed in market economies. But there are obvious difficulties in implementing subsidies and taxes on such an intangible commodity as information. Indeed, arguments for the public provision of certain kinds of information, most especially the fruits of basic research, have been based on the non-appropriability of such commodities (see Arrow, 1971b). It is not an accident that government funds are usually involved in environmental research.

In this section we take it that the government can construct an (expected) damage function – a function that relates the (expected) social damage to the pollutant level. What we wish to argue here is

(1) that environmental research and development (R&D) projects often carry with them an insurance value, so that the social costs of risks associated with such projects are often *negative*
(2) that a government should not attempt a complete diversification among R&D strategies, even if they are uncorrelated, but instead would be well advised to specialize in only a few avenues of research.

[8] We are drawing attention only to the simplest points here. The matter is a great deal more complex. For some preliminary accounts of the relation between the structure of markets and the generation and use of information, see Dasgupta and Stiglitz (1980a, b).

Suppose society is uncertain about the precise effects of environmental pollution associated with specific economic activities. For example, it may not be known whether polychlorinated biphenyls (PCBs) have a large or small effect on marine food chains. Since research on this question is under way, only time will tell which is the case. The issue to be decided now is whether to undertake, for example, a research project to discover methods for breaking PCB molecules into harmless constituents. Even if such a project were successful, the realized social benefit from it will be high only if it is found that PCBs have a large detrimental effect on marine food chains; not otherwise. This is another way of saying that the social return on such a project is inversely associated with society's social income (i.e. national income corrected for environmental effects). This means that such a project provides society with insurance against adverse environmental effects. In this case, provided the variance of the project is not too great, a risk-averse society would prefer such a project to a sure project with the same expected return that was not environmental. In other words, society would prefer such an uncertain project to a sure project even if its expected social return is slightly less than the return from the sure project – the social cost of risk associated with the project is negative.

The second point is best illustrated by the observation that research activity in general is concerned with the acquisition of information. This acquisition requires the expenditure of resources, but not all information is worth this expenditure. Nor in general does the acquisition of information eliminate uncertainty, but this is no reason for not seeking it. Even when uncertainty is not eliminated, the information obtained may alter plans, and therein lies its value. Instead of taking an action in the absence of further information, one may wish to wait until more information is available. Of course, payment has to be made for this information. At the time one pays for the information (e.g. R&D expenditure) one does not know precisely what will be required (the outcome of the R&D project). However, one knows in advance that the optimal course of action will be based on the information acquired. The value of a research project is the expected social net benefit to be obtained from it. While we have provided a verbal account, the value of information can be repre-

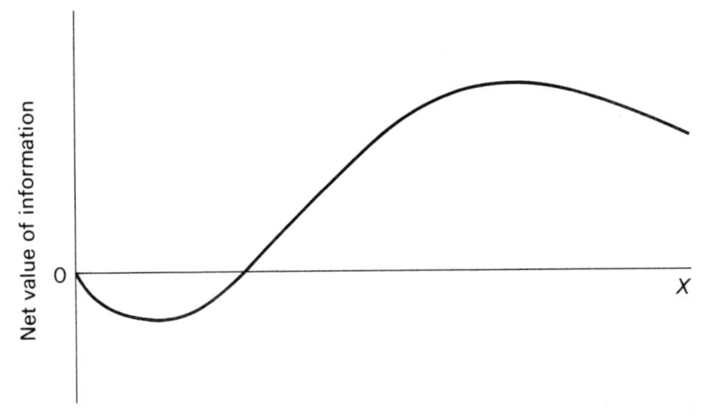

Figure 4.2

sented in a precise mathematical manner (see for example Marschak and Radner, 1972; or Dasgupta and Heal, 1979).

Suppose we were to represent environmental R&D projects of a certain kind by the degree of refinement in the experiments that define the projects. For example, all projects in the class so defined may be concerned with the effects of PCBs on marine food chains, but they may differ in the precision with which the investigator determines the effects. Suppose we were to denote the degree of precision (and therefore a research project) by x ($\geqslant 0$); thus a higher value of x denotes a more detailed experiment. We may represent the quantity of information by x; therefore, $x = 0$ is the most crude experiment of all – namely, no experiment! Suppose that the marginal social cost of information is positive. Then it can be shown (see Wilson, 1975) that under fairly weak conditions the net value of information declines in the neighbourhood of zero information (see figure 4.2). Thus if it is worth acquiring information of a certain type (as in figure 4.2), the amount of information ought to be no less than a certain positive level. But this means presumably that the decision-maker (here the government) ought to specialize in certain types of research.[9]

These arguments suggest the possibility of increasing returns in the value of information (which, incidentally, has nothing to do

[9] The possible non-concavity in the value of information was also demonstrated in an unpublished paper by Radner and Stiglitz (1975). For a simplified proof of the theorem, see Dasgupta and Heal (1979, chapter 13).

with possible lumpiness in R&D expenditure). Accordingly, a society ought to channel its R&D expenditure, not minutely into every possible avenue, but substantially into a few.

4.4 Planning mechanisms with dispersed information

In the preceding sections I have been concerned with certain aspects of what one might call 'games' against nature. In such situations the decision-maker is required to choose while uncertain about the true state of nature. What makes such 'games' relatively simple is that 'Mother Nature', it is generally thought, does not respond strategically to the decision-maker's choice. In the remainder of this chapter and in the appendix I study more complex games – those that arise in environmental management problems when there is an information gap between the decision-maker and those affected by his actions. This gap could, for example, be between the regulator and the firms engaged in environmental pollution (see sections 4.5–4.7 and the appendix). Firms typically will know more about abatement and clean-up costs than will the regulator, and may balk at providing correct information if it is not in their interest to do so. Information gaps presumably also exist between the regulator and the persons who are affected by pollutants. In fact it seems plausible that this latter information gap is even more difficult to close. While it is possible, at least in principle, for a regulator to discover firms' technological possibilities, such as abatement and clean-up costs (e.g. by engaging independent experts), determining the extent of a citizen's aversion to pollutants (i.e. learning about his mind) is an entirely different matter. Indeed, it is the potential impossibility of closing this latter gap – since individuals may well wish to give misleading information if asked – that has been central in discussions of the 'free-rider' problem in the theory of public goods (see for example Musgrave, 1959; Atkinson and Stiglitz, 1980).

The problem of devising appropriate incentive schemes in the face of information gaps has been a major concern of economists during recent years, and it is probably too early to attempt a rounded view of the findings. This is particularly so because practical applications of some of the theoretical results have so far been rare.[10] In the remainder of this section I discuss the motivation and logic underlying such incentive schemes. I shall then illustrate some of the central issues by means of an extended example running through sections 4.5–4.7 and the appendix.

In any social organization there are certain pieces of information that are known (or which will become known) only by the individuals in question; that is, they are costly (or in the extreme, impossible) to monitor publicly. These *private* pieces of information include, (a) an individual's personal characteristics (e.g. his preferences, needs, or the pollution abatement costs for a firm, etc.); that is, what kind of an entity the agent *is*, (b) the actions that he takes (e.g. how hard a person works at his task), that is, what a person *does*, and (c) localized pieces of information about the state of the world – or certain aspects of specialized technological possibilities.[11] At the same time there are certain types of information that are publicly known, or which *can* be publicly observed at relatively little cost. These may be precise pieces of information (e.g. the amount of pollution emitted by a firm) or they may be statistical information (e.g. the age distribution in a given society at a given moment of time). Thus a planning mechanism essentially selects an outcome (i.e. an allocation of goods and services) which is a function of private decisions that are based on private information and public decisions that are based on publicly known information. The idea then is to choose among planning mechanisms on the basis of their outcomes as judged by the social welfare criterion that has been adopted.[12] The planning mechanisms I have looked at so far in this book are very simple examples of this.

[10] *The Review of Economic Studies* (Symposium on Incentive Compatibility), April 1979, presents a collection of theoretical essays, as does Laffont (1979). Experimental results are reported in Bohm (1972); Randall *et al.* (1974); Barnett and Yandle (1973); and Scherr and Babb (1975).

[11] In the insurance literature the terms *adverse selection* and *moral hazard* are used to characterize the problems raised by the first and second categories of private information respectively.

[12] For a general discussion of planning mechanisms with dispersed information see Dasgupta (1980).

In the voluminous recent literature on planning mechanisms with dispersed information the aim has been to devise schemes in which the government (or planner) invites individuals and firms to send in messages (suitably chosen) to the centre and at the same time publicly announces how the totality of received messages and public observations will be translated into public decisions (e.g. the rates of taxation on individuals and firms). If the set of admissible messages is identical to the set of possible types of private information the centre wants to know, the planning mechanism is called a *direct* one. Otherwise, it is called an *indirect* mechanism (see Dasgupta, Hammond and Maskin, 1979). In the appendix (section 4A.2) we shall provide an example of a direct mechanism in which firms will find it in their interest to tell the truth about their pollution abatement costs. An outstanding example of an indirect mechanism is the one provided by Groves and Ledyard (1977) in which individuals transmit quite abstract messages to the centre and the mechanism is so devised that equilibrium outcomes have the property of sustaining efficient allocations of public goods even although individuals' true underlying preferences for these public goods remain private information.

The *relevance* of such mechanisms for environmental planning can hardly be over-emphasized. To take only one example, they have an immediate bearing on pollution management problems when private damages are private information. But the question can be asked whether social-damage functions must invariably be based exclusively on individuals' perceptions of their private damages. One can argue that this is not how people inevitably view the matter. Policies that are guided by considerations of minimum food requirements of citizens are not necessarily based on individuals' perceptions of *their* personal needs; nor should they be so. Unquestionably, needs vary across persons. But it is surely right and proper for governments to aim at ensuring some standard of food intake for all citizens even if some can live on less. A society can take the view that all citizens have a basic right to enjoying a command over certain bundles of goods and services irrespective of what individual preferences are. Thus too with environmental issues bearing on health and the risk of death. In addition, as I have argued earlier it is difficult to see why the government must respect individual beliefs about various possibilities if they happen to be wrong. In other words, what I am trying to argue here is that the economist's desire for estimating individual 'willingness to pay' to reduce the risk of environmental damages may have become obsessive. Reliance on a social damage function which is not based exclusively on individual preferences is not an 'undemocratic' act. I shall take it in what follows that the social damage function (whether or not based on individual preferences) has been estimated and that the government is concerned with the choice of policies to influence the emission of pollutants by firms.

4.5 Taxation versus regulations under uncertainty

It is intuitively clear that the effects of optimum taxation and optimum regulation are unlikely to be the same when the planner faces uncertainty about matters that are relevant to the problem at hand. In what follows I use a simple formulation to see what the relevant effects are and how they need to be assessed. In particular I argue that if the resource in question displays threshold effects, then the optimal form of 'taxation' is more like a pure regulation than a pure tax; that is, the regulator ought to impose optimal effluent standards, and not optimal effluent charges.[13]

These points can be discussed most tellingly in the context of environmental pollution. To begin with, note that environmental effects of pollution usually take time to make their presence felt. Therefore, the uncertainty about the extent of social damage resulting from pollution will not be resolved until sometime in the future. The policy chosen today then must be independent of the resolution of this uncertainty.

For example, suppose were are considering a policy to restrict the discharge of PCBs by industries into the seas. To date we are still uncertain about the capacity of zooplanktons to absorb this effluent without undue damage. It is possible that this knowledge will be gained in the future, but today's decision about how much PCB ought to be discharged must be independent of this knowledge.

[13] By a 'pure' tax I mean a marginal tax rate which is independent of the rate of emission.

In fact the planner is usually uncertain as well about the cost of pollution control. It requires specialized knowledge. Moreover, abatement programmes take time to implement, and firms may not know today precisely what the costs will be. Furthermore, as I have argued earlier, even if firms know their true abatement costs, the regulator may not, and may not be able to elicit the truth from firms unless it is in their interest to tell the truth. Thus, today's decision on the amount of pollution permitted must be independent of the resolution of this uncertainty as well.

It is now clear why regulations (i.e. effluent standards) and taxes (i.e. effluent charges) are not identical in their effects. Recall that in the pure regulation scheme the planner selects the total quantity of pollution to be emitted. Firms are prohibited from polluting in excess of this. In the pure tax scheme, the planner imposes a constant tax rate for marginal units of pollution and individual firms then decide how much to pollute. Thus, for any given realization of the social-damage function (e.g. realization of the true threshold level of the resource being damaged by the pollutant) taxes encourage too little abatement if abatement costs are in fact higher than expected and they encourage too much abatement if they are lower. The problem is reversed for the

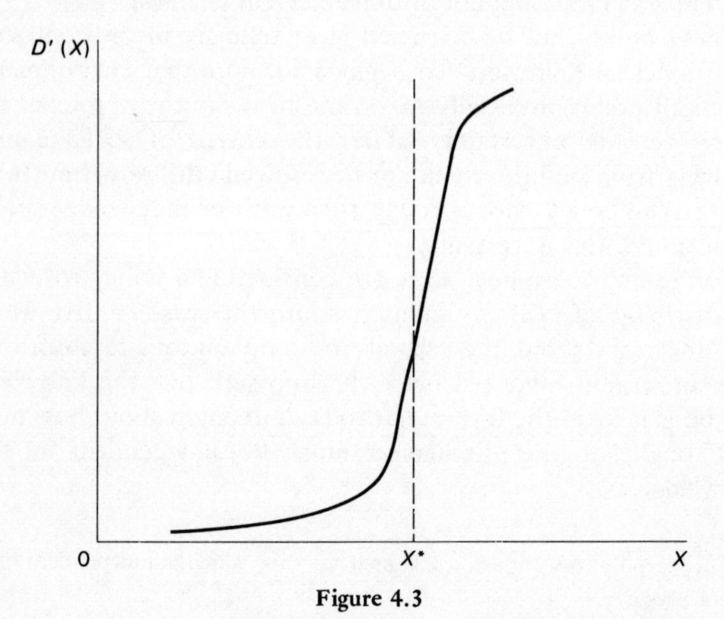

Figure 4.3

regulation scheme. Since the total quantity of pollution is decided by the planner in advance, it will be too little if costs are lower than expected and too much if they are higher.

Given that they are different in their impact, it is important to ask which is superior. As one would expect, the answer depends on the curvatures of the benefit and cost functions, and presently this will be confirmed by an example. But first it will be useful to obtain an intuitive feel for the proposition that it may well be desirable to rely on quantity restrictions rather than effluent charges (i.e. taxes) when the resource displays threshold effects.

As earlier, let X denote the total emission of a particular pollutant and let $D(X)$ be the social loss, in the sense of environmental damage caused by this emission. For the moment I am supposing that this loss function is known with certainty. Now suppose that the marginal loss function $[dD(X)/dX]$ takes the shape described in figure 4.3. Such a form seems plausible for a number of environmental problems, where X^* denotes the threshold level of pollution. That is, within a small neighbourhood of X^*, marginal damage due to the pollutant increases dramatically.

Now suppose that firms' abatement costs as a function of the quantity of pollution are unknown by the planner and are therefore functions of random variables as well. Regulation (i.e. the issue of a fixed quantity of licences to pollute) seems the better of the two schemes because the planner can ensure that the total level of pollution will be less than X^* – the level at which disaster strikes. Since cost functions are unknown to the planner, the only way to ensure against firms polluting beyond the level X^* via a pollution tax is to set a 'high' tax rate. However, a 'high' tax rate may be undesirable if there is a good chance that costs are lower than expected, because in such circumstances the amount of clean-up will exceed the amount desirable. There will be too little pollution!

The argument is still true if it is thought that there is a threshold level, and if the actual level is not known, only that it is within a range. Thus, for example, prolonged downgrading of the assimilative capacity of a medium caused by excessive levels of pollution can result in the instability of eco-systems. But it may not be known at what point the instability occurs. Here too the planner will wish to ensure against the possibility of disaster and guarantee that the level of pollution does not go much beyond the bottom value of the range. Once again, regulations can guarantee this, but pure taxes cannot, unless they are set at prohibitively high levels.

Regulations and pure taxes are polar types of plan instruments. They are an extreme case of tax functions defined on the level of effluent emission. A pure tax is a special case because the marginal rate is independent of the quantity discharged. A regulation is a zero tax rate up to the quota and an infinite tax rate for amounts in excess of the quota. It is seen that in the face of uncertainty the optimal tax scheme is one for which the tax rate is a function of the quantity of pollutants discharged and that in general it is neither of the two limiting forms just discussed. Nevertheless, for administrative reasons the planner may be forced to consider only the two limiting forms, and indeed, much of the debate on the appropriate form of intervention in economic activities involving environmental resources has centred on the relative advantages of pure taxation versus regulation.[14] The following section analyses these issues more formally in the context of a single firm emitting pollutants as a by-product of its production activity and looks briefly at the problem when more than one firm is so engaged. The appendix presents a formal analysis of this problem.

4.6 The case of a single firm

Consider once again a single firm whose net profit level as a function of the level of pollution X it emits is $B(X)$, and that the social damage from X is $D(X)$. Net social benefit $N(X)$ is taken to be $B(X) - D(X)$ and it is supposed that this is maximized at the pollution level X^* (see figures 3.1 and 3.2). It is clear that the optimum tax rate to impose on the firm is $t^* = D'(X^*)$.

Now suppose the regulator faces uncertainty about both the firm's net profit function $B(X)$ and the environmental damage function, $D(X)$. Regarding the former, it is natural to suppose that the firm knows its technology but that it is the government (regulator) which is uncertain about matters (e.g. abatement costs).

[14] Kneese and Schultze (1975) contains a good discussion of the relative merits of these polar modes which is based on institutional considerations.

Thus let $B(X, \phi)$ denote the net profit accruing to the firm when X is the level of emission and ϕ is the random variable reflecting the planner's uncertainty about the firm's technological possibilities. By hypothesis, the firm knows the true value of ϕ at the time it chooses X. However, I suppose that the planner does not know the true value of ϕ when it announces its policy.

Turning now to the social damage function D, I take it that the environmental consequences of the given pollutant are uncertain. Thus let $D(X, \theta)$ denote the social value of the damage sustained when X is the level of pollution and θ is the value of the radom variable reflecting the planner's uncertainty.

Suppose that the planner desires to choose that policy which will maximize the *expected* value of net social benefit, that is,

$$E[B(X, \phi) - D(X, \theta)] \tag{4.5}$$

where E is the expectation operator.[15] It should be noted that expression (4.5) is perfectly consistent with the regulator displaying an aversion toward risk, and we shall see this presently.

It will be supposed that the regulator can monitor the level of pollution X that the firm chooses to emit. For simplicity of exposition, assume that the random variables θ and ϕ are independent of each other. This is reasonable, since ϕ reflects uncertainties regarding the firm's technology, and θ reflects uncertainties regarding the effect of the firm's pollution on the environment. The regulator is interested in maximizing expected net social benefit (4.5). Moreover, he is aware that the firm, knowing the true value of ϕ, is interested solely in its net profits.[16] It is

[15] If $f(\bar{\theta}, \bar{\phi})$ is the probability that the two random variables realize the values $\bar{\theta}$ and $\bar{\phi}$ then by definition

$$E(B(X, \phi) - D(X, \theta)) = \sum_{\theta} \sum_{\phi} (B(X, \phi) - D(X, \theta)) f(\theta, \phi).$$

I should emphasize that when I speak of the firm knowing its own technology I mean that it knows *more* than the regulator. Whatever uncertainty the firm faces about its own technology is assumed to be expected out in its own calculations.

[16] Thus the regulator and the firm pursue different goals. It is this feature that distinguishes the problem pursued here from the theory of teams. For a thorough discussion of the latter, see Marschak and Radner (1972).

then immediately apparent that the optimum policy consists in the planner imposing on the firm a pollution tax schedule $T(X)$ which is of the form:

$$T(X) = E[D(X, \theta)] \pm \text{constant}. \qquad (4.6)$$

That is, the optimum pollution tax schedule is the expected social-damage function plus or minus a constant.[17] Faced with tax schedule $T(X)$, the firm will choose X so as to maximize

$$B(X, \phi) - T(X) = B(X, \phi) - E[D(X, \theta)] \pm \text{constant}, \quad (4.7)$$

that it, its profit, net of tax payment. Moreover, the regulator knows in advance that the firm will maximize (4.7).

Notice at once that when the regulator announces the tax schedule (4.6) he cannot predict precisely what the resulting level of pollution is going to be. This is because by assumption the regulator does not know the true value of ϕ, and as equation (4.7) makes clear, the firm's profit-maximizing choice of X depends on ϕ. Thus the imposition of the optimum tax schedule (4.6) results in an uncertainty about the amount of pollution that will eventually be emitted, thereby compounding the uncertainty about the final environmental damage. In order to maximize (4.7) the firm will choose that value of X at which marginal profit (excluding tax payment) equals the marginal tax rate.[18] That is,

$$\partial B(X, \phi)/\partial X = E[\partial D(X, \theta)/\partial X]. \qquad (4.8)$$

From equation (4.8) it is clear that the profit-maximizing X, say X^*, is a function of the realized value of ϕ. That is, $X^* = X^*(\phi)$. The regulator by hypothesis does not know the true value of ϕ, but from equation (4.8) he can calculate the response function $X^*(\phi)$. Note as well that except for the limiting case where $D(X, \theta)$

[17] The 'constant' in expression (4.6) being by definition, independent of X, is essentially a lump-sum tax or subsidy, depending on its sign. Since by assumption there are no income effects its magnitude will not affect the outcome if we ignore distributional issues. In what follows the reader may wish to ignore the constant and suppose it to be nil.

[18] We are assuming that expression (4.7) is strictly concave in X for every possible ϕ. Moreover, the random variable has been so labelled that, without loss of generality, it is supposed that for each admissible value of ϕ, there is a unique solution of equation (4.8).

is of the multiplicative form $Xg(\theta)$ (a case we have ruled out because we have supposed $D(X, \theta)$ to be strictly convex in X), the optimum pollution tax $E[D(X,\theta)]$ is not proportional to X. It follows that, except for this limiting case, the optimum tax rate on incremental pollution, namely, $\mathrm{d}E[D(X,\theta)]/\mathrm{d}X$, is not independent of the level of pollution.

We conclude that in the presence of uncertainty about abatement costs, the optimal tax schedule, $E[D(X,\theta)]$, except for special cases, is neither a quota, nor a linear tax schedule (i.e. a marginal tax rate that is independent of the level of pollution emitted). That is, in the presence of uncertainty the control of environmental pollution is best conducted with the help of tax rates that vary with the quantity of pollutants discharged by a firm. Linear tax schedules and quantity regulations are merely suboptimal limiting forms of such policies.[19]

Let us conduct an exercise with this apparatus. Suppose that $\hat{X}$ is the level of pollution at which expected marginal social profit equals expected marginal social damage (i.e., $\hat{X}$ is the solution of the equation

$$E[\partial B(X, \phi)/\partial X] = E[\partial D(X, \theta)/\partial X]).$$

Now suppose that environmental uncertainties are small so that the social damage function $D(X, \theta)$ can be approximated around the level $\hat{X}$, in the form

$$D(X, \theta) = a_1(\theta) + D_1[X - \hat{X} - a_2(\theta)] + D_2[X - \hat{X} - a_3(\theta)]^2 \tag{4.9}$$

where D_1 and D_2 are positive constants, and where, without loss of generality, it is supposed that $a_1(\theta)$, $a_2(\theta)$ and $a_3(\theta)$ are random variables with zero expected values. From equation (4.9) it is then

[19] These two limiting forms were compared and contrasted in a seminal contribution by Weitzman (1974). Notice that for this example the imposition of $E(D(X, \theta))$ as the tax schedule is equivalent in its effect to that of the imposition of the optimum state-contingent pollution tax. Thus, let $X^*(\phi)$ be the solution of equation (4.8). Then define $t^*(\phi) = \partial B(X, \phi)/\partial X$, evaluated at $X^*(\phi)$. Then $t^*(\phi)$ is the optimum state-contingent tax rate. On state-contingent prices, see e.g. Dasgupta and Heal (1979, chapter 14). The example that follows in the text is that of Weitzman (1974).

apparent that

$$E[D(X, \theta)] = D_1(X - \hat{X}) + D_2(X - \hat{X})^2 + D_2E\{[a_3(\theta)]^2\}. \quad (4.10)$$

Thus, if the environmental damage function, $D(X, \theta)$, is of the form of equation (4.9), the optimal pollution tax schedule is of the form of equation (4.10). This is, of course, neither a linear tax nor a quota. As the third term on the right-hand side of equation (4.10) is a constant, we may as well ignore it (see footnote 12). The relevant terms depend on X, the first being linear in X and the second quadratic. Notice now that if D_2 is 'small', then in the neighbourhood of $\hat{X}$ the first term on the right-hand side of equation (4.10) dominates the second term, and so

$$E[D(X, \theta)] \simeq D_1(X - \hat{X}). \quad (4.11)$$

In this case the optimal tax schedule is approximately linear, with a constant marginal tax rate D_1. On the other hand, if D_2 is 'large', even a mild departure from $\hat{X}$ results in the firm being taxed heavily, as equation (4.10) confirms readily. Confronted with such a schedule, the firm will not wish to deviate unduly from the pollution level $\hat{X}$. The effect is then not dissimilar to the case in which the planner imposes $\hat{X}$ as a quota. Thus, if D_2 is large, the optimum pollution tax schedule resembles a quantity regulation.

The intuition behind these results ought to be clear enough. If the social damage function is of the form of equation (4.9), the marginal damage function is

$$\partial D(X, \theta)/\partial X = D_1 + 2D_2[X - \hat{X} - a_2(\theta)]. \quad (4.12)$$

We have already supposed by way of simplification that the uncertainty is 'small'. Thus the range of values $a_2(\theta)$ is permitted to take is small. From equation (4.12) it is apparent that the slope of the marginal damage function (i.e., $\partial^2 D(X, \theta)/\partial X^2$) is equal to $2D_2$. If D_2 is large, what equation (4.12) tells us is that marginal social damage increases dramatically with increasing pollution in the neighbourhood of an uncertain level of pollution, $\hat{X} + a_2(\theta)$. In other words, a large value of D_2 captures the fact that the pollution in question has a threshold effect. However, the threshold level of pollution, $\hat{X} + a_2(\theta)$, is unknown, with an expected value of $\hat{X}$. Therefore, if D_2 is large, the polluting firm, faced with a tax schedule of the form of equation (4.11) will choose not to pollute in excess of $\hat{X}$ and in fact will pollute at a level slightly short of $\hat{X}$ (this last, so as to pick up a small subsidy, as given by the first term of equation (4.10)).

One can also see from this example why the planner would go way off the mark in such circumstances if he were to rely on a linear tax schedule (i.e. a constant marginal tax rate). The point is that if the regulator is uncertain about the firm's technology – for example, if he is uncertain about abatement costs – the only way to ensure that the firm does not pollute beyond $\hat{X}$ is to set a high tax rate. But a high tax rate would be undesirable if abatement cost turned out to be lower than expected, because in such circumstances the amount of clean-up will exceed the amount desirable. There will be too little pollution! On the other hand, if D_2 is small, in the neighbourhood of $\hat{X}$ the marginal damage function is approximately constant (equal to D_1), as equation (4.12) makes clear. However, if marginal social damage is known and constant, it is obviously best to allow the firm full flexibility in finding the optimum level of pollution, since the firm by hypothesis knows the true value of ϕ and the regulator, by hypothesis, does not. A constant marginal tax rate (i.e. a linear tax schedule) allows the greatest amount of such flexibility, and so it is not surprising that if D_2 is small, the optimal tax schedule resembles a linear schedule. These considerations suggest that to the extent that environmental resources display threshold effects, the optimal tax schedule designed to limit their use resembles regulations governing amount of emission, and if for administrative reasons a choice has to be made solely between the optimum linear tax schedule and the optimum quota, the latter should be chosen.

4.7 The case of multiple firms

Where a single firm is engaged in causing environmental damage, it is a simple matter to compute the form of the optimum tax schedule. In the preceding section we noted in expression (4.6) that the regulator ideally should impose a pollution tax schedule which, up to an additive constant, is the expected value of the social damage function. The intuition behind this is rather obvious. For every possible realization of the random variable ϕ, such a tax schedule, if imposed on the firm, results in the firm's net profit function, equation (4.7), being identical with the social objective function. In other words, the tax schedule is so designed that the firm's objective (net of tax payment) coincides with society's objective.[20] In such a situation, the firm's profit-maximizing response cannot help but be the response that the regulator would ideally like the firm to make. Matters are more complicated when more than one firm is involved in damaging the environment. The problem is that the damage that any one firm imposes on the environment by marginally increasing its level of pollution discharge now depends, not only on its own level of discharge, but also on the levels discharged by others. This interaction, as we shall see, causes difficulties in the computation of the optimum pollution tax schedules, though the analysis is simple enough in general terms.

Suppose then that there are N firms engaged in emitting a specific type of pollutant. Firms are indexed by i or j ($i, j = 1, 2, \ldots, N$). Let X_i be the level emitted by firm i and let us suppose that the net profit function of firm i is $B(X_i, \phi_i)$, where ϕ_i is a random variable reflecting the regulator's uncertainty about abatement costs encountered by i. As in the previous section, we shall take it that at the time i chooses X_i it knows the true value of ϕ_i but that when the regulator announces his policy he is innocent of the actual value of ϕ_i. For ease of exposition suppose that the damage suffered by the environment due to pollution depends on the sum of the levels of pollution emitted by each of the firms and a random variable θ. Thus

$$D = D\left(\sum_{i=1}^{N} X_i, \theta\right).$$

The pollutant is, therefore, a 'public bad'. Expected net social benefit, we take it, is a direct generalization of expression (4.5), being the sum of the expected profits minus the expected social

[20] That is, the imposition of the tax schedule reduces the problem to a simple example in the theory of teams. For a pioneering discussion of incentives in teams, see Groves (1973).

damage, that is,

$$E\left[\sum_{i=1}^{N} B(X_i, \phi_i)\right] - E\left[D\left(\sum_{i=1}^{N} X_i, \theta\right)\right], \tag{4.13}$$

and it is this which the regulator is determined to maximize. For the remainder of this section we shall suppose, as before, that $B(X_i, \phi_i)$ is strictly concave in X_i for all ϕ_i, and that $D(X, \theta)$ is strictly convex in X for all θ, where

$$X = \left(\sum_{i=1}^{N} X_i\right)$$

is the total emission of the pollution in question.

Let us begin by analysing what the full optimum looks like. Suppose that at the time the firms choose their levels of emission, everyone (i.e. the N firms and the regulator) knows the realized values of the N random variables ϕ_i ($i = 1, \ldots, N$). Then, clearly, in order that expression (4.13) be maximized, firm i ($i = 1, \ldots, N$) should be made to choose that level of pollution X_i which maximizes

$$\sum_{i=1}^{N} B(X_i, \phi_i) - E_\theta\left[D\left(\sum_{i=1}^{N} X_i, \theta\right)\right]. \tag{4.14}$$

Suppose, without further ado, that it does. Then firm i should be made to choose that X_i at which

$$\partial B(X_i, \phi_i)/\partial X_i = E_\theta[\partial D(X, \theta)/\partial X] \qquad i = 1, \ldots, N \tag{4.15}$$

where

$$X = \sum_{i=1}^{N} X_i.$$

Equations (4.15) are N in number, and there are N unknowns X_i to be solved for. The ith equation in (4.15) says that the ith firm should pollute up to the level at which its actual marginal profit (left-hand side of equation (4.15)) equals the expected marginal damage due to aggregate pollution, where the expectation is carried out over the remaining random variable θ. Let $\tilde{X}_i$ ($i = 1, \ldots, N$) denote the solution of the system of equations

(4.15). It will be noticed that the realized values of the random variables ϕ_i ($i = 1, \ldots, N$) are parameters for this system of equations. Thus $\tilde{X}_i$ depends on the realized values of *all* the N random variables ϕ_j ($j = 1, \ldots, N$) and not merely on ϕ_i. Thus $\tilde{X}_i = \tilde{X}_i$ $(\phi_1, \ldots, \phi_i, \ldots, \phi_N)$. This is precisely what intuition suggests. For, if it emerges that firm j's abatement cost at the margin is less than that of firm i, the former, in the interest of social welfare, should be forced to pollute less than the latter; the reverse if it emerges that i's abatement cost at the margin is less than that of j. It is therefore clear that the (full) optimum level of emission of firm i is of the form $\tilde{X}_i = \tilde{X}_i(\phi_1, \ldots, \phi_i, \ldots, \phi_N)$.

The question arises whether the full optimum can be enforced. Two distinct issues are involved here, and we have alluded to them earlier. First, it should be recognized that a knowledge of true abatement costs involves specialized technical knowledge, and while it is reasonable in many circumstances to assume that firms know their own abatement costs at the time they make their decisions, it is at least equally reasonable to suppose that the regulator does not. In this event it seems natural to allow the regulator to ask the firms to report their true abatement costs. But then recall that firms are interested only in their own private profits and not expected social benefits (equation (4.13)). If firms know in advance that their answers to the regulator's query will result in the enforcement of the optimum levels of pollution $\tilde{X}_i$, each firm will have a strong incentive to lie. Each firm would like to pretend that its marginal abatement cost is very high, reasoning that it will be allowed to pollute more than it would be allowed to were the truth known to the regulator. Its reasoning would be correct. Moreover, the regulator would know that this is how firms will reason. Therefore, he will know that the full optimum cannot be reached merely by calculating the functions $\tilde{X}_i$ and asking firms to divulge their private information. If the regulator wants the truth from firms in the environment we are considering, he must provide them with an incentive to tell the truth. The appendix to this chapter presents incentive schemes that will elicit the truth from firms.

This brings us to the second point, namely, that even if in principle the regulator can elicit the truth from firms, the cost of the transmission of this information from the individual firms to the regulator typically will not be negligible: ϕ_i may be a large set of numbers. If such transmission costs are taken into account, it may not be sensible to try and reach what we have called the full optimum, $\tilde{X}_i$. It may be better that the regulator attempt to maximize expression (4.13) without asking firms to transmit their private information, but rely instead on information that he can obtain easily.

The appendix analyses the structure of pollution taxes which will maximize expression (4.13) when two-way communication between the regulator and the firms is barred (see section 4A.3). The remainder of this section looks at some simple regulatory policies that have often been proposed in the literature.

Conceptually, the simplest by far is a direct generalization of effluent standards which was discussed earlier in this section. For the present example it would mean a pollution quota imposed on each firm. Let $\hat{X}_i$ denote the optimum quota for firm i. Since the regulator is interested in maximizing expression (4.13), $\hat{X}_i$ must be the solution of the equations

$$\partial E[B(X_i, \phi_i)]/\partial X_i = \partial E[D(X, \theta)]/\partial X \quad \text{for } i = 1, \ldots, N \qquad (4.16)$$

where

$$X = \sum_{i=1}^{N} X_i,$$

or in other words, where expected marginal profit to firm i equals the expected marginal social damage caused by aggregate pollution.

Now, in fact, there is a glaring defect with a scheme of this kind which the reader will have noticed immediately. The point is that social damage, by hypothesis, depends on the aggregate emission of pollution X. Therefore, if effluent standards are to be used, they ought to be imposed on the industry as a whole and not on each firm separately. It seems plausible that in the interest of expected social welfare it would be better if the regulator could devise a scheme in which firms chose their own levels of emission but were subject to the constraint that total emission must equal the optimum quota for the industry as a whole. The point is, of course, that the regulator ought to encourage firms with low clean-up costs to undertake more clean-up that those having high clean-up costs. But by hypothesis the regulator does not know a firm's actual clean-up costs, and so rule (4.16) does not allow for this desirable flexibility.

To make the point more clearly, suppose that the random variables ϕ_i are independent of one another and suppose furthermore that they are identically distributed. It is then clear from rule (4.16) that the optimum quota $\hat{X}_i$ is the same for every firm, say $\hat{X}$. But in fact the true value of ϕ_i typically will vary from firm to firm. It is this lack of flexibility in firm-specific emission standard schemes which has led authors like Dales (1968) to suggest an improvement, namely, a scheme in which the regulator selects the aggregate allowable level of effluent, which is then auctioned off to the firms in the form of licences. In our example, the regulator could sell $N\hat{X}$ licences to the firms.[21] If N is large, the resulting 'market' price for a licence would be akin to a pollution tax. At the resulting market price, say p^*, firms with high actual abatement costs naturally would purchase more licences than those with low actual abatement costs. This shifting of the burden of pollution control across firms is, of course, an improvement on firm-specific pollution quotas. It enables the regulator to retain control over the aggregate level of pollution and at the same time allows for a flexibility that firm-specific quotas do not display.

It will have been noticed that in the scheme just outlined the regulator sets the quota on aggregate pollution in advance. At the instant he selects $N\hat{X}$ he is uncertain about the fee, p^*, which will clear the market for these licences. At the opposite pole is a scheme in which the regulator announces a licence fee or pollution tax (or effluent charge) and firms are allowed to purchase as many licences as they like at the going fee. In this scheme the regulator does not know in advance the eventual level of pollution. The relative merits of these two schemes depend on much the same considerations that were mentioned in the preceding section. If the environmental resource in question displays threshold effects,

[21] Or alternatively, each firm could be given $\hat{X}$ transferable licences. In terms of income distribution these two procedures would not be the same though. For a reasoned assessment of the implementability of such a procedure for air-quality control, see Tietenberg (1980).

the scheme in which the regulator auctions away the optimal number of licences is preferable to the imposition of the optimal linear pollution charge.[22]

However, one will recognize that it would be better still to allow more flexibility and have the regulator impose suitably chosen firm-specific pollution-tax schedules of the form $T_i(X_i)$. For the case of a single firm, locating the optimum pollution tax schedule was an easy enough matter and, as noted in the previous section, such a tax schedule in fact sustains the full optimum. Matters are a good deal more complicated here. Suppose that the ϕ_is are independent random variables. The point to note is that the imposition of the optimal tax schedules $T_i(X_i)$ will not sustain the full optimum. The reason is easy to see: by assumption firm i knows only the true value of ϕ_i and not of ϕ_j $(j \neq i)$. Thus faced with a tax schedule $T_i(X_i)$ and a knowledge of ϕ_i, firm i will choose X_i, which will be insensitive to the realized values of ϕ_j $(j \neq i)$. However, we have already noted in this section that the full optimum has firm i polluting at the level $\tilde{X}_i$, which is a function of *all* the ϕ_js. Thus firm-specific pollution tax schedules of the form $T_i(X_i)$ cannot be made to sustain the full optimum but they can be so chosen that in terms of social benefits (equation 4.13) they lead to better results than either the pure licensing scheme or the pure pollution tax scheme. The optimum forms of such tax schedules are studied in the appendix to this chapter.

[22] A further refinement over the aggregate effluent standard scheme which we have just discussed is one in which the regulator auctions away a fixed number of licences and at the same time announces that he will pay a fixed subsidy per licence purchased by firms in excess of their actual emissions. In this scheme the regulator has to compute two parameters in order to maximize expression (4.13), the number of licences to be issued and the rate of subsidy. When optimally chosen, this scheme is superior to the two we have already discussed. For details, see Roberts and Spence (1976) and Kwerel (1977).

Appendix: Imperfect Information and Optimal Pollution Control

4A.1 Introduction

This appendix addresses the problems raised in section 4.7 and analyses the manner in which they may be solved.[23] I take it that there are N polluting firms ($i, j = 1, \ldots, N$), and that X_i is the level of pollution emitted by firm i. As before, I suppose that the private profit function of firm i is $B(X_i, \phi_i)$, where ϕ_i is a random variable whose realized value is known to i, and where B is strictly concave in X_i for all admissible values of ϕ_i. Social damage due to pollution levels X_i ($i = 1, \ldots, N$) is given by the function $D(X, \theta)$, where $X = \sum_{i=1}^{N} X_i$ and where θ is a random variable. We take it that D is an increasing and strictly convex function of X for every admissible value of θ. Net social welfare is assumed to be given by expression (4.13) which I rewrite as

$$E[\Sigma B(X_i, \phi_i)] - E[D(X, \theta)] \tag{4A.1}$$

Expression (4A.1) is to be maximized. However, the highest attainable level of expression (4A.1) depends on the class of tax schemes that the regulator can choose from. Given that ϕ_i is a variable whose value is known in the first instance only by firm i, there are incentive problems in that firms typically would like to claim that their abatement costs are high at the margin (i.e. that their marginal profitability at high levels of pollution is high). So the question arises whether the regulator can devise tax-subsidy schemes which will neutralize such biases in incentives.

The following section presents tax-subsidy schemes which will enable the full optimum to be attained despite this incentive problem. It requires that the regulator receives messages from firms and then uses them to construct tax schedules that are imposed on firms. Moreover, firms are informed about how their messages will be translated into tax schedules. I shall suppose that firms do not collude. My task will be to show that the regulator can so devise tax schemes that, (a) firms will report their true profit functions (i.e. the true value of ϕ_i), and (b) they will choose the fully optimal pollution levels. In section 4A.3 I suppose that the transmission of messages from firms to the regulator is too costly, so that the regulator is forced to impose tax schedules on firms based only on his knowledge of the probability distribution of the ϕ_is and θ. I show trivially that the full optimum cannot be attained. However,

[23] This appendix is based on Dasgupta, Hammond and Maskin (1980).

I am able to locate the optimum structure of taxes given this communication constraint.

4A.2 Two-way communication

Imagine that the regulator asks the firms to inform him of their profit functions; that is, firm i is asked to report the true value of ϕ_i. The regulator informs the firms that their reports (i.e. the reported values of the N parameters $\phi_1, \ldots, \phi_N$) and their pollution emission levels will be used to compute taxes T_i which will then be imposed on firms. Moreover, firms are told in advance of the manner in which the reported values of ϕ_i and emission levels X_i will be translated into the N taxes, T_i. The idea is to construct tax schedules in such a manner that each firm finds it in its economic interest to report the truth irrespective of what other firms do. That is, the tax schedules are so constructed that truth-telling is a dominant strategy for firms. If this can be achieved, then each firm will tell the truth and in fact the full optimum can be attained. The way to construct such tax schedules is simple enough. The idea is to construct tax schemes in such a way that for every possible set of values of the parameters $\phi_1, \ldots, \phi_N$, the net profit for each firm (net of tax payment) coincides with the social objective function (4.14). We now see how this can be done.

In what follows I suppose firms do not collude. Let $\tilde{X}_i(\phi_1, \ldots, \phi_N)$, $(i = 1, \ldots, N)$, be the full optimum; that is, the solution of equation (4.15). We want to find tax functions $T_i(X_i, \phi_1, \ldots, \phi_N)$ for $i = 1, \ldots, N$ such that if $\hat{\phi}_i$ is firm i's actual parameter value, then for any possible announcement $\phi_i (\neq \hat{\phi}_i)$ it makes to the regulator, and for any pollution level $X_i (\neq \tilde{X}_i)$ it chooses and for any possible announcement ϕ_j that firm j $(j \neq i)$ makes,

$$\begin{aligned} &B[\tilde{X}_i(\phi_1, \ldots, \phi_{i-1}, \hat{\phi}_i, \phi_{i+1}, \ldots, \phi_N), \hat{\phi}_i] \\ &- T_i[\tilde{X}_i(\phi_1, \ldots, \phi_{i-1}, \hat{\phi}_i, \phi_{i+1}, \ldots, \phi_N), \phi_1, \ldots, \phi_{i-1}, \hat{\phi}_i, \phi_{i+1}, \ldots, \phi_N] \\ &\geqslant B(X_i, \hat{\phi}_i) - T_i(X_i, \phi_1, \ldots, \phi_{i-1}, \phi_i, \phi_{i+1}, \ldots, \phi_N) \qquad (4A.2) \\ &\text{for } i = 1, \ldots, N. \end{aligned}$$

If (4A.2) is satisfied, then each firm will announce its true parameter value and also find it most profitable to pollute at the fully optimal level, $\tilde{X}_i$. A set of tax schedules that satisfies (4A.2) is, of course, of the form

$$\begin{aligned} &T_i(X_i, \phi_1, \phi_2, \ldots, \phi_i, \ldots, \phi_N) \\ &= E_\theta \left\{ D\left[\sum_{j \neq i} \tilde{X}_j(\phi_1, \ldots, \phi_N) + X_i, \theta \right] \right\} - \sum_{j \neq i} B[\tilde{X}_j(\phi_1, \ldots, \phi_N), \phi_j] \\ &\pm \text{constant.} \qquad (4A.3) \end{aligned}$$

The point then is this. While the regulator does not know the true values of ϕ_i $(i = 1, \ldots, N)$, he can compute the optimal levels of pollution $\tilde{X}_i$ for every possible set of values of ϕ_i, by solving equation (4.15). He then asks firms to reveal their ϕ_is and announces that he will impose tax schedules on firms of the form of equation (4A.3). Firms will then be allowed to choose their pollution levels and pay taxes according to equation (4A.3). Since (4A.2) is satisfied for each i if (4A.3) is imposed, each firm will find truth-telling and the optimal level of pollution emission its dominant strategy. It should, however, be noted that the government is unable to balance its budget in this scheme. This is a pervasive problem with incentive schemes of this type (see Green and Laffont, 1977).

4A.3 One-way communication

It may be felt that the foregoing scheme is unduly cumbersome, requiring as it does the transmission of a great deal of information from firms to the regulator (ϕ_i will typically consist of a great many numbers). However, we continue to assume that the regulator can monitor the emission levels costlessly. Much of the literature on environmental control has in fact addressed itself to the problem of designing optimum tax schedules based solely on emission levels. As we recognized in section 4.7, such tax schemes cannot aspire to achieve the full optimum. I now present optimal tax schedules in those circumstances where the regulator does not receive any information from firms about their private abatement costs.

Suppose that the ϕ_is are independent random variables whose probability distributions are public knowledge. The regulator's aim is to maximize (4A.1) by imposing tax schedules of the form $T_i(X_i)$ on firms.

Let $\bar{X}_i(\phi_i)$, where $i = 1, \ldots, N$, be the solution of the problem of maximizing

$$B(X_i, \phi_i) + E\left\{\sum_{j \neq i} B[\bar{X}_j(\phi_j), \phi_j]\right\} - E\left\{D\left[\sum_{j \neq i} \bar{X}_j(\phi_j) + X_i, \theta\right]\right\} \quad (4A.4)$$

A comparison of expressions (4A.1) and (4A.4) immediately makes it clear that $\bar{X}_i(\phi_i)$ is the socially optimal level of pollution for firm i subject to the informational constraint that firm i's private information (i.e., the true value of ϕ_i) remains private. Thus $\bar{X}_i(\phi_i)$, $(i = 1, \ldots, N)$ sustains a second-best social optimum. We must now locate tax functions $T_i(X_i)$ for $i = 1, \ldots, N$, such that for any $X_i \geqslant 0$ such that $X_i \neq \bar{X}_i(\phi_i)$

$$B[\bar{X}_i(\phi_i), \phi_i] - T_i[\bar{X}_i(\phi_i)] \geqslant B(X_i, \phi_i) - T_i(X_i). \quad (4A.5)$$

for all admissible values of ϕ_i. If the regulator imposes tax functions which satisfy expression (4A.5) for all i, then the second-best solution can be derived. It is clear that a set of tax schedules which satisfies (4A.5) is of the form

$$T_i(X_i) = -E\left\{\sum_{j\neq i} B[\bar{X}_j(\phi_j), \phi_j]\right\} + E\left\{D\left[\sum_{j\neq i} \bar{X}_j(\phi_j) + X_i, \theta\right]\right\} \quad (4A.6)$$

$$\pm \text{ constant.}$$

The point to note about equation (4A.6) is that while the regulator does not know the true values of the ϕ_is, he can calculate the functions $\bar{X}_i(\phi_i)$ by differentiating expression (4A.4) with respect to X_i and setting it to zero; that is, by solving the N equations

$$\partial B(X_i, \phi_i)/\partial X_i = E\left\{\partial D\left[\sum_{j\neq i} \bar{X}_j(\phi_j) + X_i, \theta\right] \Big/ \partial X_i\right\}$$

where $\bar{X}_j(\phi_j)$, $j = 1, \ldots, N$, is the solution of the maximizing problem (4A.4). Therefore the regulator can compute the tax functions of equation (4A.6). It is of course, apparent from equation (4A.6) that in general $\mathrm{d}T_i(X_i)/\mathrm{d}X_i$, is not a constant. Nor is it a firm-specific quota.

5 Dimensions of Welfare

5.1 Commodities and their labels

Earlier, I looked at the formal structure of planning exercises (chapter 3 and its appendix). It should be recognized that even though there was no explicit mention of 'time' in that discussion, time can be readily incorporated by reinterpreting the formulation. Goods, services and resource flows could be labelled not only by their physical characteristics and location but also by the *date* at which they make their appearance in the economic organization in question. This then is the thing to do: increase the dimension of the space of commodities to any extent that one's considerations require. In the face of uncertainty about future possibilities commodities ought obviously to be labelled by *date-event* pairs (see chapter 10). Likewise, when persons (or groups) are deserving of differential treatment (e.g. because of asset inequality), goods and services ought to include in addition persons (or groups) in their characterization (see UNIDO, 1972). These are an instance of *named goods*, which were introduced by Arrow (1971a) in his influential essay on the theory of externalities (see also Starrett, 1972; Dasgupta and Heal, 1979; the terminology is taken from Hahn, 1971).

To give an example of this last, consider again our formulation of the commons problem in chapter 2 (section 2.2). In expression (2.1) we could write by y_{ij} the amount of effluent emitted by country i which enters country j's damage function. Since by hypothesis exclusion is not possible it is obviously the case that $y_{ij} = y_{ik}$ for all i, j and k. The environmentally nationalistic equilibrium was based on the assumption that i had control only of y_{ii} ($= y_{ij}$ for all j) and not of y_{ji} ($j \neq i$), even although y_{ji} enters i's damage function. This was the source of the inefficiency. The cooperative solution, represented by the international cost–benefit rule (2.5), on the other hand, obtained when each i was entitled to choose y_{ji} for all j.

Admittedly, the extent to which the concept of a commodity is refined in this manner is influenced by practical considerations. It is simple to check that the number of commodities will become very large if fine distinctions are drawn.[1] But in practical affairs named goods have been with us for a long time. When public transport is supplied at a lower charge to the young and old we are appealing to this idea. So too when education and health services are provided at a differential price to identifiable groups.[2]

5.2 Social rates of discount

Consider an intertemporal planning problem faced by an organization. We take it that the organization has well-defined objectives aggregated in the form of a valuation function, which we shall alternatively call an *objective function*, or a *welfare function*.[3] We also take it that the planner has identified the controls available to him and the variety of constraints the organization is subject to. If the organization in question is the economy as a whole, and this is indeed what we shall assume below, these constraints will include the response of households, firms and others to the government's policies. Examples of planning problems were discussed in chapter 3 appendix (see section 3A.1), and chapter 4. In what follows we denote time by t and without loss of generality label 'today' as $t = 0$, the date at which the planning problem is posed. For expositional ease we shall regard time as a discrete

[1] Note that if there are two physically distinguishable commodities, five possible events and ten persons, the number of named-event goods is 100.

[2] Commodities ought to be labelled by production units as well. When private producers price a good differently from its accounting price in the public sector this labelling is explicitly done.

[3] We do this purely for expositional simplicity. See chapter 3, section 3.2 for a discussion of what is involved in a planning exercise when, as will always be the case, there *is* no social welfare function to appeal to.

variable here. In subsequent chapters we shall find it more useful to regard it as continuous. Nothing of economic substance depends on this choice.

For conceptual simplicity suppose to begin with that there is no uncertainty. Suppose as well that it is possible to implement the optimal plan – that is the solution of the planning problem – by the use of accounting prices (see chapter 3 appendix, Theorem 2). Let the planner select a given commodity as a numeraire, which we label by all its characteristics *excepting* its *date*. Let p_t be its accounting price for date t. It is a *present-value price*. It is the accounting price to be used today for the numeraire of date t. Suppose that $p_t > 0$ for all $t \geqslant 0$; that is, the numeraire is not a free good at any date. Consider two adjacent moments t and $t + 1$. The *social rate of discount* between t and $t + 1$ is defined as the percentage rate of fall in the accounting price of the numeraire over this unit interval. Denoting the social rate of discount by r_t we thus have

$$r_t = -(p_{t+1} - p_t)/p_{t+1},$$

or (5.1)[4]

$$r_t = (p_t - p_{t+1})/p_{t+1}.$$

Earlier (see chapter 3, section 3.1) it was observed that under certain circumstances the accounting price of a resource equals the increase in the maximum value of the planner's valuation function were the economy endowed with an extra unit of the resource. From equation (5.1) it follows then that under such circumstances r_t equals the social rate of indifferent substitution between the numeraire at dates t and $t + 1$.[5]

[4] In the face of future uncertainty let $p_{s,t}$ denote the (present value) accounting price of the numeraire at date t and event s. Then the social rate of discount over the interval $(t, t + 1)$ is defined as:

$$r_t = \left(\sum_s p_{s,t} - \sum_s p_{s,t+1}\right) \Big/ \sum_s p_{s,t+1}$$

[5] Stating this formally let X_t be the numeraire at t and W the social welfare function. Under conditions identified in chapter 3 appendix (section 3A.1)

In chapter 3, section 3.4, we noted as well that under these circumstances one may use the gradient of the social welfare function at any state of the economy as a system of accounting prices at that state. The gradient can thus be used for evaluating the worthwhileness of a small change. It follows that under these circumstances one may regard social discount rates as social rates of indifferent substitution of the numeraire between adjacent dates even when the economy is far from the optimum.

It is sometimes thought that the choice of social rates of discount involve solely moral considerations, in particular notions of intergenerational justice.[6] This is not correct. Representing as they do a set of accounting prices, their status is no different from that of any other accounting price. As I noted in chapter 3 and its appendix, accounting prices depend not only on social objectives (and this is where moral considerations do enter) but also on the constraints that the economy is faced with, which include a description of where the economy happens to be at; that is, accounting prices reflect both welfare judgments and feasibility constraints. Excepting for special circumstances, namely when the economy is at a steady state (i.e. when relative accounting prices are constant over time) social discount rates depend as well on the numeraire chosen. But, of course, the choice of policies is not affected by the numeraire.

Much has been written on social discount rates and the arguments that are involved in 'estimating' them (see for example Baumol, 1968; Arrow and Kurz, 1970; and Lind 1982). It is sometimes held that they ought to be nil, since otherwise one would be discriminating against the claims of future generations.

---

we have

$$p_t = \partial W / \partial X_t$$

at the optimum. Thus equation (5.1) implies that

$$r_t = (\partial W / \partial X_t) / (\partial W / \partial X_{t+1}) - 1;$$

the social rate of indifferent substitution.

[6] For a discussion of alternative notions of intergenerational justice see Dasgupta and Heal (1979, chapter 9). Neher (1976) contains an illuminating discussion of resource exploitation under recurrent majority voting.

This is essentially the argument used by Professor Georgescu-Roegen in his criticism of Harold Hotelling's analysis of the optimal depletion of exhaustible resources (see Hotelling, 1931; Georgescu-Roegen, 1979). Much depends on what the numeraire is. If some index of per capita aggregate consumption is chosen as the numeraire and this is expected to grow, then this might be used as an argument for discounting future flows of the numeraire, since future generations will have more of it (see Dasgupta and Heal, 1979, chapter 10). But quite independent of this there is a case for discounting even future *welfare*, for the reason that future generations (at least those in the distant future) may not exist. The possibility of future extinction looms large if for no other reason than the redoubtable Second Law of Thermodynamics, a law which Professor Georgescu-Roegen himself has skilfully invoked to decry the manner in which economists are prone to modelling production possibilities (see Georgescu-Roegen, 1970, 1971). No doubt there is a chance that future generations will exist no matter how distant into the future we peer, the chance being smaller the farther we peer. But this is an argument for including all future generations in a planning exercise, not an argument for awarding their welfare claims equal weights.

5.3 Measures of social product

In practice it is imperative that one aggregates and it is convenient to keep various social goals separate. *Per capita aggregate consumption* is invariably appealed to as *one* of the indices of the level of well-being in an economy. Not surprisingly, it is this aggregate which is often used as a numeraire (see UNIDO, 1972). In what follows I shall do the same and on occasion refer to social rates of discount as *consumption rates of interest* so as to remind the reader of what the numeraire is.[7] What ought to be the ingredients of such an aggregate is dictated as much by what is convenient as by anything else. Here I shall suppose that in the procedure for this aggregation the prices that are used take existing

[7] In Little and Mirrlees (1974) the numeraire is uncommitted government income.

externalities into account. (Alternatively, one could keep existing 'externalities' as a separate category and include it as a correction to aggregate consumption when estimating the value of social product.) In an economy where it is judged that the rate of investment is not optimal one would need to weight (aggregate) investment by its accounting price (which would be in excess of unity if the economy is investing too little) and then add it to consumption to arrive at an index of aggregate product. (At a finer level of analysis, where one wants to draw attention to the *composition* of investment, one would wish to impute separate accounting prices to different forms of investment.) But this would not be an index of social product, since we will still not have allowed for distributional considerations. To include these one may take per capita aggregate consumption as the benchmark and award differing premia to the consumption levels of different groups: the premia being positive or negative depending on whether the group's consumption level is lower or higher than the benchmark – to capture the idea that incomes accruing to richer groups ought to be awarded lower weights. (Of course, if the rich *invest* more this feature would be caught via the premium on aggregate investment; see below.) Finally one would need to deduct for depreciation of capital assets which include, among other things, the *depletion* of various types of *natural resource* stocks (and also the quality degradation of such stocks). We arrive at an approximate measure of net social product when these features are included (see UNIDO, 1972; Dasgupta and Heal, 1979, chapter 8; Sen, 1979).

To illustrate this suppose Y_t^i is the disposable income of group i ($i = 1, \ldots, N$) at date t and suppose C_t^i is its consumption level. If C_t is aggregate consumption; p_t the accounting price of aggregate investment; $w(C_t, C_t^i)$, ($\gtreqless 0$) the premium awarded to the consumption of group i; I_t the level of government investment and D_t the rate of aggregate depreciation, then net social product, Y_t, at t in this approximation is:

$$Y_t = C_t + p_t\left(I_t - D_t + \sum_{i=1}^{N} (Y_t^i - C_t^i)\right) + \sum_{i=1}^{N} w(C_t, C_t^i)\, C_t^i. \tag{5.2}$$

(If, on the other hand, one wants to capture inequalities in *income* and not consumption, the distributional weights ought to be based on disposable income and then applied to the income levels of these groups in equation (5.2).)[8]

Distributional weights are often thought to be arbitrary and therefore not worthy of inclusion. They do involve moral judgments, but they are not arbitrary. They have the same conceptual status as social rates of discount which *are* widely regarded as worthy of being used in the control of resources. No doubt views differ on such weights. But then so would they differ on the choice of social discount rates if people pondered over the matter. What is paradoxical is the claim that such weights are arbitrary and that therefore they ought to be set at zero. It is not clear what 'zero' is if it is not a number. The discussion in chapter 3, section 3.2, is relevant here.

There is, however, a serious shortcoming in equation (5.2) as a measure of social product if, as we are doing here, such measures are given welfare connotations. I am thinking here of the various types of social overhead capital which affect welfare directly. Stocks of local public capital goods such as public transport, health, sanitation and educational facilities are prime examples. So too are capital stocks that constitute the machinery for warfare which, it is universally held, yield direct benefits in the form of national security. Admittedly the direct welfare effects of such overhead capital are unusually difficult to evaluate (see chapter 3, section 3.2). That is not, of course, an argument for ignoring them. To do so involves considerable peril, for if governments are allowed to ignore them they cannot be expected to provide a justification for one pattern of public expenditure over another. There is no item in a government's budget which is subject to so little public scrutiny as the accumulation of armaments. Measuring their increments solely by the prices at which armament contracts are negotiated, and not being obliged to place any value to their services *vis-à-vis* those obtained from other forms of social over-

[8] Note that the above formulation does recognize the fact that in industrial countries much investment is undertaken by the corporate sector from retained earnings. We would need to introduce the corporate sector as a separate group.

head capital is possibly a means of discouraging public debate. Welfare indices shorn of any information on the stocks of various forms of social overhead capital and amenities, *and* on which groups have access to them, are not to be taken seriously.[9]

5.4 The value of resource stocks and social overhead capital

This last set of considerations, the direct welfare effects of certain types of capital assets, has a strong bearing on environmental economics. In chapter 1 we noted that persistent pollutants such as detergents and pesticides have an impact on welfare not only as a flow but also as a stock. As a flow DDT is useful in agriculture as an input; as a stock it is hazardous for health (see also chapter 8). Likewise fisheries and aquifers are useful not only for the harvest they provide: as a stock they are directly useful, since harvesting and extraction costs are low if stocks are large (see chapters 6 and 7). Likewise, forests are beneficial not only for the flow of timber they can supply: as a stock they prevent soil erosion and maintain a genetic pool (see chapter 2, section 2.4; chapter 9). Then of course there are stocks of natural resources that are valued for the amenities they directly provide (e.g. places of scenic beauty) and species that one feels ought to be preserved on moral or aesthetic grounds. They are often merit goods.

This then is the point: like social overhead capital, stocks of natural resources are most often directly valuable (or, as in the

[9] A common explanation for what is almost universally felt to be excessive global expenditures on armaments is that, roughly speaking, nations are locked in a non-cooperative equilibrium of the kind explored in chapter 2, section 2.2; or in other words, something mildly resembling the outcome of a Prisoners' Dilemma game. This does account for the bias towards excessive expenditure, but not the magnitude of the bias. Any attempt to explain this last along these lines must recognize the fact that the *perceived* rate of armaments obsolescence is remarkably high: a marginal technological improvement by one nation rendering, obsolescent entire vintages of weapons of its rivals. Galbraith (1974, p. 153), offers a different explanation of the armaments race between the United States and the Soviet Union, which is based on the idea that there is tacit collusion between what he calls the 'technostructures' in these countries.

case of pollutants, damaging). Unlike bulldozers and lathes they do not merely have indirect welfare effects as a source of future service flows.

The evaluation of the direct welfare effects of social overhead capital and certain natural resources presents unusual difficulties. It would not do to value stocks such as educational facilities by the utility gain of the users. Individuals have a complex set of relationships with commodities and services whose value cannot be measured solely by utility consequences. A blind man has no use for paintings. However, there is nothing that one can do to give him the option of relating to paintings. Likewise, an illiterate man may have no use for education. Nor is it necessarily the case that he would be happier *were* he to be educated. The value of education, presumably, is to be measured not only by its utility consequences but also by the additional range of relationships he can have with people and things - something, one may argue, he has a right to. It should therefore be emphasized that when we talk of the 'welfare effects' of social overhead capital we mean a great deal more than its utility consequences. Given the complex nature of such welfare effects it is not surprising that estimates of net social product inevitably exclude them. It was noted in chapter 3, section 3.3, that a way to capture such rights is to set targets for such forms of capital formation and environmental resource conservation. The moral is banal: no single index can possibly hope to capture all welfare considerations. Attempts at constructing 'quality of life' indices are bound to prove self-defeating. It is much better to look at a *vector* of indices - each index reflecting a separate consideration - when judging the performance of an economy. In practice this is indeed what is at times done by social commentators.[10]

5.5 Social rates of return

For the sake of conceptual clarity it is none the less useful to suppose, as we argued in chapter 3 and its appendix, that

[10] In a well-known essay Nordhaus and Tobin (1972) have attempted to measure net national product by taking into account a variety of considerations that are usually left out. Samuelson (1979) calls such measures NEW, for Net Economic Welfare.

there *is* a welfare function capturing various social goals. This enables one to distil the implications of different considerations for the choice of policies. The central implication of the fact that various types of social overhead capital and resource stocks have direct welfare effects is that in estimating social rates of return on such stocks one ought to include these effects. To put it in a slightly different way, if these 'stock effects' are not included, then one ought to aim at accumulation rates at which social rates of return on desirable stocks fall short of the social discount rate. For pollutants the reverse is the case. Since this is a matter we shall confront repeatedly in the chapters that follow I illustrate it here by means of a stylized example so as to see what the issue is.

Suppose there is a single durable commodity whose stock at date t we denote by S_t. The maximum net flow of output of this commodity is given by a function $H(S_t)$ whose general properties are depicted in figure 5.1. Let C_t denote the rate at which the commodity is consumed. It follows that the net rate of accumulation of the stock is given by the difference between output and consumption which, assuming continuous time, is:

$$\mathrm{d}S_t/\mathrm{d}t = H(S_t) - C_t. \tag{5.3}$$

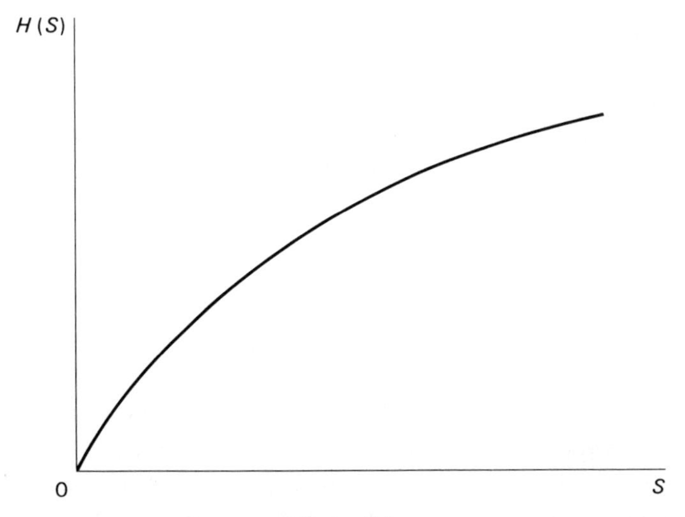

Figure 5.1

We suppose that the flow of social welfare at t is not only a function of the consumption rate C_t but also of the stock of this durable commodity. This we write as $U(C_t, S_t)$, which we suppose here for simplicity to be strictly concave (see chapter 3) with the property that $\partial U/\partial C > 0$, so that consumption is desirable. Finally we take it that the social welfare function today is the sum of the discounted flow of social welfare, where the discount rate, m (>0), captures, albeit in an approximate manner, the possibility of future extinction. Thus, the social welfare function today takes the form

$$\int_0^{\infty} U(C_t, S_t)\, e^{-mt}\, \mathrm{d}t.$$

Let us choose 'consumption' as our numeraire. Then it follows from the discussion in section 5.2 that the social rate of discount r_t, at t is:

$$r_t = m - (\mathrm{d}(U_c)/\mathrm{d}t)/U_c \tag{5.4}$$

(U_c is a short hand for $\partial U(C, S)/\partial C$).

From equation (5.3) it is clear that the productivity of the stock is $H'(S)$. But this is not the social rate of return on investment. To compute this one must add to it the direct welfare effect of the stock which, in terms of our chosen numeraire, is U_s/U_c (where $U_s = \partial U(C, S)/\partial S$). In other words, the social rate of return on investment is $H'(S) + U_s/U_c$. It is greater than the 'productivity' of capital if the direct welfare effect of the stock is beneficial; the reverse if it is detrimental. But now note that for an investment policy to be socially optimal it must be the case that physical assets are accumulated in such a manner that the *net* social rate of return on each equals the social rate of discount. For our example this social cost–benefit rule reads as:

$$r_t = H'(S_t) + U_s/U_c. \tag{5.5}$$

(For further details see Arrow and Kurz, 1970.) Equation (5.5), which is fundamental in social cost–benefit analysis, is widely referred to as the Ramsey Rule in honour of Frank Ramsey, who established a special version of it (see Ramsey, 1928).

Repeatedly I shall obtain adaptations of this rule in the chapters that follow. Note first that if $U_s > 0$ (the direct welfare effect of the stock is beneficial), $r_t > H'(S_t)$; that is, the stock ought to be accumulated up to a point where its productivity is less than the social discount rate; the reverse if $U_s < 0$. It is only if the stock has no direct welfare effect that its productivity ought to equal the social discount rate. Note finally that social product in this optimizing economy reads as:

$$Y_t = C_t + dS_t/dt + (U_s/U_c)\, S_t. \tag{5.6}$$

It is the value of social overhead capital, as captured by the final term in the right-hand side of equation (5.6), which is missing in expression (5.2).

5.6 Population as social capital

The type of social capital which raises the deepest conceptual problems is unquestionably the population that comprises a society. Here, the comparison of policies needs to be made on the basis of their impacts on a population which is itself subject to choice. Such a phrasing of the problem, based as it is on the mode in which arguments in welfare economics are conducted, is in fact questionable, as we shall see. Social scientists as a general rule have revealed a preference for valuing a person's life in terms of his 'consumption', his contribution to 'production', and the various 'side-effects' his existence may have on the lives of others; and for some, his effect on some abstract entity, like his race, or caste, or class, or even possibly the state.

Population is of course not only a modern concern. Even in classical times it would appear to have been much discussed. Plato, characteristically, gave thought to the matter and concluded that the number of *citizens* in the ideal city state is 5040; arguing that this is exactly divisible by every number up to 10, and indeed, having as many as 59 divisors which, presumably, would allow for the population to 'suffice for purposes of war and every peacetime activity, all contracts for dealings, and for taxes and grants' (see Plato, 1970, p. 205). In a different vein Rousseau also admitted no difficulty with the size of the population a government ought to aim at. For he says:

> I am always amazed that one obvious mark should be consistently misconstrued, and that men should be of such faith

> as not to agree about it. What is the goal set themselves by all political organizations? – Surely it is the maintenance and prosperity of their members. And what is the most certain sign that a people is being maintained and rendered prosperous? – the size of the population. There is no need to go further in our search. Other things being equal, the government under which . . . the citizens do most increase and multiply is infallibly the best. (Rousseau, 1946, pp. 356–7)

This passage undoubtedly appears quaint to us, if for no reason than that present-day circumstances in many countries are so utterly different from those which Rousseau faced. Nevertheless, on occasion governments have been known, even in recent years, to profess to some variant of such a view, most especially perhaps when programmes for controlling birth rates have not borne fruit.

The modern conception of optimum population is, however, thoroughly utilitarian in character. There are two broad variants of this, based on whether it is the *average*, or the *total*, level of well-being that is to be maximized. Since it is some variant of average utilitarianism, as formulated by Mill, Cannan, Wicksell, Robbins and Wolfe, which dominates thinking in most parts of the secular world, we discuss it first (for a review see Gottlieb, 1945).

The idea, in its simplest form, is to consider an economy in a stationary state, where aggregate consumption is constant over time. Stocks of capital are assumed to be given and the variable to be controlled is the size of the population. Output, as a function of population is taken to be of the form drawn in figure 5.2, so that the associated *average* product curve is bell shaped. The optimum population size is the one at which average product (and hence average consumption) is maximized; that is, where the average product of labour equals its marginal product.

A central disturbing feature of this solution is the assumption that stocks of capital equipment and natural resources are a datum for all time. Presumably investment is also subject to choice, and quite patently choice of an investment policy is linked to that of a population policy. Variations of average utilitarianism in an intertemporal setting have been studied by Ohlin (1967) and Pitchford (1974). Ohlin (1967) posed the problem of optimum

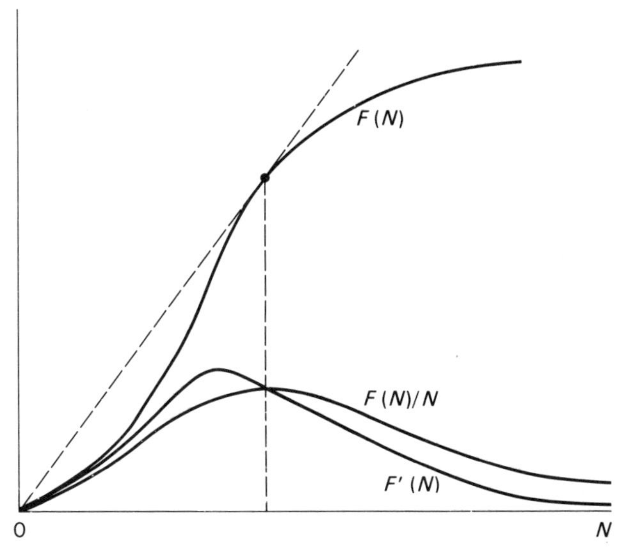

Figure 5.2

population policy as one of locating that rate of growth of population and capital formation which will maximize the percentage rate of growth of per capita national income. As one of a number of social indices growth rates are worth considering, and indeed, they are commonly appealed to. As a single objective there is nothing to commend it. Patently, conceptions of social welfare are far more complex than can be captured by a single index of this kind.

A formulation much nearer to the spirit of average utilitarianism is the one in Pitchford (1974), who studied optimum investment and population policies when the social objective function is the sum of the discounted flow of utility, where utility is solely a function of per capita consumption. It is essentially this framework which some years earlier had been used by Enke (1966) to develop a methodology for social cost–benefit analysis of family planning expenditure. Enke identified the value of a prevented birth by the discounted value of the difference between an additional person's lifetime consumption and his lifetime output. His conclusion was startling: the return to investment in family planning in several developing countries (e.g. India) is about 100 times the return to other forms of investment. Enke's figures cannot be taken seriously, most especially because of his presumption that there is a close connection between family-planning expenditure and the number of prevented births (see Cassen, 1978, for a review of the literature). A problem that plagues this entire area of discourse is the extent to which one is ignorant about the manner in which various considerations affect the choice of family size in those circumstances where it is subject to choice. Children are not only a consumption good; they are a form of investment for parents, a particularly valuable form of investment for those near the edge of subsistence, with no prospects for old-age pension and no insurance for ill health and death. There is, of course, a distinction between male and female children as potential sources of family income (the prevelance of female infanticide in certain parts of India testifies to a vigorous distinction there). In an oft-cited work May and Heer (1968) estimated that an average couple in India in the 1960s needed to have 6.3 children in order to be 95 per cent sure of having a surviving son when the father reached the age of 65. Clearly the mortality rate (especially infant mortality rate) and the extent to which people are unprotected from personal disasters are amongst the determinants of the birth rate, and it is this that demographers have in recent years pointed to (see for example, Cassen, 1978, chapter 2). The private return to having children is much greater than the social return in many parts of the globe.[11]

5.7 Classical utilitarian views on population

While it is some variant of average utilitarianism which dominates thinking in much of the world, the problem of optimum population as seen strictly through utilitarian spectacles assumes a different form. Characteristically, it was Henry Sidgwick who gave an explicit formulation of this.

[11] The kinds of material incentives for limiting family size that merit consideration quite obviously depend on, among other things, the types of social services that a community has chosen to make available. In China today one form of material incentives is the quality of housing.

> For if we take Utilitarianism to prescribe, as the ultimate end of action, happiness as a whole, and not any individual's happiness, unless considered as an element of the whole, it would follow that, if the additional population enjoy on the whole positive happiness, we ought to weigh the amount of happiness gained by the extra number against the amount lost by the remainder. So that, strictly conceived, the point up to which, on Utilitarian principles, population ought to be encouraged to increase, is not that at which average happiness is the greatest possible ... but that at which the product formed by multiplying the number of persons living into the amount of average happiness reaches its maximum. (Sidgwick, 1907, pp. 415–16).

It was this formulation which was revived in the important work of Meade (1955). To illustrate it consider once again an economy whose production possibilities are given by figure 5.2. The stocks of capital equipment are given and we restrict our attention to stationary states. Let $Z = C/N$ denote average consumption. Assuming that individuals are identical and that consequently they are identically treated, the Meade formulation takes the social welfare function to be of the form $NU(Z)$, where $U(Z)$ is the utility function of the representative individual.[12] It is then immediate that provided it is not zero, the optimum population size in this framework is given by the solution of the equation

$$U(Z) = U'(Z)(Z - F'(N)). \tag{5.7}$$

The social cost-benefit rule (5.7) brings out both the strengths and the weaknesses of utilitarian formulations. When an additional person is created the social gain, as seen through classical utilitarian spectacles, is his utility level. But there is a loss, incurred by others, which consists of the value of the difference between his own consumption and his contribution to output. The social cost-benefit rule (5.7) says that the population size society ought to aim at is one at which the gain equals the loss.[13]

[12] For simplicity of exposition we suppose that U depends solely on Z and that $U'(Z) > 0$, and $U''(Z) < 0$.

[13] For an axiomatic foundation of a generalized form of utilitarianism, of

Given an exogenous investment programme, Meade's Rule (5.7) indicates the population which is optimal relative to it. Similarly Ramsey's Rule (5.5) indicates the investment programme which is optimal relative to a given population programme. But the optimum number of descendants is surely dependent on planned bequests. More generally, and what is ignored in the Ramsey–Meade formulations, optimal investment and population programmes are interdependent and should be determined jointly. A synthesis of these two rules, in which the relevant intertemporal tradeoffs are explicitly evaluated according to the dictates of Classical Utilitarianism, has been provided by Dasgupta (1969) and Lane (1977).

5.8 Person-affecting utilitarianism

Many would today regard utilitarianism to be founded on a special doctrine of rights: the right on the part of individuals to have their welfare included in the social calculus; the sum of utilities being merely a particular aggregation of these rights. (For an axiomatic basis for utilitarianism, see Maskin, 1978.) Viewed in this manner utilitarianism does not seek to maximize total happiness as such, but the total happiness of actual people: 'We are in favour of making people happy, but neutral about making happy people' (Narveson, 1973, p. 73). Sidgwick's doctrine seems distinctly at variance with one's moral intuition. It treats people on par with potential persons. But people have rights, potential persons do not. Clearly then people should count for more than potential ones. Indeed, it is hard to see why the present generation should be obliged to add to its numbers for the sake of total utility if in doing so its own welfare is reduced. For whose rights would be transgressed by their not adding to the numbers? No one's. Indeed, side-effects apart, unmodified utilitarianism could be used to condone the extermination of an individual if this is a means to creating an exceptionally happy person. Clearly this will not do. It is this distinction between existing and potential persons which led

---

which the average and the classical versions are special cases, see the illuminating work of Blackorby and Donaldson (1980).

Narveson (1967) in an important article to develop what can be interpreted as a quasi rights-based version of utilitarianism. Narveson's doctrine would have us choose policies that improve the well-being of people (via, say, a utilitarian calculation). Indeed it condemns the creation of persons who are imprisoned in lives of misery, not because creating such a person 'harms' him (prior to being conceived the person did not exist!), but because the act results in there being a wretched life. But the doctrine is *neutral* about the creation of people with positive welfare.

At first blush such a modified version of utilitarianism may appear to be precisely what one is after. Unfortunately, as Parfit (1976) has noted, under a seemingly natural interpretation of Narveson's doctrine – an interpretation that Narveson himself may have intended – there are difficulties. To illustrate it suppose that there are two people in existence with welfare levels 4 and 6. There are three possible policies, A, B, and C. Under A and B a third individual is created with welfare levels 1 and 4 respectively, and the welfare levels of the existing pair are unaffected. Under C (do nothing) no additional person is created. Thus the welfare levels under A, B and C are (4, 6, 1), (4, 6, 4) and (4, 6) respectively. Now Narveson's doctrine demands that all three persons must be counted when a comparison is made between A and B. Under both average and total utilitarianism B is clearly preferred to A. But the doctrine is neutral between A and C and between B and C, because existing people are equally well off under all three policies and it is posited that the potential person will enjoy positive welfare no matter whether A or B is chosen. If, as Parfit would have us do, Narveson's idea of neutrality is interpreted as *social indifference*, one should be indifferent between A and C, and between B and C. But B is preferred to A. So social indifference is not transitive, and this is distinctly awkward.

One might be tempted to argue though that neutrality really amounts to *non-comparability*, for the doctrine is founded on the welfare claims of people. With this interpretation Narveson would rank B over A, but would regard both A and C and B and C as non-comparable. Intransitivity is thereby avoided in the example, but at a price: population policies are not *completely* ordered, only *partially* so (see chapter 3). We should have perhaps not expected otherwise, for the insistence on a complete ranking of alternatives is overly demanding. Not all moral problems have answers. Unfortunately even this is not an escape route for Narveson. For suppose now that policies A, B and C lead to welfare levels (5, 11, −1), (6, 8, 1) and (7, 6) respectively. Narveson would have us rank C over A (a wretched life is created under A) and, if total utilitarianism is invoked over identical populations, would regard A and B socially indifferent. This would imply that C is preferred to B. But under our present interpretation of neutrality, B and C are non-comparable. This, too, is awkward.

5.9 Rights-based population policies

A more extreme form of a rights-based doctrine applied to population and investment policies was explored in Dasgupta (1974). There the idea was to endow each generation with a zone of control, in the simplest illustration the size of the next generation and the level of investment. An intertemporal profile of population and investment was regarded there as optimal if, (a) each generation that comes into being during the pursuit of the programme regards its investment level and its procreation commitment to be in its own interest when all other generations that are created along the programme are expected to abide by the programme, and (b) no individual born along the programme has a negative welfare level.[14] Formally, condition (a) was interpreted as an intergenerational Nash equilibrium. The appeal of the doctrine lies in the fact that the claims of only those who are born along a programme are taken into account when judging its merit. Clearly as well, unlike Narveson's doctrine it does not suffer from the problem of intransitivity of the social ranking. To be sure it yields only a partial ranking of policies. But this, as we have noted earlier, is not an argument against it. The problem with such a rights-based doctrine, rather, is that it is so *exclusively* rights-based. A programme may well satisfy both (a) and (b) and yet have large numbers of people throughout generations with low (but positive) welfare. And this would be found preferable, under

[14] We are considering a deterministic model, so that (b) can be guaranteed. Otherwise (b) must be formulated in some 'expected' sense.

such a doctrine, to a programme which does not satisfy (a) but along which all who are born are very well off in terms of welfare. The point is of course that one wants to include considerations that are *both* rights-based *and* welfare based, and a comfortable accommodation is hard to find.

Many would find such difficulties of no great practical moment, for in a great many parts of the world it would seem clear that a lowering of the growth rate of population can be urged on the basis of one of several moral doctrines. While this is comforting to the man of affairs it is nevertheless important to ask which considerations one is in fact appealing to in the choice of policies. Otherwise it is difficult to know how far one should push in the pursuit of one programme rather than another, what opportunities one ought to forego in the drive towards lowering the rate of population growth.[15] The inconclusiveness of our discussion is not a matter of irrelevance in the world we know. It merely illustrates how complex our moral sensibilities are.[16]

[15] The response that the difficulties inherent in arriving at a criterion for population policies are of no great consequence because in many regions population growth ought obviously to be pruned, is similar to the claim that in poor countries there is no need for developing criteria for the selection of investment projects because *any* productive investment is desirable there. What this claim misses is that one needs to know what investment opportunity is foregone when a choice is made, and how to value it.

[16] Hare (1973) in his review of Rawls (1972) asserts the Rawls' theory of justice subscribes to population policies that maximize the well being of the worst-off member of the grand assembly of potential souls, and therefore that it would encourage large population sizes at low welfare levels. This is taken as a serious weakness of Professor Rawls' theory. Quite apart from the fact that Rawls says nothing about population policies that would emanate from his doctrine, the theory is not based on anything as bizarre as a congress of souls. A legitimate criticism of the theory is that it *is* silent on population policies. If one reflects that almost every policy has an impact on the composition of future population (the exact timing of a conception affects it!) it is a telling shortcoming.

6 Fisheries and Aquifers: The Stationary Case

6.1 Introduction

Studying a set of interacting populations is hard work. Analytical results are difficult to come by.[1] It is therefore not surprising that systems analysis has, for the most part, failed to yield the kinds of sharp qualitative insights that economists typically search after. Much of the literature has concentrated on single-species models; that is, species in isolation in stable environments. In this and the following chapter I shall study the optimum management of such isolated renewable resources and compare this with the competitive outcome when the resource is common property.[2] In this chapter I shall, for the main part, limit myself to *stationary* states, to be defined below. Indeed, I shall find that for the models to be developed optimal stationary policies are the ones that ought to be pursued in the long run. In the following chapter I shall therefore say something about optimal *transient* policies.

But first we must study *feasible* intertemporal policies. We therefore begin with natural growth functions of renewable resources.

6.2 Growth functions of renewable natural resources

We consider a regenerative natural resource in a stable environment. We ignore chance factors and suppose that the system

[1] So far as I am aware specific characteristics of the optimum mode of harvesting from even such a simple system as the Volterra–Lotka 'predator–prey' model are not known. Clark (1976) and Clemhout and Wan (1981) contain several general features of such models.

[2] In other words, among other things, I shall be providing an intertemporal version of the ideas developed in chapter 2, sections 2.1–2.3.

is deterministic. Let S_t denote the resource stock at date t. In the case of fisheries, S would denote the biomass of the fish species in question, measured in, say, tonnes.[3] In the case of isolated groundwater basins S would be measured in, say, acre-feet. Animal and bird populations can also be studied usefully by the methods to be developed below. However, I shall restrict my attention to fisheries and isolated groundwater basins when illustrating the theory.

In what follows I shall treat time as a continuous variable. I consider a stable environment and average over seasonal fluctuations. In general, then, the rate at which the resource rejuvenates must be a function of the stock level. Let $H(S)$ be the natural rate of growth of the stock – that is, the rate of rejuvenation in the absence of human predators – if S is the stock.[4] It follows that in the absence of human encroachment the equation representing ecological balance is:

$$dS_t/dt = H(S_t) \tag{6.1}$$

Various special forms of $H(S)$ may now be considered.

1. If $H(S) = 0$, the resource is a pure exhaustible one, like fossil fuels.
2. For isolated groundwater basins it is customary to assume $H(S) = A$, a positive constant. A is the rate at which the basin in question is recharged – the rate of natural replenishment. To be sure, this is only an approximation, for aquifers do have a maximum capacity, and so at large values of the basin stock there will be seepage of water out of the basin, with the consequence that the net rate of recharge will typically be a function of the stock level. Nevertheless, over a large range of the basin level a constant rate of replenishment is a good approximation (see Domenico, 1972).
3. For small populations in a stable environment (e.g. fruit flies) it is plausible that the *percentage* rate of natural growth is

[3] The biomass would be a sufficient statistic if, in particular, one could ignore the age distribution. In what follows I shall ignore the latter. (See chapter 11.)

[4] The effect of non-human predators is implicitly captured in the function $H(S)$.

constant. In this case $H(S) = AS$, where A, a positive constant, is the percentage rate of growth.[5]

4. A large number of studies of fisheries have assumed $H(S)$ to be quadratic in S and, in particular, to have the form:

$$H(S) = AS - BS^2 \qquad A, B > 0. \tag{6.2}$$[6]

In figure 6.1 we have drawn the growth functions in 2–4. Notice that the quadratic form (6.2) implies that growth is positive even when the stock is a very small positive number. Species with such a property are said to have a high biotic potential. On the other hand, there are species for which the rate of growth is negative when the stock is low, the point being that mating encounters are that much rarer then. A simple extension of the quadratic form (6.2) can capture this feature; for we may write:

$$H(S) = \begin{cases} -K + AS - BS^2;\ K, A, B > 0, & \\ \text{and } A^2 > 4BK, & \text{if } S > 0. \\ 0 \quad \text{if } S = 0. & \end{cases} \tag{6.3}$$

In figure 6.2 we depict some of the general characteristics of the quadratic function (6.3). We motivate these characteristics first. The idea is that for very small stocks (below $\underline{S}$) the rate of rejuvenation is negative, since mating encounters are rare (for equation (6.3) note that

$$\underline{S} = [A - \sqrt{(A^2 - 4BK)}/2B\,].)$$

$\underline{S}$ can be regarded as the *threshold* level below which the population is doomed.[7] Over a range $(\underline{S}, \hat{S})$ the rate of growth increases,

[5] A vast literature, addressing itself to long-run economic growth potentials, has used this hypothesis to characterize the growth of human populations. For a survey of such growth models, see Solow (1971) and Wan (1971).

[6] The quadratic (or logistic) function, discussed originally by Lotka (1956), was introduced into the economics of fisheries by Shaefer (1954) (see also Beverton and Holt, 1957). Bell (1978) contains an excellent recent review of the literature. In section 6.8 I shall summarize a case study of a lobster fishery by Henderson and Tugwell (1979) which uses the growth function (6.2).

[7] We recognize that it is possible on occasion to generate artificial spawning and thus revive a dying fishery.

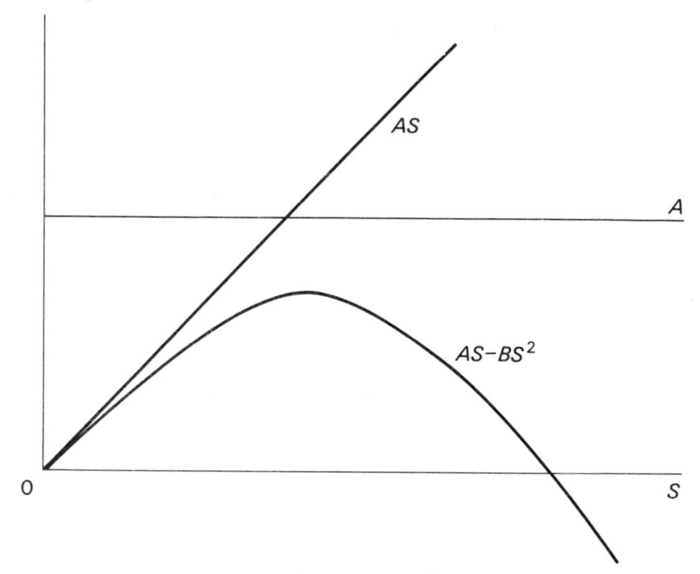

Figure 6.1

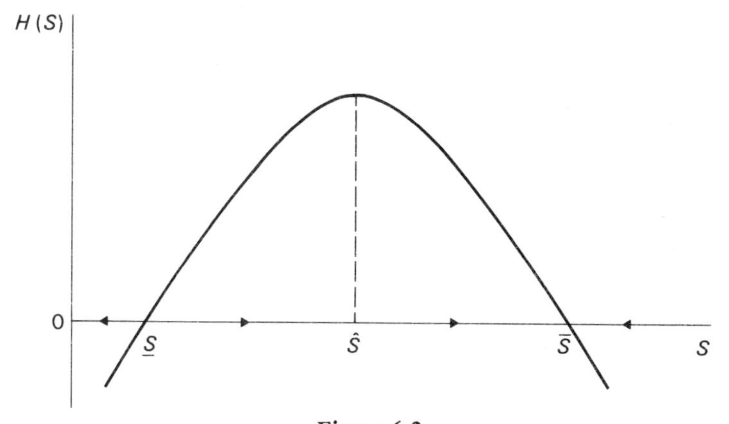

Figure 6.2

but at a diminishing rate. In this population interval conditions are really favourable for the species. The size is sufficiently small, so that despite a constant exogenous flow of food supply population growth increases with size, though at a diminishing rate. Beyond $\hat{S}$ (for equation (6.3) note that $\hat{S} = A/2B$) the population is so large that the fact that the food supply is constant makes itself felt sharply. In the interval $(\hat{S}, \overline{S})$ (for equation (6.3) note that

$$\overline{S} = [A + \sqrt{(A^2 - 4BK)/2B}])$$

growth is still positive, but the rate of growth declines with the population size, and it declines at an accelerating rate). Beyond $\overline{S}$ the population is simply too big. The net rate of reproduction is negative. We formalize these general characteristics in equation (6.4), and regard this as case 5.

> There exist stock levels, $\underline{S}$ and $\overline{S}$ (with $\overline{S} > \underline{S} \geqslant 0$) such that $H(0) = H(\underline{S}) = H(\overline{S}) = 0$, $H(S) > 0$ for $\underline{S} < S < \overline{S}$, and $H(S) < 0$ for $0 < S < \underline{S}$ and $S > \overline{S}$. Furthermore, $\mathrm{d}^2H(S)/\mathrm{d}S^2 < 0$ for $\underline{S} < S < \overline{S}$. (See figure 6.2.) (6.4)

In the fisheries literature much attention has been given to the quadratic form (6.2). But there are empirical investigations that assume other functional forms, which nevertheless satisfy (6.4) (see for example Pella and Tomlinson, 1969; Spence, 1974). In what follows we take it, unless we say otherwise, that $H(S)$ satisfies (6.4). Using (6.4) in equation (6.1) it is clear that $\underline{S}$ and $\overline{S}$ are the two *stationary* stocks.[8] Of these, $\overline{S}$ is *stable* and $\underline{S}$ is *unstable* (see figure 6.2).[9] This implies that if unencroached over a long period one would expect the stock to be at $\overline{S}$, which may therefore be referred to as the *natural* equilibrium level of stock. Note finally that the rate of growth is maximum at $\hat{S}$.

Thus far a resource in its natural environment. It remains to introduce resource exploitation by human predators. This is the next task.

6.3 Harvest costs

Let X_t $(\geqslant 0)$ denote the rate at which the resource is harvested at t. Then the dynamical equation representing the stock becomes

$$\mathrm{d}S_t/\mathrm{d}t = H(S_t) - X_t. \tag{6.5}$$

[8] That is, $\mathrm{d}S_t/\mathrm{d}t = 0$ at $S = \underline{S}$ and $S = \overline{S}$. So is $S = 0$ a stationary stock level, but it is an uninteresting one.

[9] Thus, if the stock differs slightly from $\underline{S}$ it moves away from $\underline{S}$, but if it differs slightly from $\overline{S}$ it moves towards $\overline{S}$. In particular, note that if the stock

Since X_t can be controlled, the dynamical system (6.5) is a controlled one. If $X_t = H(S_t)$ then $dS_t/dt = 0$, and so the stock does not change. This is the case where the rate of harvest equals the net reproduction rate. If $X_t = H(S_t)$ for $t \geqslant 0$ then we say that X is a *stationary catch policy* – 'stationary', because the catch rate is constant over time. From figure 6.2 it is clear that if $\underline{S} < S < \overline{S}$ then a stationary catch policy can be pursued; not otherwise. Of these, $H(\hat{S})$ is the maximum. $H(\hat{S})$ is called the *maximum sustainable yield* (MSY) a concept which looms large in the fisheries' literature.[10] It may be thought that MSY is a desirable target; and indeed it has for long been so regarded. Subsequently we shall see that it almost never is a desirable target.

Extracting a resource is not a costless activity. Fishing requires labour and equipment. Pumping water from an aquifer requires inputs as well. For simplicity one may aggregate the inputs. In the fisheries literature this aggregate is often called *effort*. Let E_t denote the effort level at t. Then in general the production function relating effort, the stock and the yield may be expressed as

$$X_t = G(S_t, E_t),$$

where

$$\left. \begin{array}{l} G(0, E) = G(S, 0) = 0 \qquad \partial G/\partial S \equiv G_S > 0 \\ \partial G/\partial E \equiv G_E > 0 \qquad \partial^2 G/\partial S^2 < 0 \end{array} \right\} \quad (6.6)^{11}$$

and

$$\partial^2 G/\partial E^2 \leqslant 0.$$

---

ever falls below $\underline{S}$ – say due to overfishing – the resource will get exhausted in finite time.

[10] The concept of maximum sustainable yield corresponds to the Golden Rule of Accumulation in the growth literature. For an introduction to the latter concept, see for example Wan (1971). For a selection of essays assessing the former, see Roedel (1975).

[11] We ignore technological progress in harvesting and therefore do not allow G to depend explicitly on time. The last two inequalities mean non-increasing returns to each factor in the production function.

The dependence of the yield on the size of the stock is something one would expect – the larger the stock then, *ceteris paribus*, the greater the yield. In the case of fisheries this occurs because less time is involved in locating the resource if the stock is large. In the case of an aquifer a larger deposit means a higher water table and therefore less pumping costs.

For a wide class of functional forms for G it is possible to invert it and express E as a function of S and X. In this case write

$$E = C(S, X) \quad \text{with } \left.\begin{aligned} \partial C/\partial S \equiv C_S < 0 \\ \partial C/\partial X \equiv C_X > 0 \end{aligned}\right\} \tag{6.7}$$

as the effort function; $C(S, X)$ being the minimum effort necessary to obtain a yield of X when S is the stock. If the marginal cost of effort is constant, then we may normalize and set this marginal cost equal to one. In this case $C(S, X)$ is a cost-function. We shall assume this to be the case. Thus $C(S, X)$ will denote the instantaneous cost of harvesting at the rate X when S is the stock.

It is often useful to simplify and suppose that costs are linear in harvest, and therefore that $C(S, X) = L(S)X$, say; where $dL(S)/dS < 0$. In this case marginal harvest cost is $L(S)$ and it equals average harvest cost.

A functional form for (6.6) that has been used widely in the fisheries literature is the Cobb–Douglas one

$$X = G(S, E) = \alpha S^a E^b \quad \text{with } \alpha > 0 \text{ and } 1 \geqslant a, b > 0 \,. \tag{6.8}$$

From equation (6.8) it follows immediately that

$$E = C(S, X) = \beta S^{-a/b} X^{1/b} \quad \text{with } \beta > 0,\ 1 \geqslant a, b > 0,$$

or more succinctly

$$E = C(S, X) = \beta S^{-\gamma} X^{\mu} \quad \text{with } \beta > 0,\ \gamma > 0 \text{ and } \mu \geqslant 1, \tag{6.9}$$

as the cost function.

A special case of this, often appealed to (see Bell, 1978), is $\mu = 1$. In this case $E = \beta S^{-\gamma} X$, and so again, cost is linear in yield.

6.4 Free entry into common property resource

Suppose the market for the resource is competitive. Let p (> 0) be the market price. In this section we propose to extend our analysis of common property resources (see chapter 1 and 2) to an intertemporal setting and see the manner in which such resources are exploited over time. Towards this we simplify and take it that free entry by firms into a common-property resource results in the market price equalling the *average* cost of yield at each moment. This implies that the industry makes zero profit at each instant. Implicit in this assumption is the hypothesis that the adjustment process characterizing the entry and exits of firms into the common-property resource is instantaneous. If industry-wide profits were to be positive at any instant, firms would enter to wipe out profits. Likewise, if they were to be negative there would be a sufficient number of exits to wipe out losses. Thus we assume that

$$p = C(S_t, X_t)/X_t. \tag{6.10}$$

Given an initial stock S_0, equations (6.5) and (6.10) therefore characterize the dynamics of the free entry common-property resource. This system is a special case of one studied by Smith (1968). In what follows I simplify further to highlight the kinds of considerations that merit study.

Suppose the industry cost function is of the Cobb–Douglas form, equation (6.9). In this case the zero-profit condition, equation (6.10) reads as

$$\beta S_t^{-\gamma} X_t^{\mu - 1} = p \qquad \beta, \gamma > 0,\ \mu \geqslant 1. \tag{6.11}$$

The case where $\mu = 1$ is easiest to dispose of. It is also of considerable interest because it implies that cost is linear in harvest rate. Thus marginal and average harvest costs coincide. In this case equation (6.11) reduces to

$$S_t = S = (\beta/p)^{1/\gamma}, \tag{6.12}$$

and thus the instantaneous zero profit condition is consistent only with the stock $(\beta/p)^{1/\gamma}$. For the adjustment mechanism to make sense we must now suppose that $(\beta/p)^{1/\gamma} > \underline{S}$. For the stock level in equation (6.12) to be maintained we must also have $X_t =$

$H((\beta/p)^{1/\gamma})$. This is therefore the constant rate of catch with free entry under our hypotheses.

We now consider the case $\mu > 1$. Eliminating X_t from equations (6.5) and (6.11) yields

$$dS_t/dt = H(S_t) - (p/\beta)^{1/(\mu-1)} S_t^{\gamma/(\mu-1)}. \qquad (6.13)$$

Equation (6.13) is an ordinary non-linear differential equation in one variable S_t, and it is simple to analyse its solution. In figures 6.3 and 6.4 I present the two broad categories of cases. Notice that the right-hand side of equation (6.13) is the difference between two expressions, each a function of the stock. In figure 6.3 we consider the case where p/β is sufficiently low that the curves representing these two functions cut each other. The figure identifies two points of intersection, S_f and S_f' (with $S_f < S_f'$). These are the two stationary points of the differential equation (6.13) for this parametric case. Notice now that if $S > S_f'$ then the right-hand side of equation (6.13) is negative and therefore the stock will decline. Likewise, if $S_f < S < S_f'$, then the right-hand side of equation (6.13) is positive and therefore the stock will increase. This proves that if $S_0 > S_f$, then free-entry into the common-property resource does not spell its ruin. In finite time the industry will settle down to a stationary state along

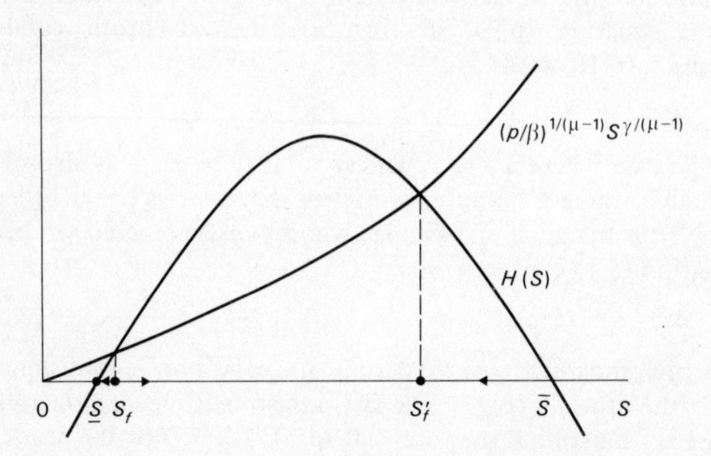

Figure 6.3

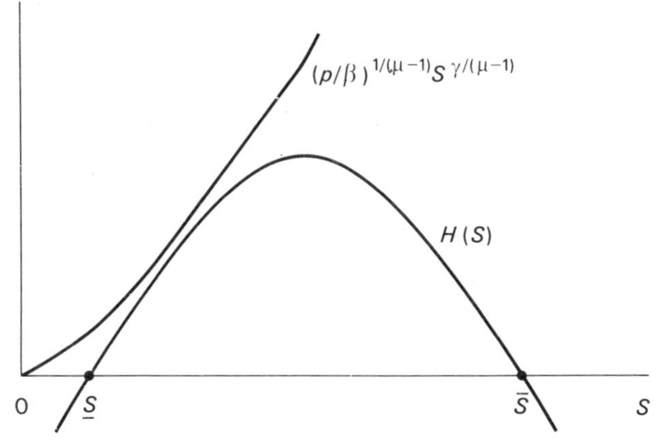

Figure 6.4

which the harvest rate is $H(S_f')$. However, if for some reason $S_0 < S_f$, the resource is indeed doomed; for, the right-hand side of equation (6.13) is negative if $S < S_f$, and so the stock will decrease, and in finite time the resource will be exhausted.

Figure 6.4 depicts the case where (p/β) is so large that the curves do not intersect. From the figure one can see immediately that the right-hand side of equation (6.13) is negative for all values of S. This means that no matter what the size, the stock will decline under free entry, and indeed, that in finite time the resource will be exhausted. We conclude that if the resource is highly valued freedom in the commons leads to its exhaustion; not otherwise. Our observations in chapter 2, section 1, have therefore been borne out. The intuition behind the result is immediate. If the resource is very valuable, free entry leads to excessive catch; in the sense that the harvest rate exceeds the natural rate of rejuvenation no matter what the size of the stock. This means that the net rate of regeneration is negative. The resource is doomed. However, if the resource is not that valuable then for a range of stock levels the harvest rate at which industry profit is zero is less than the current rate of natural regeneration. This enables the stock to grow.

The foregoing, highly simple, model of an unregulated common-property resource would appear to bring out the main analytical issues. I turn therefore to an exploration of the optimal rate of harvest. I shall then compare the two analyses to look at the structure of taxation which, if imposed, will ensure that a free entry common-property resource is optimally harvested.[12]

6.5 Optimal stationary policies for fisheries

I begin with a fairly general formulation of the planning problem and then restrict myself to optimal stationary policies. In chapter 7 I shall return to the formulation and attempt to characterize the entire optimal policy.

Using the notation of chapter 3 let $B(X)$ denote the flow of social benefit enjoyed when the harvest rate is X. If the market in which the resource is sold is approximately competitive, and if the market price (p, say) approximately reflects its social value then $B(X) = pX$. But for the moment we do not necessarily suppose this to be the case. We merely suppose that $B(X)$ is a concave function; (that is, non-increasing marginal social benefit from yield). We simplify and assume that the social rate of discount is a positive constant, r. Similarly we take it that $C(S, X)$ is the social cost of harvesting X when S is the stock. Write

$$N(S_t, X_t) \equiv B(X_t) - C(S_t, X_t).$$

Then $N(S_t, X_t)$ is the flow of *net* social benefit at date t and $e^{-rt} N(S_t, X_t)$ is the present discounted value of this flow. We add all present discounted values and arrive at the social objective function:

$$\int_0^\infty e^{-rt} N(S_t, X_t)\, dt.$$

[12] For an example of a process by which productivity may decline in common land see Jodha (1980). The case in question is the desertification of the arid zone in the state of Rajasthan, India. Jodha identifies an increase in subsistence requirements of the farming community and a rise in the profitability of land exploitation from cropping and grazing as the central reasons. It is this latter cause which, in an extreme form, is captured in the model in the text. Jodha argues that ironically, it was in fact the government's land reforms in this area, unaccompanied by investment in improving the productive base, which has triggered the process.

In the following chapter we shall pose and analyse the full planning problem. Here we restrict ourselves to characterizing the conditions that an optimum stationary policy must satisfy.

In order to see what characterizes an optimum stationary policy, note first from equation (6.1) that $dH(S)/dS$ is the *marginal productivity* of the stock. Write

$$dH(S)/dS = H'(S).$$

Then $r - H'(S)$ can be regarded as the *net* social rate of discount that ought to be used in discounting *marginal* benefits from exploiting the resource in question. Now $N_X(S, X) \equiv B_X(X) - C_X(S, X)$ is the change in the current flow of net social benefit if the rate of harvest is increased marginally – i.e. current marginal net social benefit. The question to ask now is this: what additional cost would be imposed on future generations if the current rate of harvest were to be increased marginally? This is simple to calculate. The consequence of increasing current harvest marginally is a marginal decline in the stock. Along a stationary policy this implies that harvest costs will increase marginally for all future generations. This additional cost at each future date is

$$-\partial C(S, X)/\partial S \equiv -C_S(S, X).$$

Discounted at the *net* social rate of discount, $r - H'(S)$, the present value of this flow of additional costs is

$$-C_S(S, X)/(r - H'(S)).$$

For a stationary policy to be judged optimal this additional cost must equal the additional benefit from increasing current harvest marginally. That is:

$$N_X(S, X) \equiv B_X(X) - C_X(S, X) = -C_S(S, X)/[r - H'(S)]. \tag{6.14}$$

(See chapter 5, equation (5.5).)[13]

[13] See e.g. Clark (1976). 'Optimal' rules of exploitation, such as equation (6.14), should be contrasted with recurrent 'democratic' exploitation rules such as those analysed by Neher (1976). Lewis and Neher (1980) contains a discussion of the relation between the two in some specific circumstances.

Equation (6.14) is one equation, but it contains two unknowns, S and X. We would seem to be one equation short; not so. Since we are studying a stationary policy the system must satisfy

$$H(S) = X. \tag{6.15}$$

An optimal stationary policy must satisfy equations (6.14) and (6.15).

Equation (6.14) represents a fundamental principle in the economics of renewable natural resources. It has been much discussed in the literature.[14] We proceed to note several points that are pertinent about it.

First, one must check that the pair of equations (6.14) and (6.15) possesses a solution. If not, an optimum *stationary* policy simply does not exist (see chapter 7). For the remainder of this chapter I assume it does. The second point to note is that the solution may not be unique. This certainly causes complications; for if it is accepted that an optimum stationary policy is what ought to be aimed at in the long run, a multiplicity of solutions implies that we do not know without further thought *which* of these solutions one ought to converge to. This too is an issue I shall consider in chapter 7. However, for expositional ease we suppose in the remainder of this chapter that there is a unique solution; this we label as (S^*, X^*).

Third, note that the left-hand side of equation (6.14) represents the *shadow* (or *accounting*) price of the unharvested resource (see chapter 3, sections 3.1 and 3.4). Equation (6.14) is a social cost-benefit rule for stationary policies and it says that if the untapped resource is imputed a value equal to the right-hand side of equation (6.14) then it ought to be extracted up to the point where net social benefit of extraction equals this shadow price. This leads us immediately to the fourth point, that so long as $-C_S(S, X) > 0$, which is what we have assumed here, it must be the case that $r > H'(S)$; for the resource is not in infinite supply: its shadow price is positive. If in the extreme case $C_S(S, X) = 0$ – i.e. harvesting costs are independent of stocks – then $r = H'(S)$; for otherwise the right-hand side of equation (6.14) would be

[14] For a rigorous mathematical analysis of the economics of renewable resources, see Clark (1976).

zero, which would imply that the shadow price is zero, which is an absurdity. It follows that in this extreme case the condition $r = H'(S)$ yields the optimal stationary stock and the stationarity condition $X = H(S)$ yields the harvest rate. The shadow price is simply $N_X(S, X)$. (See chapter 5, section 5.5.)

The fifth point to note is that except by fluke the optimal policy is *not* the maximum sustainable yield (MSY). To see why this must obviously be so, recall that MSY is obtained at the point $H'(S) = 0$. Now, there are two reasons why MSY is not a desirable policy, and they pull in opposite directions. One is that future benefits are being discounted at a positive rate (r). Therefore, as the argument in chapter 5, section 5.5, implied, if $C_S(S, X) = 0$, then for a stationary policy to be optimal the social rate of return $H'(S)$ must equal the social rate of discount, r. Thus $H'(S) = r > 0$; a point we have noted as well in the previous paragraph. In this case it is optimal to aim at stock less than the one sustaining MSY. The other reason, which implies that *ceteris peribus* a larger stock is better, is embodied in the assumption that $C_S(S, X) < 0$: aiming at a higher stock is desirable because future harvesting costs are thereby reduced. The force of these two considerations is caught in equation (6.14). Indeed, if harvesting costs decline dramatically as the stock is increased it is entirely possible that the optimal stationary stock is in excess of the one that sustains MSY; that is, $H'(S) < 0$; and therefore a stock at which the marginal productivity is *negative*! (See section 6.9.)

Even supposing that the pair of equations (6.14) and (6.15) possesses a unique solution it is not possible to say how the optimal stationary policy varies with the parameters underlying the planning model. Except, of course, when one imposes further structure on the functional forms. We examine one such distinguished case studied by Burt (1967b) in the process of developing the optimal rate of extraction from groundwater basins (see Burt, 1964, 1966, 1967a, 1967b)).

6.6 Groundwater basins: An example

It was noted in section 6.1 that for isolated groundwater basins the assumption of a constant rate of recharge is a good approximation.

In this case $H(S) = A > 0$, where A is the rate of recharge. But then $H'(S) = 0$ and equation (6.14) reduces to the form:

$$B_X(X) - C_X(S, X) = -C_S(S, X)/r. \tag{6.16}$$

Suppose

$$\left.\begin{aligned} &B(X) = \alpha X - \beta X^2 \text{ and } C(S, X) = (\gamma - \delta S)\,X, \\ &\text{where } \alpha, \gamma, \delta > 0 \text{ and } \beta \geqslant 0. \end{aligned}\right\} \tag{6.17}$$

It is plain that since the rate of recharge is constant the only reason one would wish to have larger storage is because of the reduction in withdrawal costs. In fact on using equation (6.17) in equations (6.15) and (6.16) it is simple to confirm that the optimal policy (S^*, X^*) is

$$X^* = A \text{ and } S^* = (2\beta A + \gamma - \alpha + \delta A/r)/\delta. \tag{6.18}$$

From equation (6.18) it is immediate that; (a) an increase in the social rate of discount reduces optimal stationary storage, (b) the higher the rate of recharge A the higher the storage level, (c) an increase in the social value of water (α) reduces optimal stationary storage, and (d) if $\gamma + 2\beta A > \alpha$, then an improvement in pumping technology (i.e. an increase in δ or a decline in γ) reduces optimal stationary storage.

These observations may appear obvious. The remarkable fact is that they are not necessarily true under more general circumstances!

Much of the hydraulics literature concentrates on the factors determining recharge rates and water table-levels of aquifers. Rainfall, subsoil structure, underground streams etc., are obvious determinants. So are surface-water streams and canals. Withdrawal of surface water can reduce the groundwater table level and thereby increase extraction costs. In a classic case study Brown and McGuire (1967) attempted to estimate the optimum mix of groundwater and surface-water withdrawal in Kern County, California. Likewise, the building of irrigation canals often raises the groundwater table level and thereby reduces extraction costs. So much so that groundwater withdrawal may increase after the introduction of the canal system. Indeed, cropping patterns may change radically thereby in a manner not envisaged by the canal builders (see Chopra, 1981).

6.7 Optimal taxation

Suppose there is free-entry into a common-property resource such as a fishery and suppose that the resource is marketed at the price p. Suppose further that free-entry results in zero-profits; i.e. equation (6.10) is satisfied. We wish to locate the structure of taxes which, if imposed, will result in the industry harvesting at the optimum stationary rate. To avoid extraneous issues from our point of concern we suppose that $B(X) = pX$ – that is, the social value of the harvested resource is identified with its market price. It is now an easy matter to see what properties the corrective tax must satisfy. In fact the tax will in general have two components. First, it will be recognized that the unregulated industry by hypothesis treats the unharvested resource as a free good, whereas we know that its shadow price is positive. Indeed we know that this shadow price equals the left-hand side of equation (6.14). This is the first component. The second component arises only if harvesting costs are *not* linear in the rate of harvest, so that marginal and average harvesting costs differ. The unregulated (free-entry) equilibrium (equation (6.10)) has the industry equating market price of the harvest to the average cost and unless this equals marginal cost there is a dissipation of rents. Smith (1968) calls the wedge between marginal and average costs a *crowding* externality. (The reduction in future harvesting costs due to a lowering of current harvesting rates he calls a *stock* externality.) It follows that a specific tax rate equalling the sum of these two distortions is the corrective tax. That is, letting τ denote the specific tax one has

$$\tau = [C_X(S, X) - C(S, X)/X] - C_S(S, X)/(r - H'(S)). \qquad (6.19)^{15}$$

An equivalent way of arriving at equation (6.19) is this. Suppose τ is the specific tax that is imposed on each unit harvested. Then, since firms sell the commodity at the price p

[15] It should be borne in mind that the right-hand side of equation (6.19) should be estimated at the optimum stationary values of X and S: i.e. at (X^*, S^*).

they now receive $p-\tau$ per unit. Therefore, in equilibrium we have instead of equation (6.10) the condition

$$p-\tau = C(S, X)/X. \tag{6.20}$$

But plainly, τ must be so chosen that equations (6.14) and (6.20) are identical. This implies that τ must satisfy the formula in equation (6.19).

6.8 Fisheries: Some observations

The literature on the economics of fisheries is enormous. Given the importance of fish resources, this is not surprising. It is estimated that in 1973 the world's harvest of fish was about 65.7 million tonnes, of which about 55.94 million tonnes (or about 83 per cent in mass) was from ocean fisheries. The total harvest was valued at over 18 billion US dollars (see FAO, 1973).[16] By 1978 world seafood exports had reached the figure of nearly 11 billion US dollars.[17] Mexico, Peru, India, Thailand, Indonesia and South Korea, for example, earn more than 100 million US dollars annually from fish exports. Not only have specific fisheries been scrutinized closely for their performance and potentials, there have been several attempts at global aggregation, to say something about the world's fishfood potentials. For example, Ryther (1969), in an oft-cited article, has suggested that the maximum sustainable annual yield from the world's ocean fisheries is about 100 million tonnes.[18] Ryther's estimate is among the lowest figures that have so far been suggested; but it is within the general range of other estimates.[19] At the extreme aggregate

[16] Japan, China, USSR and USA continue to remain the largest harvesters.

[17] The 1979 world catch amounted to about 71.3 million tonnes, of which 63.8 million tonnes was from marine fisheries (see FAO, 1979).

[18] Strictly speaking the figure of 100 million tonnes does not refer to MSY but, rather, to maximum potential harvest, since a good fraction of the fisheries' production has to be left unharvested on ecological grounds. Thus, Ryther (1969) estimates that the world's potential total fish production is about 240 million tonnes annually.

[19] FAO (1969), for example, estimates it to be about 120 million tonnes.

level then, the annual rate of harvest would seem to be a good deal less than maximum sustainable yield (MSY). The matter is different, of course, if one were to disaggregate and consider individual fish species, and even more so if one disaggregates further and studies individual fisheries. Thus, for example, while annual harvests of tunas, sardines and herring-like fish, shrimp, clams and scallops (1973 landings estimated at 1.71, 4.34, 1.11, 0.62 and 0.22 million tonnes respectively) fall short of their MSYs (estimated at 2.39, 5.97, 1.49, 1.44 and 1.49 million tonnes respectively), they exceed their respective MSYs in the case of groundfish, halibut and mackerel (11.84, 0.12 and 3.01 million tonnes respectively in 1973 versus their corresponding MSY values of 11.73, 0.06 and 2.74 million tonnes).[20] Now the analysis in section 6.4 demonstrated that even if unregulated, a common-property resource does not get ruined if harvest costs relative to the value of the harvest is not too low. Furthermore, the analysis of section 6.5 implies that a harvest rate falling short of MSY is, on its own, no necessary cause for jubilation – the harvest rate could well be far from optimal. Likewise, we shall see in the following chapter that if initial stocks are large the optimum policy will be to deplete the stock somewhat, which may well imply that for a while the rate of harvest exceeds MSY. Therefore the figures quoted above, on their own, do not convey much information. The presumption that there is excessive fishing in unregulated common-property fisheries comes rather from theoretical considerations of the kind offered in sections 6.4 and 6.5. Such a presumption has led Cooper (1975, 1977) to attempt to estimate the tax revenue that ought to be generated from international marine fisheries. Cooper assumes that marginal and average costs of harvest are equal so that, as would then be implied by equation (6.19), the optimal tax rate is of the form

$$\tau = -\,C_S(S, X)/(r - H'(S)). \qquad (6.21)$$

The procedure often appealed to for estimating excess harvesting costs due to free-entry is to compare yields per unit input in recent years with those at some earlier period when, it is thought, there was no overfishing. Using what is essentially this procedure

[20] See Bell (1978, p. 127).

Crutchfield and Pontecorvo (1969) estimated that excess cost figures amounted to about 80 per cent of total resource costs in the Alaskan salmon fishery during the 1950s. Since then excess cost figures have been estimated for a number of common-property fisheries. On the basis of these, Cooper has assessed that, as a minimum, there is on average an excess cost of about 20 per cent on about 60 per cent of the world's marine fishing (see Cooper, 1977, pp. 108–10). This, and annual harvest figures enable him to obtain an estimate of the numerator of the right-hand side of equation (6.21). Estimates of the denominator are necessarily *ad hoc*. But Cooper (1977) argues that the optimum tax on international marine fisheries ought approximately to generate an annual revenue of 2.5 billion US dollars. Being a global commons it is a natural suggestion that such a tax be administered by the United Nations, possibly as a contribution to its Development Fund.

Such estimates of global fisheries are necessarily pretty crude. But they are useful, if only because they stem from correct arguments and suggest rough orders of magnitude. More careful empirical studies have been conducted for specific fisheries for which time series data are available. In the following section I summarize the findings in one such study and so illustrate the theory that has been developed in this chapter.

6.9 Application to the lobster fishery

In an interesting and careful study Henderson and Tugwell (1979) have made an empirical investigation of the lobster fishery in two catchment areas of Canada: Port Maitland and Miminegash. In what follows I summarize their findings with regard to the former only.

Henderson and Tugwell assume that the growth function of the lobster fishery is of the quadratic form of equation (6.2), and on the basis of data for the period 1954–69 estimate that

$$H(S) = 1.80167S - 0.00051S^2, \qquad (6.22)$$

where the mass S in equation (6.22) is measured in units of thousands of pounds. It is now an easy matter to check that the

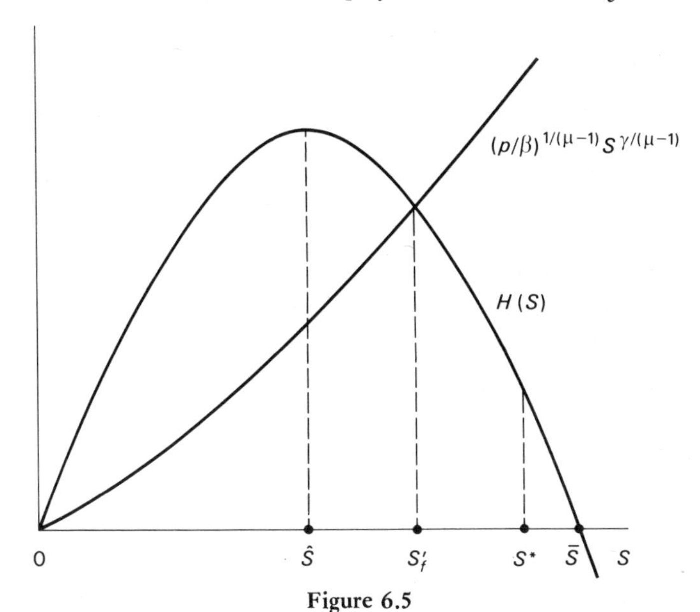

Figure 6.5
($\hat{S}$ = 1.77 million lbs; S'_f = 2.49 million lbs (see figure 6.3); S^* = 3.05 million lbs; $\bar{S}$ = 3.53 million lbs.)

stock that sustains maximum sustainable yield is 1.77 million pounds (see figure 6.5).[21]

The production function for lobster catch is assumed to be of the Cobb–Douglas form (6.8) and Henderson and Tugwell estimate it to be

$$X = 2.26\, S^{0.44} E^{0.48}, \tag{6.23}$$

where effort, E, is measured in units of thousand lobster traps.[22] With these estimates the authors calculate the stationary values of both the free-entry and the optimal solutions – the theory of which have been developed in sections 6.4 and 6.5 respectively. Henderson and Tugwell base their calculations on prices prevailing in 1961. Lobster price, p, is taken to be 485 US dollars per thousand pounds and the marginal cost of effort is taken to be 1421 US dollars per thousand traps. Using these figures in

[21] The natural equilibrium stock $\bar{S}$ (see figure 6.2) is 3.53 million pounds.

[22] For details of their estimation procedure, see Henderson and Tugwell (1979).

equations (6.10) and (6.15) they conclude that other than the origin there is a unique solution – the stable stationary point to which the *unregulated* industry converges (S_f' in figure 6.3) – and the lobster stock at this solution is 2.49 million pounds with an associated annual catch of 1.33 million pounds (see figure 6.5). Henderson and Tugwell compare this with the actual average figures (over the period 1959–63), of 2.47 million pounds of stock and 1.18 million pounds of annual harvest – suggesting thereby that the free entry stationary solution is a good approximation to what was prevailing in this fishery during this period. Using equations (6.22) and (6.23) and the price figures in equations (6.14) and (6.15) they find that the solution is unique and that the optimal stationary stock, S^*, for this fishery is 3.05 million pounds, yielding an annual harvest of 0.75 million pounds (see figure 6.5). Finally, unregulated and optimal effort levels are computed to be 450 000 and 110 000 lobster traps respectively.

It is in fact a simple matter to compute the tax per unit catch which will sustain the optimum stationary policy for a common property fishery. On using equation (6.19) Henderson and Tugwell estimate that $\tau = 270$ US dollars per thousand pounds. This is about 56 per cent of the price of 485 US dollars per thousand pounds, implying that the distortion created by a lack of regulations is substantial. This is, perhaps, to be expected. The 'Cobb–Douglas coefficients' 0.44 and 0.48 in equation (6.23) imply that there are strong diminishing returns both to biomass (S) and effort (E). Therefore both the 'crowding' externality – the term $(C_X - C/X)$ in equation (6.19) – and the 'stock' externality – the term $-C_S/(r-H'(S))$ in equation (6.19) – are large. Therefore the corrective tax is large.

Other details apart, these numerical results show that free entry does not lead to the fisheries' ruin. Indeed, the stationary stock under free entry exceeds the MSY stock. The fishery is thus well preserved. However, there *is* excessive fishing at the unregulated solution, in the sense that the optimum stock is still larger. The catch is certainly greater than the optimum, but then so is the effort applied. The latter costs more than the gains obtained from larger harvests. We conclude that the estimates suggest that there are serious cost advantages in allowing the stock to grow in size.

7 Fisheries and Aquifers: The Transient Phase

7.1 Introduction

In the previous chapter I established social cost–benefit rules for the management of renewable resources, such as fisheries and groundwater basins. For simplicity, the rules were restricted to those that identify optimal stationary policies. It is clear of course that except by fluke the initial stock – that is, the inherited stock at the date the social management problem is posed – will not equal the level that sustains such a policy. In this chapter, therefore, I look into the implications of this.[1] Intuition suggests that for a wide range of plausible cases optimal stationary policies are really long-run goals. For the immediate future the right policy would, one supposes in such cases, be to allow the stock to adjust (optimally of course!) until it attains the long-run target. In what follows I identify a class of such cases, and refer to the adjustment period as the transient phase. This explains the title of this chapter.

7.2 The problem

I continue to use the notation introduced in chapter 6. The harvest rate at date t is denoted by X_t and the stock by S_t. The flow of net social benefits is shown by

$$N(S_t, X_t) \equiv B(X_t) - C(S_t, X_t)$$

[1] A thorough mathematical account of such optimum control problems is in Clark (1976). Brown (1974), Spence (1974) and Spence and Starrett (1975) are important early contributions to this range of issues.

and it is assumed that $B(X)$ is concave; that is, marginal social benefit is non-increasing in yield.[2] In many applications $B(X)$ is increasing in X. I shall take it, for simplicity, that average harvesting cost is independent of the harvest rate. This means that I can write

$$C(S_t, X_t) = L(S_t) X_t$$

In figure 7.1 I characterize the general features of the average cost function, $L(S)$, that I shall assume holds. As a function of the stock average cost is assumed to decline at a declining rate.

As before, let r (>0) denote the social rate of discount, and S_0 the stock inherited at $t = 0$, the date at which the optimum harvesting policy is being calculated. The welfare criterion is the sum of the discounted values of the flow of net social benefits: that is $\int_0^\infty e^{-rt} N(S_t, X_t)\, dt$. The variable that the planner is assumed to control directly is the harvest rate X_t. It follows (see equation (6.5)) that the planner's choice of X_t indirectly affects future stocks via the 'growth' equation:

$$dS_t/dt = H(S_t) - X_t, \tag{7.1}$$

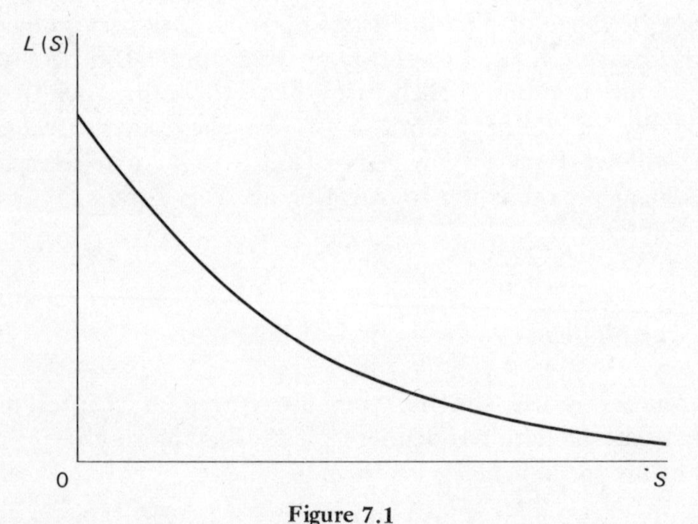

Figure 7.1

[2] As in the previous chapter we are assuming for simplicity that the net benefit function does not depend explicitly on time. In particular, this means that there are no improvements in harvesting techniques.

where, I take it, that the natural rate of renewal, $H(S)$, satisfies the conditions specified in condition (6.4) (see also figure 6.2). For simplicity of exposition only we shall assume that there is an upper bound to the rate at which harvesting can feasibly be carried out. This upper bound we denote as $\bar{X}$ (>0) and we suppose that $\bar{X}$ exceeds the maximum sustainable yield.[3] Thus $0 \leqslant X_t \leqslant \bar{X}$ for all $t \geqslant 0$. We may now express the planner's problem as follows:

$$\left.\begin{array}{l}\text{Choose } X_t\ (0 \leqslant X_t \leqslant \bar{X}) \text{ for } t \geqslant 0 \text{ so as to} \\ \text{maximize } \int_0^\infty e^{-rt}\,[B(X_t) - L(S_t)\,X_t]\,dt, \text{ subject} \\ \text{to the constraint (7.1); where } S_0 \text{ is given as datum.}\end{array}\right\} \quad (7.2)$$

Two broad category of cases are now worth distinguishing: (a) where $B(X)$ is proportional to X, and (b) where $B(X)$ is strictly concave in X; that is, marginal benefit is a diminishing function of X. In the following section we consider the case where $B(X)$ is proportional to X. Such a benefit function is plausible in many circumstances (a small fishery exporting its harvest) and we shall find that provided certain additional assumptions are satisfied, the optimal harvesting strategy in such a case is precisely what conservationists often advocate: a moratorium on catch for a limited period. In section 7.4 I shall comment on the implications of assuming that $B(X)$ is strictly concave.

7.3 Most rapid approach paths

Suppose that $B(X) = pX$, where $p > 0$. Here, p will be interpreted as the accounting price of the yield. Recalling that $\underline{S}$ ($\geqslant 0$) is the threshold level (see condition (6.4)), we now assume that $p > L(\underline{S})$, and that $H'(\underline{S}) > r$. Since by hypothesis $L(S)$ is a decreasing function of S (see figure 7.1), $p > L(\underline{S})$ implies that p exceeds unit harvesting costs at all stocks in excess of the threshold. The second

[3] It should be emphasized that this assumption is made solely for expositional ease. Nothing of substance emerges if we do not assume this. Notice that if time were treated as a discrete variable such an upper bound would automatically be given by the size of the stock.

assumption; viz. $H'(\underline{S}) > r$, means that the resource is sufficiently productive at the margin near the threshold.

We look once again at stationary optima. They are solutions of equations (6.14) and (6.15). Since we have $X = H(S)$ along a stationary path, we may re-write equation (6.14) for the present model as:

$$r = H'(S) - [L'(S)\,H(S)]/[p - L(S)]. \tag{7.3}$$

Equation (7.3) is a single equation in one unknown. We begin by considering those cases for which the equation has a *unique* solution, say S^*, and where $\bar{S} > S^* > \underline{S}$. In the previous chapter we assumed that even when the initial stock is not equal to it, S^* is the long-run optimal stock. That this is indeed so has been proved by Spence and Starrett (1975). But we still need to know what is the best approach to this target stock. This is described below.

Since

$$N(S_t, X_t) = [p - L(S_t)]\,X_t,$$

the net benefit function is proportional to the harvest rate. This means that marginal net benefit is independent of the harvest rate; viz. $(p - L(S_t))$. This suggests immediately that if $\underline{S} < S_0 < S^*$ - so that one may claim that the resource has been over-harvested in the past - the best mode of getting to S^* is by refraining from harvesting the resource until the stock attains the target level. The great attraction of this policy is that it enables the stock to grow at the fastest possible rate and, therefore, allows the target to be reached in the shortest possible time.[4] In Spence and Starrett (1975) it is demonstrated that this is in fact the optimum policy.

Suppose instead that $S_0 > S^*$. The long-run goal is to reduce the stock to S^*. The fastest way of reaching this target in this case is to harvest at the maximum feasible rate $\bar{X}$.[5] It can in fact be shown (see Spence and Starrett, 1975) that this is indeed the best

[4] If $X_t = 0$, then $\mathrm{d}S_t/\mathrm{d}t = H(S_t)$, and so this minimum time is

$$\int_{S_0}^{S^*} \mathrm{d}S/H(S).$$

[5] Since by assumption $\bar{X}$ exceeds the maximum sustainable yield, the stock will indeed be run down if $\bar{X}$ is the chosen rate of harvest. The minimum time

mode of getting to S^*. Since in either case the transient phase involves reaching the target stock S^* in the shortest possible time, we call it a *most rapid approach path* (see Spence, 1974; Spence and Starrett, 1975).

Most rapid approach paths have much to commend them. They are simple to understand and easy to compute. Their limitations we shall comment on in the following section. But the foregoing result; viz. the optimality of most rapid approach paths for the model being considered here gives an analytical underpinning to the conservationists' claim that there ought to be moratoria on the harvesting of seriously depleted stocks. By identifying conditions under which such proposals have merit one also learns something about those circumstances where they do not.

So far so good. Under the assumptions made so far, the most rapid approach to the target stock S^* is the best policy. But what if the optimality condition (7.3) possesses *multiple* solutions? Which solution should the planner aim at? I turn to this issue now.

Continue to assume that $p > L(\underline{S})$ and that $H'(\underline{S}) > r$. We shall also suppose without much loss in generality that *all* the solutions of equation (7.3) lie between $\underline{S}$ and $\overline{S}$ (see figure 7.2). Consider two of them, labelled S_a^* and S_b^*, and suppose, without loss of generality, that $S_a^* < S_b^*$. Consider the case where

$$(p - L(S_a^*))\, H(S_a^*) < (p - L(S_b^*))\, H(S_b^*);$$

that is, the flow of social benefits at the larger stock exceeds that at the lower one. Now this might suggest that the larger solution ought to be aimed at. This is not necessarily so. For suppose $S_0 < S_a^*$, as in figure 7.2. Then clearly the minimum time involved in getting to S_a^* is less than that required to get to S_b^* and it may be a good deal less. Admittedly, the advantage of sitting at S_b^* over S_a^* is that the flow of social benefits is greater at the former. But

---

required to attain S^* is in fact

$$\int_{S_0}^{S^*} \mathrm{d}S/(H(S) - \overline{X}).$$

This follows from the fact that $\mathrm{d}S_t/\mathrm{d}t = H(S_t) - \overline{X}$, when $X_t = \overline{X}$. Integrating this yields the result.

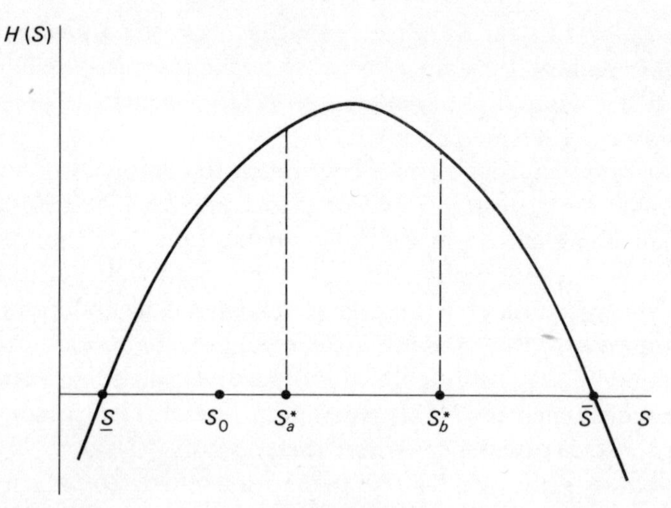

Figure 7.2

the disadvantage is the greater time spent in getting there, during which period, under the most rapid approach policy, there is no harvest. Moreover, we are discounting future benefits at a positive rate r. Thus the loss may well exceed the gain. When this is so, the smaller stock, S_a^*, ought to be aimed at. However, if the initial stock is large, it may well be optimal to aim at the larger solution S_b^* in the most rapid manner. This at once provides a clue as to how to locate the optimal harvesting policy: compute in turn the present discounted sum of net social benefits obtained along the most rapid approach paths to each of the solutions of equation (7.3). The optimal policy is the one with the greatest present discounted value (for a proof, see Spence and Starrett, 1975).[6]

The foregoing result implies that initial conditions – or, to put it in other words, inherited circumstances – not only influence what

[6] Thus, for example, if $S_0 < S_a^* < S_b^*$, then S_b^* and S_a^* are to be ranked according to

$$\int_{T_a}^{\infty} e^{-rt}[p - L(S_a^*)]\, H(S_a^*)\, \mathrm{d}t \gtreqless \int_{T_b}^{\infty} e^{-rt}[p - L(S_b^*)]\, H(S_b^*)\, \mathrm{d}t,$$

where T_a and T_b are the minimum time periods involved in getting from S_0 to S_a^* and S_b^* respectively.

the optimum policy is for the *immediate* future; in general even the *long-run* goal depends on the initial circumstances, a point which probably acquires still greater significance when applied to the field of environmental pollution (see chapter 8).

7.4 Commentary

I have identified a class of planning problems whose solutions consist of proceeding as rapidly as possible to a stock size worth maintaining and then staying there forever. Such policies are of interest not only because they are optimal under the circumstances postulated in the previous section. They are also simple, and therefore possibly easier to explain and to implement than are policies that approach the desired target stock level less dramatically. In addition, the conclusions of section 7.3 is of interest because it demonstrates sharply the fact that environmentalists' interest in the preservation of species is not necessarily in conflict with economic goals; and indeed, that even a moratorium on the harvesting of endangered species can often be recommended solely on commercial grounds.

Of course, if the discount rate r is high enough, or the regenerative capacity of the resource low enough (i.e. $r > H'(\underline{S})$) then it would be economically profitable to exhaust the resource in finite time (see Clark, 1973). In this case the conservationists' goal is in direct conflict with the implications of the economic criterion assumed in the previous section. If the social goal is to preserve the species then one way of incorporating this is to impose a 'no-extinction' constraint in problem (7.2); that is, a lower bound on the stock below which the resource must not be allowed to fall. (See chapter 5, sections 5.3 and 5.4.) This is often the manner in which pollution control problems are posed. (See problem (8.9) in chapter 8 and William Nordhaus' formulation of the carbon dioxide problem discussed in chapter 8, section 8.10.) The solution to this problem is to run the resource down until the no-extinction constraint becomes binding and then either stay there or let the stock rise again and then repeat the process. Which of the two policies is optimal depends on the parameters of the model.

All this is one side of the coin. The other side is the loss of employment in, say, a fishery, if a moratorium is imposed; and this, in many circumstances, may matter greatly. The welfare criterion in problem (7.2) is insensitive to this issue. It has to be admitted that there are circumstances where it makes little sense to take this issue into account. There are industries that patently will not collapse if they are prohibited from catching those species that are endangered. To take only one example, unemployment in the whaling industry, as Spence (1974) has argued, will not necessarily rise dramatically if there is a moratorium on the slaughter of blue whales, for the industry does not specialize in blue whales. Nevertheless, it must also be admitted that there are industries for which a moratorium will prove a great burden, especially if it is of long duration.

The idea then, is to introduce an employment premium. The way to do this is to reduce the accounting wage rate. The effect of this, for the model being considered, is to scale down the entire average cost schedule, $L(S)$, by a factor. For a large class of interesting cases it is simple to show that this *reduces* the optimum stationary stock and therefore the moratorium period.[7] But a moratorium is a moratorium and a mere reduction in its duration is not exactly consoling if there is no way to compensate people when they are thrown out of work. The obvious way to capture this concern is to use an income distributional weight in the objective function of the planning exercise (see chapters 3 and 5 and UNIDO (1972)). If the weight depends on the income – the

[7] To see this, let $\alpha L(S)$ be the average cost function, with $\alpha > 0$. As before, we assume that $p > \alpha L(\underline{S})$. Suppose that equation (7.3) possesses a unique solution S^*, and consider the case where $S^* > \hat{S}$, where $\hat{S}$ is the stock that sustains maximum yield (MSY). From equation (7.3) we may conclude that

$$\begin{aligned} -\,dS^*/d\alpha = {} & [-(r-H'(S^*))\,\alpha L(S) + \alpha L'(S^*)\,H(S^*)]/ \\ & \times [-H''(S^*)\,(p-\alpha L(S^*)) - (r-H'(S^*))\,\alpha L'(S^*) \\ & + \alpha L''(S^*)\,H(S^*) + \alpha L'(S^*)\,H'(S^*)] < 0. \end{aligned}$$

Thus, a reduction in the scale factor, α, reduces S^*, the optimum stationary stock. Mishra and Beyer (1976) make a systematic use of accounting prices in their evaluation of a state financed project designed to exploit the Ratnagiri fishery in Maharashtra, India.

smaller the income the larger the weight – then the effect of its introduction is to have a social benefit function $B(X)$ which is *strictly* concave; that is, while $B'(X) > 0$, we have $B''(X) < 0$.[8] The long-run stationary optimum is, in this case, a solution of equation (6.14). But the approach to this stationary optimum is less draconian than the most rapid approach path. Even if the resource in the past has been severely depleted the optimum policy in the immediate future will typically be to engage in some harvesting, albeit at a low rate to begin with so as to enable the stock to regenerate. The disadvantage of such a policy is the greater time needed to reach the optimum stationary stock. But this is more than matched by the gain, which is that social benefits are reaped even in the immediate future. It is intuitively clear why this is typically so. Since $B''(X) < 0$, *marginal* social benefit from yields is highest when yield is nil. If marginal benefit is very large at zero yield it cannot be optimal to have no yield even for a short while.[9] As I have remarked before, planning exercises ought to be flexible enough to accommodate the various kinds of considerations that are judged important. This inevitably introduces a taxonomic element into the exercises. Far better this than sure-fire prescriptions that do not survive scrutiny.

[8] Of course, the benefit function $B(X)$ in problem (7.2) may be strictly concave due to reasons that have nothing to do with income distributional considerations. In some applications $B(X)$ may be the area under a 'willingness to pay' curve which is downward sloping.

[9] Propositions of this sort are proved in Brown (1974) and Clark (1976).

8 The Economics of Pollution Control

8.1 A simple classification of pollutants

Ecologists have found it useful to construct a two-way classification of pollutants in accordance with whether they are *qualitative* or *quantitative*.[1] The first category (which includes chlorinated hydrocarbon pesticides, such as DDT; industrial chemicals, like the PCBs; and certain herbicides) consists of synthetic substances that are produced and released into the biological environment solely as an outcome of human activity. The latter, on the other hand, consists of substances such as mercury, nitrates, phosphorus and radiation, that are naturally present in the environment, but whose presence, either as stock or as flows, are augmented by human activity.

For economic analyses of pollution this particular two-way classification is not very helpful. The ecologist's motivation for it though would seem to be the following: many qualitative pollutants are biologically active; they stimulate physiological activity in ecological systems. But since by the definition of qualitative pollutants organisms have had no previous experience with them, these substances are often not biodegradable. They are among the most tenacious of molecules, and several of them are suspected of causing serious long-term damages.[2]

In the economics literature on pollution control it has been customary to focus attention on the concentration of pollutants themselves, and to regard them directly as economic 'bads'. This

[1] See Ehrlich *et al.* (1977, p. 629).

[2] A more direct two-way classification of wastes consists therefore of degradable and non-degradable pollutants. There are several quantitative pollutants that are non-degradable. See Kneese and Bower (1968, chapter 2).

is a perfectly reasonable procedure. We followed it in chapter 4, and shall do so again in this chapter. But it is conceptually useful to bear in mind, and I noted this in chapter 1, that the emission of pollutants into an ecological system results in a *reduction*, either in the *quality* or in the *size* (or both), of resource stocks that are positively valued. Eutrophication of lakes is an example containing elements of both. The discharge of nitrogen and phosphorus (e.g. in the form of inorganic fertilizers) into aquatic eco-systems leads to the growth of various algae. This in turn results in the generation of foul odour and taste in drinking water. It can at the same time lead to a depletion of dissolved oxygen, and thereby to loss in fish stocks. In very many instances, though, it is only the quality of a valued resource which is affected by the emission of pollutants. Ambient air-quality standards are based on quality indices of the air. For water, a quality index much in use is the dissolved oxygen level, which is related to the biochemical oxygen demand (BOD), via what is known as the Streeter–Phelps equation (see Kneese and Bower, 1968, p. 20).[3] But since such quality indices, by their definition, reflect the concentration of pollutants of various kinds that are present in the resource in question, one may as well focus attention on the pollutants themselves in the construction of formal models.

Pollutants are created as by-products of production, consumption and as intermediate products in the process of production.[4] A good example of the first is provided by the pulp and paper industry. Cigarette smoke is an oft-cited example of the second. Pesticides, herbicides, and chemical fertilizers are obvious examples of the last. Here I wish to introduce the kinds of considerations that must typically be taken into account in the analysis of intertemporal economic problems arising from pollution. A general formulation is, therefore, precisely what is desired at this stage, so that it can incorporate a wide variety of features. At the same time it is sensible here to keep the formulation as uncomplicated as possible. In doing this we begin by supposing that the pollutant

[3] BOD measures the quantity of dissolved oxygen that would be depleted by a specific quantity of organic waste at a standard temperature over a specified period.

[4] I am concentrating my attention on man-made pollution and not 'natural pollutors' such as volcanoes.

appears as a by-product of production. Subsequently we shall note that the formulation can absorb the case where the pollutant is an intermediate good in production.

8.2 The emission–output ratio

Let us suppose that we are concerned with production at a particular location. Let Y_t denote an aggregate index of output at t, whose production is under scrutiny. If P_t is the *rate of discharge* of pollutants associated with this output, then we may suppose that

$$P_t = \alpha Y_t, \tag{8.1}$$

where α is the emission–output ratio. Presumably, this ratio can be influenced by choice of technology. Thus, for example, in the case of coal-based electric power plants one may introduce stack-gas scrubbers to remove the sulphur dioxide (SO_2) produced during coal combustion.[5] Likewise, sewage treatment plants, designed to raise the quality of household and industrial sewage to a level suitable for discharge into rivers, lakes and coastal waters, are among the most important examples of the model we are constructing here; although, strictly speaking, household waste ought to be regarded as a by-product of consumption. Alternatively, one may look for different input mixes in the production of Y_t which generate less pollution; for example, switching to solar energy for the generation of domestic heating and thereby reducing SO_2 emission; or, in the case of crop production, substituting the use of pesticides by alternative techniques which involve, among other things, special planting combinations, the use of repellents and hormones, and the introduction of beneficial insects. In the former case pollutants are produced as a by-product of production (or consumption), but are treated before being

[5] To give an example of such coefficients, in 1976 the emission standards in force for new fossil fuel-based steam–electric power plants in the USA consisted, among other things, of 0.80 pounds of SO_2 per Btu heat input as a maximum 2-hour average emission from the combustion of liquid fossil fuels, and 1.2 pounds for those using solid fuels. See Ehrlich *et al.* (1977, p. 551).

discharged into the atmosphere. In the latter case choice of a suitable mix of inputs reduces the amount of pollution that is generated – something that is often called the choice of a 'clean technology'. In either event, the idea is that the emission–output flow coefficient, α, can be reduced by the expenditure of resources.[6]

We are concerned here with the flow of pollutants discharged into the surrounding medium. Thus we suppose that with each technique of production there is an associated value of α. We now use an accounting device which will prove most useful for exposition and which will not diminish the generality of the formulation. We shall suppose that if there is no attempt at pollution control there is a best technology for producing the output. That is to say, this is the technology which the producer will choose if he is not constrained either by emission charges or by emission standards. To produce a given flow of output Y_t using this technology involves a stream of costs. This cost stream we keep in the background for the moment. But we now suppose that to *reduce* the emission–output coefficient from the level associated with this technology involves an *additional* flow of costs which we discount at the consumption rate of interest (or the social rate of discount) to arrive at a capitalized figure. This additional investment outlay we call I, and we suppose that the emission–output ratio is a function of I. Thus $\alpha = \alpha(I)$. Again, to have an interesting problem we take it that α is a declining function of I (i.e. $d\alpha/dI < 0$), to capture the fact that the emission–output ratio can be reduced by increasing investment. We should emphasize that $\alpha(I)$ is the net emission–output ratio. Thus it includes the pollution that is created by the undertaking of the anti-pollution investment I. (The question can be asked whether the pollutants generated by abatement schemes themselves are likely to be large. Via an interesting case study of the St Louis airshed, Kohn (1975) has shown that it can be negligible.) Note in particular from our accounting convention that $I = 0$ is associated with the production technology that would be chosen by the producer in the absence of any environmental regulations. By this convention the emission–ouput ratio associated with this technology is $\alpha(0)$. In figure 8.1

[6] Another way of reducing α is to divert the effluent to a different medium where it is less harmful. This case too is caught in our formulation.

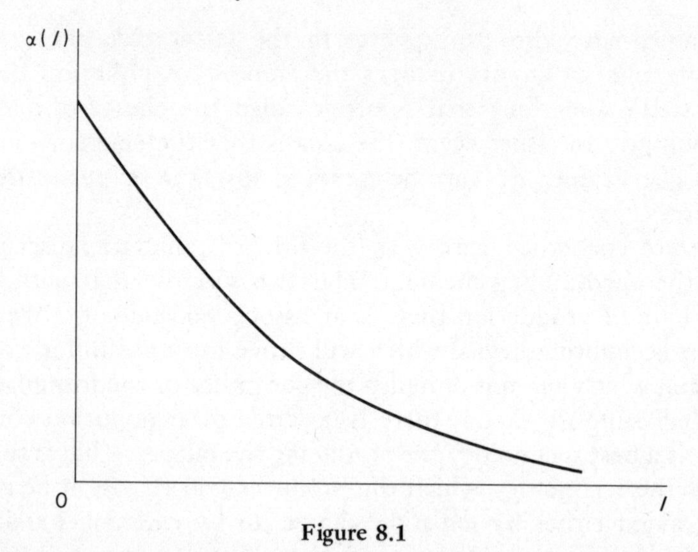

Figure 8.1

we have drawn a stylized version of the function $\alpha(I)$. The diagram displays the phenomenon of *increasing marginal cost* of pollution control (i.e. $d^2\alpha/dI^2 > 0$); a feature which appears to be fairly pervasive (see Kneese and Schultze, 1975, chapter 2).[7,8]

[7] Thus, Kneese and Schultze (1975, pp. 19–21), write:

> As a virtually universal phenomenon, the greater the percentage of pollutants already removed from an industrial process, the higher will be the cost of removing an additional amount ... for example, when 30% of the BOD has been removed from the waste discharges of a typical large meat-processing plant, the cost of removing an additional pound is 6 cents. But once 90% of the BOD is removed, another pound costs 60 cents; above 95%, the cost rises to 90 cents ... In one analysis, the total ten-year cost of eliminating 85 to 90% of water pollution in the United States was estimated at $61 billion. Achieving 95 to 99% freedom from pollution would add *another* $58 billion, bringing total costs to $119 billion, or about 1% of national income. A 100% objective (zero discharge) would demand an *additional* $200 billion.

These broad figures are economy wide. A number of good case studies in which the costs of pollution-abatement measures are estimated for various specific industries are to be found in Leone (1976).

[8] It may be argued that there is no need for a trade-off, that technologies exist that are both cheaper *and* cleaner, and that bad practices have resulted

8.3 Clean-up costs and natural amelioration rates

I now proceed to characterize the manner in which the pollution concentration changes with time. I denote the concentration level in the medium under study by S_t at date t. Thus, for example, if it is the stock of SO_2 in the air which is under discussion we may measure S_t by the number of micrograms of SO_2 per cubic metre at t. Ignoring seasonal variations and exceptional local circumstances, and taking the discharge of *other* pollutants into the medium as given, we may take it that the net rate of change of the stock of the pollutant in question is a function solely of the rate of discharge, P_t, and the concentration level itself. This we write as $H(P_t, S_t)$ and, therefore, that

$$dS_t/dt = H(P_t, S_t). \qquad (8.2)^9$$

It is appealing to simplify the functional form H and suppose that it is 'additive separable' in P_t and S_t. This is often a good approximation, and so I assume that

$$H(P_t, S_t) = G(P_t) + J(S_t),$$

---

in the prevalence of inferior technologies in both these senses. The formulation in the text does not contradict this thesis. It merely supposes that inefficient techniques of production have been disbanded and that we are comparing alternative techniques that *do* involve a trade-off.

[9] This is the counterpart of the growth equation for renewable resources, such as fisheries. See equation (6.1). I emphasize that I am simplifying here considerably for expositional ease. As I have mentioned in the text H depends not only on P_t and S_t, but also on activities elsewhere by possibly other agencies that alter the medium into which the pollutant under scrutiny is discharged. I considered these general issues in chapter 2, section 2.4 when formalizing the problem of land management. Therefore I ignore these complications here by considering these other activities as *given*. The question of *synergism*, which was mentioned in chapter 4, is quite something else and will be incorporated in the text below. In certain special cases $H(P, S) = 0$ for all P and S to denote the fact that the stock does not change. This is so for noise pollution, for noise does not accumulate as a stock. The Streeter–Phelps equation, referred to in the text, is an example of equation (8.2) (see Streeter and Phelps, 1925).

where G and J are known functions.[10] Thus, the growth equation (8.2) reduces to the form

$$dS_t/dt = G(P_t) + J(S_t). \quad (8.3)$$

In what follows I shall suppose solely for expositional ease that $G(P_t) = P_t$, and therefore that the natural rate of degradation of the pollutant depends solely on the concentration level. There are important cases though where this is not true. But nothing of substance will be lost by this simplifying move.

We are concerned with pollutants that are rendered harmless by natural processes with the passage of time. In some important extreme cases the process may be painfully slow, as with chemicals such as the PCBs, and pesticides like DDT and mirex; they are 'non-degradable'.[11] For these limiting cases one may approximate and write $J(S) = 0$. Others, such as herbicides like 2,4-D, are degraded by soil bacteria within months. For these $J(S)$ is negative. Often enough, ecologists draw attention to those cases where pollutants depreciate over time provided their concentration is not too large. For such cases $J(S)$ – the natural depreciation rate of the pollutant in the medium in question – is *negative* if S is not too large, but is *nil* if S is large enough, as in figure 8.2.

We shall consider pollutants that do not multiply once released (unlike, say, harmful bacteria) and so we take it that J is never positive. Since J is *not* the percentage rate of depreciation, but is the rate of depreciation itself, one takes it that in the case of degradable pollutants the absolute value of $J(S)$ increases with S, at least so long as S is not too large. In figure 8.2 the example that has been drawn is one for which $J(S)$ decreases with increasing S until the stock attains the level $\bar{S}$, from which point J increases rapidly to zero, that is beyond $\bar{S}$ the rate of depreciation is painfully slow. Examples of such cases are often emphasized in the ecological literature (see Ehrlich *et al.*, 1977).

[10] We are considering the deterministic case here. If we wish to introduce uncertainty, we may proceed by supposing, as we did in chapter 4, that $H = H(P_t, S_t, \theta_t)$, where θ_t is a random variable at date t.

[11] Under experimental conditions the persistence of insecticides such as toxaphene have been noted to be as high as 45 per cent of the original deposit even after 14 years in as open a medium as soil.

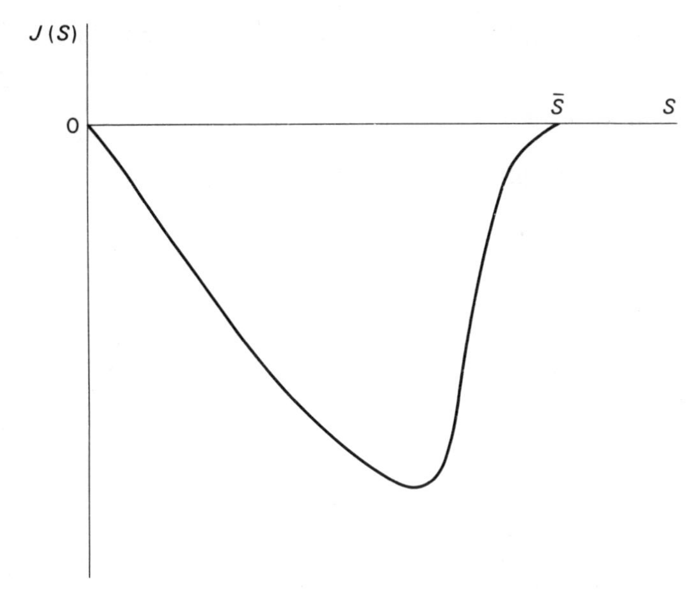

Figure 8.2

For those cases where it is judged that $\bar{S}$ is 'large' it is often convenient to ignore the range beyond $\bar{S}$ and to simplify and suppose that the pollutant depreciates at a fixed percentage rate, say δ, where δ is a positive number. In this case we have

$$J(S_t) = -\delta S_t, \tag{8.4}$$

so that equation (8.3) reduces to the familiar form

$$\mathrm{d}S_t/\mathrm{d}t = P_t - \delta S_t \qquad (8.5)^{12}$$

We shall not need to restrict ourselves to the form of equation (8.4), nor indeed the case depicted in figure 8.2, but if the reader finds these special forms helpful for conceptual purposes, there is no harm in thinking in terms of either of them. The point I wish now to formalize is yet another kind of pollution control: namely neutralizing discharged effluent in the medium in question. Artificial aeration of water bodies with low oxygen content is an obvious example. But this involves expenditure – what are often called *clean-up costs*. Thus let E_t denote costs incurred at t in reducing the stock of pollutant by artificial means. We may as

[12] Keeler *et al.* (1972) use this formulation, as do many others. It should be noted that equation (8.4) is the functional form of *radioactive decay*.

well incorporate this clean-up cost directly into the 'decay function' J and write it as $J(E_t, S_t)$ – where we must suppose, to have an interesting problem that $\partial J/\partial E < 0$, to capture the fact that pollution degradation can be augmented by expenditure. Consequently, the growth equation (8.3) now reads as:

$$dS_t/dt = P_t + J(E_t, S_t). \qquad (8.6)^{13}$$

8.4 Social damage due to pollutants

Thus far, a description of the system under study. I now come to the normative issues. I consider damages first. Recall that the pollutant may be detrimental to welfare either as a flow (e.g. noise) or as a stock (e.g. DDT), or both. It may damage welfare directly (e.g. the effect of smog on health, or the contamination of drinking water); or indirectly, by being detrimental to production elsewhere (e.g. crop reduction due to salinization of irrigation water, and the pollution of fish stocks, or the corrosion of metals by SO_2 in the air). Such a damage function we write as $D(S_t, P_t)$ and we shall subtract this from the flow of social benefits associated with output Y_t. Thus $D(S_t, P_t)$ denotes the *flow* of social damage when S_t is the concentration level and P_t the emission rate at date t.[14] As I remarked in chapter 4, the measurement, not to mention the valuation, of such damages poses some of the most difficult problems in environmental economics. There is usually not only a great deal of uncertainty about the physical or biological effects of pollutants; the valuation of these effects can be deeply problematic. The discussion in chapter 3, section 3.2 is relevant here. (For a good discussion of such measurement problems, see Mäler and Wyzga, 1976, and Freeman, 1979.)

It should be noted that the damage function, as has been formulated above, absorbs a wide variety of cases. The costs associated with operating water-treatment plants is a case that merits

[13] For the radioactive decay case of (8.4) one may simplify and suppose that $\delta = \delta(E)$, with $d\delta(E)/dE > 0$. Thus, (8.5) reads as $dS_t/dt = P_t - \delta(E_t)\, S_t$, a convenient form with which to work.

[14] The damage function may well depend explicitly on time t, to capture, say, the fact that the population in the locality in question is increasing or decreasing. We ignore this here for simplicity of exposition.

mention. If the production of the output under study involves the contamination of a source of drinking water, and if measures are taken to treat the *flow* of drinking water, then the damages attributable to the pollutant in the source are the costs of water treatment.

In many important cases damages depend solely on the pollutant stock – noise being a major exception. For expositional ease I concentrate on such cases; thus $D = D(S_t)$. In figure 8.3. I have presented a stylized version of such a damage function (see also chapters 3 and 4). For the purposes of illustration I present the case where due either to threshold effects or to the phenomenon of synergism, damages as a function of pollution stock display what scientists often call a *non-linear dose–response relation*. The terminology is unfortunately far-less precise than one would have expected from scientists, because the case they wish to emphasize, and which is implicitly caught in figure 8.3, is a *special* kind of non-linearity, one for which marginal damage is very large in the neighbourhood of some stock level $\bar{\bar{S}}$, and is small elsewhere. Thus, for example, below a certain level of pollution trees survive in smog. So do fish in waters in which the dissolved oxygen is above a certain threshold. Neither survives beyond the threshold. Likewise, SO_2 and certain kinds of atmospheric particulates are,

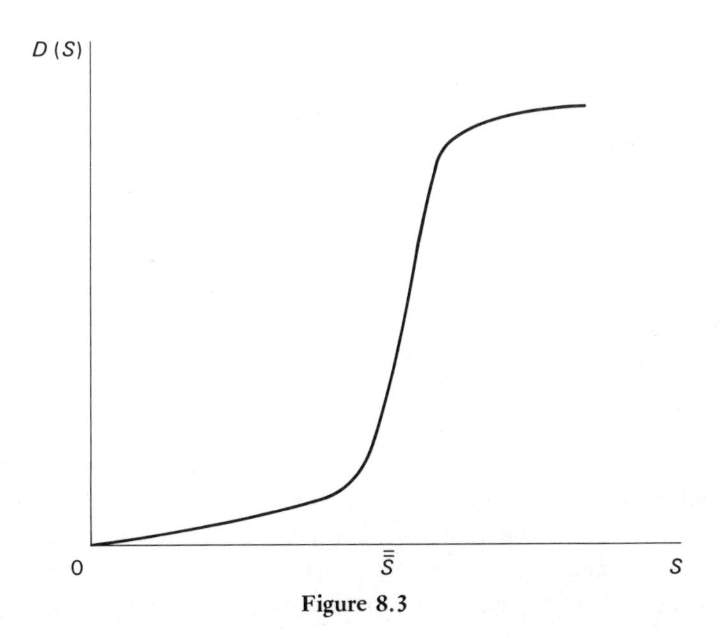

Figure 8.3

together, hazardous for health at concentrations below the levels at which each on its own is dangerous. We might then be considering the case where the particulates are already present in small concentrations and SO_2 is the pollutant being discharged into the atmosphere.

It should be emphasized that it is not being claimed that all pollutants display threshold effects. The formulations of pollution control problems that follow do *not* depend on the presence of such effects. I have highlighted threshold effects in figure 8.3 simply because they have been much discussed. In any case, small dosages of pollutants experienced over a prolonged period are exceedingly difficult to quantify in terms of a dose–response relationship. Where this is so one simply must acknowledge uncertainty and appeal to the kinds of consideration that were invoked in chapter 4.

Now it may be thought that since by definition $D(S)$ is the *flow* of social damages when pollution level is S, figure 8.3 does not really capture the non-linear dose–response relation scientists are often concerned with. For it can be argued that, in highlighting such relations scientists wish to point out (possibly temporary) *irreversibilities* that occur due to the destruction of socially valued resource *stocks* (such as forests or fish) when pollutants exceed threshold levels. Nevertheless, one can confirm that the policy implications arising from the case under study are similar to those arising from a non-linear dose–response relation. To see this notice from figure 8.3 that marginal damage is very high in the neighbourhood of the pollutant level $\bar{\bar{S}}$. Moreover, the flow of damage beyond $\bar{\bar{S}}$ is large, though *marginal* damage is small. Likewise, for concentrations below $\bar{\bar{S}}$ the flow of damage is small and marginal damage is small. It is therefore clear that a socially optimal policy will involve, among other things, keeping the pollution level from ever reaching $\bar{\bar{S}}$.

8.5. Social benefits from production

I come finally to the net social benefits associated with the output Y. Since by our accounting convention all costs that are not directed at pollution control have been separated out, they have now to be taken into account. Thus let $B(Y)$ denote the flow of net social benefits when production flow is Y. Since production costs have been included in the calculation of net social benefits, $B(Y)$ will typically be decreasing at large output levels. In figure 8.4 a stylized form of the social benefit function is presented (see also chapter 3).

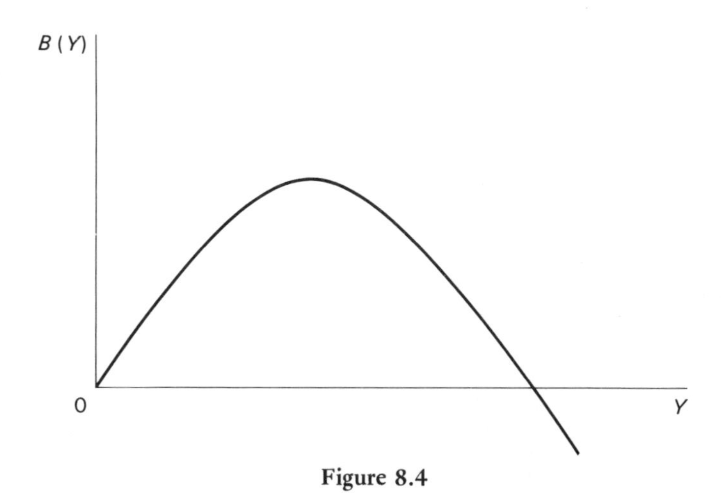

Figure 8.4

8.6 The environmental planning problem: Alternative formulations

We are now in a position to piece together the various bits of our construction and pose the planning problem of which the problem of pollution control is only a part. Let r (>0) denote the consumption rate of interest (or the social rate of discount). The variables in our model which a planner can control are clearly (a) the capitalized value of pollution abatement costs, I; (b) the output of the product over the planning horizon, Y_t; and (c) clean-up expenditures over the planning horizon, E_t. The flow of net social benefits at date t is clearly $B(Y_t) - D(S_t) - E_t$, and the present discounted value of this at the initial date is therefore $[B(Y_t) - D(S_t) - E_t]\, e^{-rt}$. The criterion of welfare is the sum of the discounted present values of net social benefits over the future. Thus the planner's problem is the following:

$$
\left.
\begin{array}{l}
\text{choose} \\
\quad I, Y_t, E_t \qquad (t \geqslant 0) \text{ so as to} \\
\text{maximize} \\
\quad \displaystyle\int_0^{\infty} [B(Y_t) - D(S_t) - E_t]\, e^{-rt}\, \mathrm{d}t - I, \\
\text{subject to the constraints} \\
\quad \mathrm{d}S_t/\mathrm{d}t = \alpha(I)\, Y_t + J(E_t, S_t), \qquad I, Y_t, E_t \geqslant 0, \\
\text{where } S_0 \text{ is given.}
\end{array}
\right\} \quad (8.7)
$$

[15]

Simple though it is, the formulation in (8.7) would appear to reflect the essential features of problems associated with the economics of pollution control. It is on the basis of such formulations that rules for social cost–benefit analysis of pollution control programmes need to be developed. In section 8.9 I will highlight the rules for social cost–benefit that problem (8.7) generates. Often enough though, because among other things, of the deep uncertainties that are involved in the estimates of damage functions, short cuts are undertaken in formulating pollution-control problems. Thus for example, an upper limit to concentration levels may be selected – possibly on the basis of thresholds – and if

[15] The reader may wonder how the formulation here is related to the 'materials balance' approach to environmental planning. The answer is that the latter is not really an *approach* as such; the term having been coined to emphasize the fact that a characteristic of all activities is that 'environmental materials' balance; that is, the wastes discharged into the environment must equal the resources absorbed from the environment minus the augmentation of fixed capital. It is an accounting device based on the conservation of matter-energy principle, designed to ensure that economic activities are correctly described. In our formulation the principle is implicitly incorporated in the benefit and damage functions and the amelioration function J. For details of the materials-balance approach, see Kneese *et al.* (1972). d'Arge and Kogiku (1973) incorporate this directly in an intertemporal optimization model. Useful collections of non-technical essays on environmental problems are Enthoven and Freeman (1973) and Dorfman and Dorfman (1972).

the inherited level of concentration is less than this, cost–benefit analysis is then directed at maximizing social surplus subject to the constraint that the concentration level never exceeds this upper limit. The advantage of this formulation is that one avoids having to introduce damage functions in the analysis. Here, standards act as constraints on the planning exercise (see chapter 3, section 3.3). Examples are water quality and ambient air standards (see e.g. Davies, 1973). For the model under discussion such a formulation would be as follows: let S^* be the chosen upper limit, and suppose S_0 is less than S^*. Then the planning problem is:

$$\left.\begin{array}{l} \text{choose} \\ \quad Y_t,\ I \text{ and } E_t \qquad (t \geqslant 0) \text{ so as to} \\ \text{maximize} \\ \quad \displaystyle\int_0^\infty [B(Y_t) - E_t]\, e^{-rt}\, dt - I, \\ \text{subject to the constraints} \\ \quad dS_t/dt = \alpha(I)\, Y_t + J(E_t, S_t), \qquad S_t \leqslant S^*, \text{ all } t \geqslant 0, \\ \text{and } I, E_t, Y_t \geqslant 0; \text{ all } t \geqslant 0; \text{ where } S_0 \text{ is given.} \end{array}\right\} \quad (8.8)$$

(Notice that (8.8) does not have a damage function.)

Problem (8.8) is a reasonable manner of posing a pollution control question if S^* is a threshold level of the kind depicted in figure 8.3. Indeed, if the damage function possesses the characteristics of figure 8.3 in a sharp form (with $\bar{\bar{S}} = S^*$) there is not much difference between the control problems (8.7) and (8.8).

A major source of difficulty arises with this latter approach if the existing concentration level, S_0, happens to exceed the level, S^*, that is judged intolerable. In this case cost–benefit analysis is typically directed at locating the least-cost mode of attaining the target within a specified period. For our model the problem would be posed as follows: assuming that it is feasible suppose that it is desired that the target be met within T years. Then the planning problem is:

$$
\left.
\begin{array}{l}
\text{choose} \\
\quad Y_t, I, \text{ and } E_t \qquad (t \geqslant 0) \text{ so as to} \\
\text{maximize} \\
\quad \displaystyle\int_0^{\infty} [B(Y_t) - E_t]\, e^{-rt}\, \mathrm{d}t - I, \\
\text{subject to the constraints} \\
\quad \mathrm{d}S_t/\mathrm{d}t = \alpha(I)\, Y_t + J(E_t, S_t), \quad S_t \leqslant S^* \quad \text{for } t \geqslant T, \\
\text{and } I, Y_t, E_t \geqslant 0; \text{ all } t \geqslant 0; \text{ where } S_0 \text{ is given and} \\
S_0 > S^*.
\end{array}
\right\} \quad (8.9)
$$

The problem with (8.9) is, of course, that T is arbitrarily chosen. In particular, if T is small, maximum social surplus will be small: either I or E_t (or both) will need to be raised dramatically, or output will have to be curtailed in order to drive the concentration level down to S^* by year T. Without engaging in sensitivity analysis it is not possible to judge how costly one choice of T is as compared to another. One may call the solution of problem (8.9) a *target-oriented programme*.

8.7 United States environmental protection acts: An illustration

It is worth distinguishing between formulations (8.8) and (8.9). In section 8.10 I shall report on a simulation exercise on the CO_2 problem which is cast in the form of (8.8). Problem (8.9) is interesting, though, because it is in terms of such a formulation that one can interpret and see the underlying logic in target-oriented environmental programmes that governments occasionally embark on. Thus, for example, the 1970 Clean Air Amendments in the USA considerably expanded the role of the federal government in setting and enforcing ambient air quality standards by appealing to a level of ambient concentration below which it is judged that no health damages occur. In discussing these amendments Kneese and Schultze (1975, pp. 51–2) note that:

> Congress directed the Environmental Protection Agency (EPA) to use scientific evidence to determine threshold values for pollutants assumed to have them, and then to set those values minus 'an adequate margin of safety' as 'primary standards'. These standards, which relate to injury to human health, are to be met first. More rigorous standards, to be met later, relate to public 'welfare' and aims to protect property, crops, livestock, and public transportation from pollutants. The states were to prepare implementation plans assuring that the primary standards would not be violated anywhere in the state after mid-1975. These plans to meet primary standards were supposed to have been completed by the beginning of 1972; deadlines for the secondary standards were more flexible.

They then go on to write:

> Perhaps the most striking feature of the new legislation was in the amendments to the National Emission Standards Acts, ... which established specific emission standards (α in our notation) for automobiles. These include limits on hydrocarbons (HC) and carbon monoxides (CO) for new car models in 1975 and an additional standard for oxides of nitrogen (NO_x) to be met in 1976 ... the act effectively calls for a 97% reduction, compared with uncontrolled conditions. (Kneese and Schultze, 1975, p. 52).[16]

In the case of water-pollution control Kneese and Schultze note that the 1972 Water Pollution Control Act Amendment for the USA begins by asserting two national goals: (1) 'that the discharge of pollutants into the navigable waters be eliminated by 1985', and (2) 'that wherever attainable, an interim goal of water quality which provides for the protection and propagation of fish, shellfish, and wildlife and provides for recreation in and on the water be achieved by July 1, 1983'. In the context of our formulation here it would seem that the first goal states that by 1985 the value of α must be driven to zero, whereas the second goal pertains to a target water-quality level to be attained by 1983. In view of this,

[16] Expressed in grams per mile these emission standards (α) were determined to be 0.41 HC, 3.4 CO and 0.04 NO_X.

it should perhaps not be surprising that Kneese and Schultze (1975) in their excellent monograph provide a sustained critique of the United States pollution-control programme. Their complaint for the most part is that prior to passing the environmental legislations no systematic exercise was performed to calculate the costs involved in meeting stated targets and to conduct sensitivity analyses with a view to computing the amounts that could be saved by relaxing the targets somewhat; for example by increasing T in our formulation (8.9) – the date by which the target quality standard must be met – or indeed, by reducing the target quality standard; that is, by increasing S^*.[17]

In the following two sections I shall bring out various features of the pollution control problem as formalized in (8.7) and highlight some of the general properties of the solution to it. In section 8.10 I report on a simulation exercise due to Nordhaus (1977) on the carbon dioxide problem, which is cast in the form of problem (8.8).

8.8 Some prototype policies

While relatively simple, the formulation of pollution-control, as captured in problem (8.7), nevertheless accommodates a wide variety of considerations that have been aired over the past decade and a half. We discuss them here.

In problem (8.7) the social objective is the sum of the present discounted values of the flow of net social surplus. Quite obviously, the nature of the optimal programme depends on the characteristics of the various functions appearing in problem (8.7) and also the pollution level S_0 that the economy has inherited from the past. In particular, it depends on the availability of 'pollution-free' technologies, the extent to which pollutants ameliorate under natural conditions, the social value of output and the social damages caused by pollution. Without specifying these

[17] The amounts may well be large. Kneese and Schultze (1975, p. 70), estimate that the cost difference between achieving the less ambitious goals in the earlier legislations in the USA and the ones in the 1970 and 1972 amendments on air and water quality standards may well be of the order of 250 billion US dollars.

reasonably precisely one cannot tell what the solution to problem (8.7) actually looks like. Nevertheless, one can discuss the broad categories of solutions that would emerge under different specifications. Since some of these categories have been discussed extensively in the environmental literature I mention them below.

It will be recalled that the social objective in problem (8.7) is

$$\int_0^\infty [B(Y_t) - D(S_t) - E_t]\, e^{-rt}\, \mathrm{d}t - I.$$

In table 8.1 below we list four broad categories of policies that would appear to yield a high value to this objective under differing specifications of the various functions in problem (8.7).

The first category of policies is characterized by the pursuit of limited economic activity and modest expenditures on pollution control. Limiting output would imply a modest emission of pollutants. Granted that such a policy yields only modest levels

TABLE 8.1

Policy	*Output* Y	*Pollution control expenditure:* E, I	*Level of pollution*
Limited growth and modest depollution effort	medium	medium	medium to low
High growth rates and vigorous depollution programmes	high	high	medium to low
High growth rates and negligible pollution control programmes	high	low	high
Low growth and negligible pollution control programmes	low	low	?

of direct welfare $B(Y)$; but it does mean that only a moderate expenditure on pollution control is required to result in low pollution damage $D(S)$.

The second class of policies consists in pursuing vigorous economic activity, from the fruits of which substantial sums are incurred on pollution control so as to limit the concentration of effluents. It would be misleading to suggest that it is in terms of an advocacy of these two classes of policies that one distinguishes 'environmentalists' from those who are not. Eminent environmental economists have supported the latter while commenting on the environmental programmes pursued in the United States (see Kneese and Schultze, 1975, p. 77). What one may infer, though, is that the enviromental debate during the past decade and a half strongly questioned the desirability of the third broad class of policies in table 8.1 which consists of a high level of economic activity together with negligible expenditures on pollution-control programmes - policies that were in effect being pursued until environmental issues gained prominence. However, a glance at problem (8.7) suggests that one cannot tell, *a priori*, whether this third class of policies may not be optimal. For notice that what society loses via social damages $D(S)$ *may* well be more than compensated by gains from large output and low expenditures on pollution control. What the environmental debate does draw attention to is the suspicion that the social damages are likely to be so vast that this class of policies simply cannot be desirable.[18]

To be sure, we are painting the tension between these views in broad strokes. To be sure also, there have been additional strands in the environmentalists' literature which cannot be captured in as aggregative a model as the one we are discussing here. In any case, for certain types of production in certain locations one policy may be optimal; not so for others. One simply cannot tell in advance. Nevertheless, the construct we are discussing here can indeed support the objections that have been raised to the view that poor

[18] However, for illustrative purposes economists have developed theoretical models in which such a policy is indeed optimal. See Keeler *et al.* (1972) in which a model of pollution is developed in which this is the case. Keeler *et al.* call this a Murky Age; murky, though optimal!

societies ought to curb their aspirations for growth because of the environmental implications – the fourth class of policies in table 8.1. The point is that if output is very low there is simply too little social surplus available for financing programmes that are required for the treatment of even the most common forms of waste which cause serious social damages. We have placed a query regarding the concentration of pollution in this fourth category simply because, while it may involve negligible *industrial* pollutants, it may typically involve suffering both because of low output and high doses of other forms of pollution. It cannot be emphasized strongly enough that some of the worst forms of environmental degradation are associated with low income, not high. Deterioration of health due to inadequate sanitation, not to mention inadequate diet, is a burden that the poor bear, not the rich. In the face of this, a call for curbing the growth rates that LDCs aspire to, appears at the very least, as an indication of misplaced human concern.

8.9 Cost–benefit rules for optimal pollution control

The planning exercise, problem (8.7), is in general difficult to solve analytically. At the technical level the first point to note is that, as figures 8.2 and 8.3 display, the problem is in general 'non-convex' (i.e. (8.7) is not a concave planning problem; see chapter 3 appendix), so that *marginal* social cost–benefit analysis as a means of *locating* the optimal policy is not a reliable procedure. I discussed this issue in chapter 3 and its appendix. Often enough, such 'non-convexities' prohibit the planner from relying exclusively on shadow prices (i.e. *pollution charges*) as a mode of decentralization (see especially chapter 3 appendix and the examples presented there). Where this is the circumstance, there is a clear case for centralized coordination and control by way of *pollution standards*. In chapter 4, I compared charges and standards in the context of a planning exercise in which the government has incomplete information about damages and about technology. The point here is different; in this chapter I have assumed no such incomplete and differential information. The desirability of standards as a mode of control can arise from 'non-convexities' and not incomplete information.[19] Nevertheless, there are many circumstances where a variant of Theorem 2 in chapter 3 appendix can be used so that I can characterize a solution of problem (8.7) in terms of charges. In what follows I assume that this can be done. Furthermore, for expositional ease I restrict myself to optimal *stationary policies* where, by definition, the economic variables are constant over time.[20]

Since the pollutant is undesirable we would expect its shadow price to be negative; that is we would expect charges to be imposed on them – not subsidies. Let p denote the *emission charge*, where p is positive. We can now obtain the social cost–benefit rule for production Y. It goes as follows: the present discounted value of output at date t is $e^{-rt}B(Y)$; and the present discounted value of the social cost imputed to this output is the effluent charge associated with this output. This latter is

$$pPe^{-rt} = p\alpha(I)Ye^{-rt}.$$

Output at t ought therefore to be chosen so as to maximize, not $e^{-rt}B(Y)$, but $e^{-rt}[B(Y) - p\alpha(I)Y]$. It follows that the cost–benefit rule for the production of Y is:

$$\mathrm{d}B/\mathrm{d}Y = p\alpha(I). \qquad (8.10)^{21}$$

The rule for clean-up expenditure is likewise simple to characterize. The present discounted value of clean-up cost at date t is $e^{-rt}E$. The social benefit from this expenditure is $-e^{-rt}pJ(E, S)$, the social value of reduced concentration (this is positive because J is

[19] To be sure, there are administrative problems in relying on standards. For a good discussion of this see Kneese and Schultze (1975). As we are concerned with *analytical* issues here we ignore such problems.

[20] In many such planning problems the solution of problem (8.7) will, in the long run, tend to a stationary state, no matter what the initial concentration level, S_0, is; but not necessarily. Though it may look easy enough, characterizing the solution of problem (8.7) is hard analytically. We addressed ourselves to this question in a different context in the previous chapter.

[21] Unless the optimum is to produce nothing, i.e. $Y = 0$, in which case the rule is $\mathrm{d}B/\mathrm{d}Y < p\alpha$ at $Y = 0$. This can readily happen at specific locations, where it may be best not to engage in production of this sort and to move the location of production. Since there is then not much to say about this case we ignore it.

negative; see figure 8.2). Thus clean-up expenditure at date t ought to be chosen so as to maximize $e^{-rt}[-pJ(E, S) - E]$. This yields the rule:

$$-p\ \partial J/\partial E = 1, \qquad (8.11)$$

(Unless $E = 0$ is optimal, in which case $-p\ \partial J(E,S)/\partial E < 1$ at $E = 0$; i.e. marginal cost exceeds marginal benefit at $E = 0$.)[22]

The investment rule for pollution control is likewise simple to obtain. An investment outlay, I, is equivalent to expenditure in perpetuity of rI per period.[23] When P is the emission rate, the *social damage* due to this output is valued at

$$e^{-rt}pP = e^{-rt}p\alpha(I)Y.$$

Therefore the present value of net social loss at date t due to I is $e^{-rt}[p\alpha(I)Y + rI]$. Notice that this entire expression is positive. The aim in undertaking pollution control is to minimize this loss. It follows that the rule determining optimal investment in pollution control is:

$$-pY\ \mathrm{d}\alpha(I)/\mathrm{d}I = r. \qquad (8.12)$$

(Unless $I = 0$ is optimal, in which case $-pY\,\mathrm{d}\alpha(I)/\mathrm{d}I < r$ at $I = 0$. Note that $\mathrm{d}\alpha/\mathrm{d}I < 0$, figure 8.1.) Quite clearly, firms would not undertake pollution control measures unless emission charges or emission standards were imposed on them.

Recall next that I am characterizing an optimal stationary state. Stationarity implies that equations (8.1) and (8.6) yield:

$$\alpha(I)Y = -J(E, S). \qquad (8.13)$$

I now come to the final optimality rule, central to the social management of pollution. It is the direct counterpart of the optimal fisheries' rule, equation (6.14), derived in chapter 6. It will substantiate the early claim in chapter 1 that pollution problems bear a strong family resemblance to the problems of manag-

[22] This last will be the case when technological possibilities of cleaning up pollutants after their discharge are limited, as for example with gaseous emissions into the atmosphere.

[23] Walter (1975, p. 65), presents estimates of environmental control costs per dollar of final sales in various United States industries for the year 1971.

ing renewable resources such as fisheries. To derive this final optimality rule I note that pollutant concentration is a capital stock with negative social value $-pS$. From problem (8.7) it is obvious that the social rate of return to holding this 'asset' can be expressed as the sum of two terms, $\partial J(E, S)/\partial S$, $(\equiv J_S(E, S))$ and $[\mathrm{d}D(S)/\mathrm{d}S]/p$, $(\equiv D_S(S)/p)$. The first term denotes the increased rate at which the pollutant disappears, and the second term the damage that is inflicted on future generations from a unit more of concentration – an intergenerational externality. But r is the social rate of discount. Therefore the optimal programme must be characterized as well by the condition:

$$r = D_S(S)/p + J_S(E, S). \qquad (8.14)^{24}$$

(See chapter 5, equation (5.5).)

There is an alternative argument which can be appealed to for deriving equation (8.14) and which will make transparent the similarity between the optimality rules (6.14) and (8.14). (See chapter 5, section 5.5.) In order to develop this argument notice that $B_Y(Y)/\alpha(I)$ is the change in the current flow of net social benefit if the rate of pollutant emission is increased marginally. The question to ask now is this: what additional cost would be imposed on future generations if the current rate of emission were to be increased marginally? To compute this notice that the consequence of increasing the current rate of emission is a marginal increase in the concentration of pollution. Along a stationary policy this implies that pollution damages $(D(S))$ will increase marginally for all future generations. This additional cost at each future date is $D_S(S)$. Now $J_S(E, S)$ is the increased rate at which the pollutant disappears; that is, $J_S(E, S)$ is the 'marginal productivity' of the pollutant. Furthermore, r is the social rate of discount. Thus $r - J_S(E, S)$ can be regarded as the *net* social rate of discount that ought to be used in discounting the flow of *marginal* social damages due to the concentration of pollutants. It follows that the present value of the flow of additional social damages is $D_S(S)/[r - J_S(E, S)]$. For a stationary policy to be judged optimal this additional cost must equal the additional benefit from increasing the rate of emission marginally.

[24] The first term on the right-hand side of equation (8.13) is positive and the second term is negative.

That is:

$$B_Y(Y)/\alpha(I) = D_S(S)/[r - J_S(E, S)] \tag{8.15}$$

Using equation (8.10) we note that equations (8.14) and (8.15) are identical.[25]

Compare the optimality rules (6.14) and (8.15). They possess the same structure and they highlight the fact that at a formal level pollution control problems have the same underlying structure as the problems of controlling renewable resources, such as fisheries and groundwater basins.

We are required to solve for *five* unknowns, p, Y, I, E and S from *five* equations (8.10) to (8.14). If a solution does not exist it means that even in the long run an optimal policy does not tend to a stationary state. For simplicity of exposition, therefore, we suppose that a solution exists. It should then be noted that there may be multiple solutions. The implication of this, as we noted in a different context in the previous chapter, is this: it suggests that the long-run characteristics of the optimal plan – i.e. the stationary state to which the plan converges, if it does – may well depend on what pollution level the economy starts with. That is, *history matters*.[26] It is often thought that if two societies have similar objectives and possess similar technologies they will have similar *long-run* goals. The foregoing argument suggests that this is not

[25] The optimality conditions, equations (8.10) to (8.12) and (8.14), can as well be derived directly from a Lagrangean formulation if we appeal to Theorem 2 in chapter 3 appendix. We wish to locate a *stationary* optimum. Suppose that the antecedent clause in the theorem is true. Then if $p(>0)$ denotes the multiplier associated with the constraint (8.13) the Lagrangean of the planning problem, at any arbitrary date can be expressed as:

$$B(Y) - D(S) - E - rI - rpS - p(\alpha(I)\,Y + J(E, S)),$$

and the choice variables are Y, E, I and S. Differentiating the Lagrangean partially with respect to these four variables in turn and equating them to zero yields the four optimality conditions.

[26] This is a general characteristic of optimal control problems in which stock variables enter the instantaneous net benefit function, as is the case with problem (8.7) and the models discussed in chapters 6 and 7 (see Arrow and Kurz, 1970). In addition, the model has non-convexities. Multiple solutions will often emerge.

necessarily so. History matters, in the sense that if they have inherited different pollution levels they may well wish to aim at substantially different goals. That is, their long-run stationary policies may differ greatly. Notice finally that if the pollutant displays threshold effects – either in terms of the damage inflicted (figure 8.3), or in terms of the amelioration rate (figure 8.2) – these threshold levels will typically be avoided along the optimal programme.

8.10 The carbon-dioxide problem: An application

The combustion of fossil fuels results in the emission of carbon dioxide (CO_2) into the atmosphere. It would appear that about 50 per cent of this remains there. It is known that CO_2 in the atmosphere produces a greenhouse effect, so that other things being the same, an increase in CO_2 concentration results in an increase in the mean global surface temperature. The current concentration of CO_2 in the atmosphere is about 330 parts per million. It is thought that if the use of fossil fuels grows at about 3 to 4 per cent per year the atmospheric concentration of CO_2 will rise to a level between 365 and 385 parts per million by the year 2000. In a well-known study Manabe (1971) estimated that, other things being constant, this will result in an increase in the mean global temperature by 0.3 °C to 0.6 °C. In a subsequent study, Manabe and Wetherald (1975) argued that a doubling of atmospheric concentration of CO_2 would result in an increase in the mean global temperature by 3 °C. Taken on its own, 3 °C, not to mention 0.6 °C, may not appear as a significant increase. Unfortunately, it is thought that even a 0.6 °C increase is sufficiently large to bring about changes in atmospheric circulation and the melting of sea ice; that is to say, it is feared that there is significant *climatic amplification* associated with increase in the mean surface temperature of the earth. The impact on agriculture could be deleterious, and the effect would be world-wide. It is for such reasons that the carbon-dioxide problem is taken very seriously by scholars with varied dispositions.

In an interesting and important recent study, Nordhaus (1977) has estimated efficient ways of allocation energy resources so as to ensure that CO_2 concentration in the atmosphere never exceeds a given multiple of the current level.[27] The point is that while alternative energy sources, such as fission and solar energy, are currently more expensive than fossil fuels, they have no significant CO_2 emissions.[28] Nordhaus' simulation study is based on a problem rather like problem (8.8). He chose a planning horizon of 200 years, a discount rate of 10 per cent per year, and his central analysis was conducted on the basis of an upper limit to the concentration level being twice the existing one.[29] It is assumed that there is no effective technology for removing CO_2 from the atmosphere by artificial means. The only way therefore that remains for controlling CO_2 emission is a judicious mixture of output control and a move towards more expensive energy sources; that is, in the notation of this chapter, controlling both Y_t and I. It should be noted that since the model does not incorporate a non-convex damage function, as in figure 8.3, nor a non-convex natural amelioration function, as in figure 8.2, Nordhaus' planning model does not have the non-convexities of the type that prohibit an appeal to shadow prices. In fact the problem, as he poses it, is a linear programming one, and he obtains the intertemporal structure of CO_2 taxes which could in principle be used for implementing the optimal plan.

We shall not present details of Nordhaus' highly original study. Table 8.2 reproduces his results. The table is self-explanatory and so we merely highlight the more interesting results. Notice first from the first two rows that total energy consumption is not significantly constrained by the imposition of the carbon constraint. Indeed, in year 2100 the simulation run projects an *increase* in US energy consumption as a consequence of the constraint from 395×10^{15} Btu to 405×10^{15} Btu. However, from the second pair of rows one notices that CO_2 emissions are severely curtailed in *later* years along the optimal programme when the

[27] Nordhaus (1980) provides a revised and more elaborate account of the CO_2 problem. Since the analytical apparatus is much the same in the two studies I discuss the earlier, briefer account in what follows.

[28] It is not overlooked that nuclear fission poses other environmental problems.

[29] In the notation of problem (8.8) in the text, we have $S^* = 2S_0$.

TABLE 8.2

	Actual	*1980*	*2000*	*2020*	*2040*	*2100*
Energy consumption in USA (10^{15} Btu/year)						
Uncontrolled CO_2 (i.e. $S^* = \infty$)	{71}	76	92	155	250	395
100% increase CO_2 ($S^* = 2S_0$)		75	92	142	160	405
Global carbon emissions (10^9 tons/yr)						
Uncontrolled CO_2	{4.0}	6.9	10.7	18.4	40.1	45.4
100% increase CO_2		6.9	10.7	16.6	16.0	4.9
Carbon emission tax (p_t $/ton at 1975 prices)						
Uncontrolled CO_2	{0.00}	0.00	0.00	0.00	0.00	0.00
100% increase CO_2		0.14	1.02	8.04	67.90	87.15

Source: Nordhaus (1977)

CO_2 constraint is imposed. This suggests that it is only in later years that the optimal programme is characterized by a major shift to costly input mixes. This is readily explainable. The upper limit on the concentration chosen being *twice* the current level means that there is a lot more of CO_2 emission that the programme allows. Given that one is discounting future costs it is quite natural that a move towards expensive but 'clean' sources of energy ought to come some time in the future – in the simulation exercise in fact it comes some 60 years from now. The last row of the table is revealing. It shows that the CO_2 emission tax becomes significant only at about the middle of the next century.[30]

I have noted that major impacts of a CO_2 concentration constraint of twice the prevent level begin occurring about 60 years from now; not until then. Nevertheless, it is instructive to calculate the social cost of imposing the constraint on CO_2 concentration level. To do this one computes the maximum value of the social objective in problem (8.8) under the assumption that $S^* = \infty$ (the unconstrained problem) and then subtract from this the maximum value for the case $S^* = 2S_0$. This is a useful exercise to perform precisely because the upper bound to the concentration level is, in any such exercise, somewhat arbitrarily chosen. Nordhaus calculates that at 1975 prices this cost is about 87 billion US dollars. This is not an unduly large figure; but it is arguable that the upper bound has been chosen too generously, given the gravity of the problem and the risks that are involved. For this reason Nordhaus computes the social costs incurred if the constraint on CO_2 concentration is only 50 per cent in excess of the current level (i.e. $S^* = 3S_0/2$). It is of the order of 540 billion US dollars in present value terms. This *is* a large sum. However, as with all global environmental problems, the question remains: how is international agreement to be reached among diverse nations?

[30] In 1975 the prices per ton of carbon-based fuels were about 25 US dollars a ton for coal, 100 US dollars a ton for petroleum, and 200 US dollars a ton for natural gas.

9 Forests and Trees

9.1 Forest externalities

Forest management generates a large array of externalities of the kinds discussed in chapters 1 and 2. Watershed forests, for example are not only a source of timber, they also preserve soil cover on site and protect soil downstream from erosion, smooth the supply of water for agriculture from irregular rainfall and prevent water reservoirs and irrigation systems from sedimentation.[1] Likewise, tropical rain forests, in addition to these services, provide a habitat for a diverse genetic pool, and influence local and regional climate substantially. The severity of the monsoon floods in Northern India in 1978 was at least partly due to the deforestation that has taken place around the upper reaches of the Ganges over the past few decades. One of the fears expressed by environmentalists about deforestation of the Amazon basin (the last of the 'great forests') is over its possible impact on global climate (see also chapter 8, section 8.10). Moreover, ecologists are at pains to remind us of the myriad of living species that inhabit forests. The value of a forest typically exceeds the value of the timber it nurtures, and on occasion exceeds it greatly.

The measurement of the external benefits that a forest confers poses vast problems at both the conceptual and the practical level.

[1] Das (1977) reports, to give an example, that the capacity of the Nizamsagar Reservoir in India has more than halved from about 900 million cubic metres to less than 340 million cubic metres, largely as a consequence of deforestation in the watershed. This fall has had serious impact on the availability of irrigation water in the neighbouring lowlands which grow sugar cane and rice.

For example, in chapter 2 (section 2.4), I noted that the state of forest cover in a watershed affects future productivity of soil in the lowlands (see equation (2.11)). But, as was noted in equation (2.11), there is considerable ignorance about the quantitative effects of deforestation. To be sure this is not an argument for ignoring such external effects; and indeed, integrated regional development plans attempt to quantify such interactions, albeit in a tentative way. In earlier chapters (especially chapters 2, 3 and 4) I studied alternative schemes for encouraging activities that confer external benefits and discouraging those that inflict disbenefits on others. Our general conclusions there clearly hold for forestry. But since massive deforestation in one country may have *global* environmental effects, the implementation of judicious policies in such cases poses additional problems. If the rate of deforestation of the Amazon basin is to be reduced, what incentives ought Brazil to be provided with, and by whom? The point is that the resolution of unidirectional transfrontier externalities – which is what is involved here – might be expected to pose even greater difficulties than the management of global common-property resources such as deep sea-bed nodules and open-sea fisheries. (For some evidence, see Walter (1975).) Admittedly, the reciprocal externalities involved in the exploitation of sea resources are not exactly symmetrical, unlike the example in chapter 2. Nevertheless, the problems raised by the sea being a common property are a shared one. There are additional political problems involved in the resolution of unidirectional externalities arising from activities such as deforestation precisely because of the stark asymmetry. It may be in the national interest to engage in deforestation: the land may have alternative uses (e.g. for mining or ranching) which, from the point of view of the nation, are socially more profitable.[2] However, the transfrontier damages caused by deforestation may be severe. Voluntary restraint may be too much to expect. As the analysis of chapter 2 (section 2.4) implies, in such situations one possibility that suggests itself is for compensation to be paid by the international community to the nation in question for reducing the rate of deforestation. This

[2] We are not, however, claiming that the current rate of deforestation of the Amazon basin has much to commend itself. See chapter 2, section 2.5.

would be an international subsidy.[3] One thinks of this – rather than an international tax on the country for each square mile of forest that is felled – because international law, as it stands, awards 'pollutors' rights' on such a question: a nation having the right to fell its forests.[4] The discussion in chapter 2 is relevant here.

9.2 The value of forest products

The world's forests, covering some 40 million square kilometres, contain about 340 billion cubic metres of timber (see Persson, 1974). The value of the world's production of forest products today is over 115 billion US dollars per year, of which the amount traded internationally exceeds 40 billion US dollars. The rate at which the forests are being exhausted is quite uneven across regions, and for certain types of forests the rate is high. Thus, for example, the tropical rain forests are being denuded at the rate of over 100 000 square kilometres per year.[5]

It is useful to recognize that the greatest cause of global deforestation today is not the market for wood products, but rather, the need for wood fuel and agricultural land. It is estimated that fully 50 per cent of the trees cut down in the world is for fuel use. Furthermore, it is thought that some 12 to 24 million acres of forests are depleted annually for agriculture alone (see Sommer, 1976).[6] The need for wood fuel has unquestionably increased

[3] In effect this policy was pursued by UNESCO in their financing of the transportation of the ancient tombs from near the High Dam in Aswan.

[4] The Declaration on the Human Environment signed at the United Nations Stockholm Conference in June 1972 states that nations have an obligation to 'ensure that activities within their jurisdiction or control do not cause damage to the environment of other states or of areas beyond the limits of national jurisdiction'. But this is not binding.

[5] Simple calculations imply that if this rate persists all the tropical forests will be destroyed in 80 to 90 years. This kind of calculation is provided solely for giving an indication of the current rate of deforestation, not a prediction of what will happen.

[6] FAO (1978) reports that the Ivory Coast lost more than 30 per cent of its forest cover during the decade 1956–66 to shifting agriculture. Of the 40 million exploitable hectares of forest in Indonesia, 12.5 million hectares are already under exploitation, 4 million are under concession and about 10 million are the subject of inventory for future concessions.

sharply with the cost of kerosene during the past decade. Firewood is collected most often, as in the Sahel, from trees and shrubs that are common property. For this reason the increased demand for wood fuel has not readily provided an incentive, via prices, to persons and groups to transfer land from other uses to forestry.

It is because of the pervasive externalities forests provide that throughout the world much forest land is under government jurisdiction, either at the federal or the state level. But vested interests often triumph and governments often mismanage. What I wish to do in this chapter is to provide an analytical framework for the social evaluation of forests; and I shall do this, for simplicity, by studying a forest in isolation; that is valuing it solely in terms of its timber yield. As has already been noted, in its full complexity, the determination of the social value of a forest is probably an impossible task. Forests are often a key sector of a complete eco-system (see chapter 2, section 2.4), so that studying a forest in isolation invariably is a road to wrong answers. Fortunately though, one expects that it leads to *biased* answers, because, for the main part forests provide external *benefits* to the rest of the eco-system. Thus, if we were to evaluate the economic benefits of a forest in isolation, that is, without taking into account its beneficial effects on the rest of the eco-system, we are most likely to obtain a figure well below the true expected economic benefits derived from a forest.

9.3 Growth functions of trees

Consider an area of forest land which, it is proposed, is to be developed for other purposes (e.g. ranching or farming). Assume that the forest is socially managed and that it provides a source of timber. In judging whether alternative development of this area is justifiable one needs to estimate the social opportunity cost of this alternative development. As I am, for simplicity, studying the forest in isolation, this social opportunity cost is the maximum social value of the flow of timber that can be obtained from the forest. It is this that I will wish to estimate.

Trees are felled for their timber, and I suppose that the shadow price of timber – net of the cost of felling – is a constant, p, per cubic metre, and without loss of generality, that planting a seed is costless.

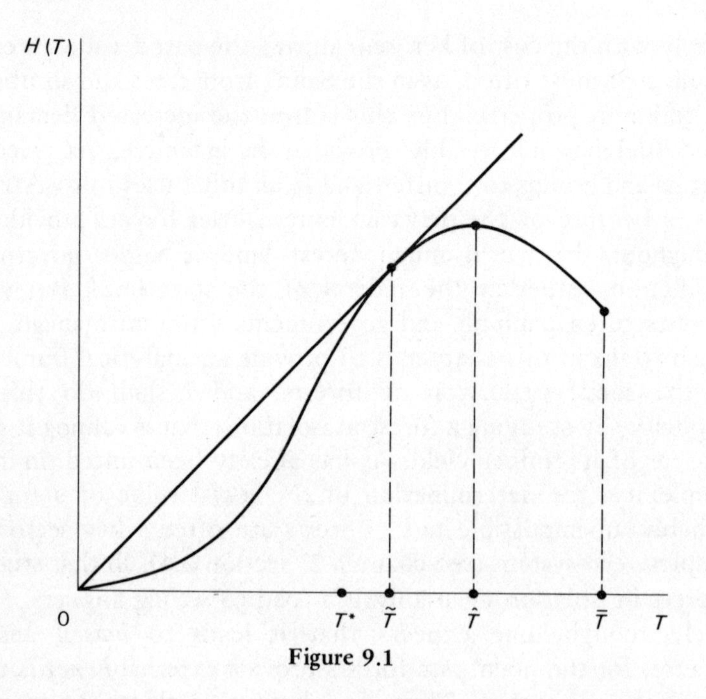

Figure 9.1

If a seedling is planted at date t the amount of timber obtainable from it T years later is written as Y_{t+T}, and it is assumed that this is solely a function of T; i.e.

$$Y_{t+T} = H(T). \tag{9.1}$$[7]

Figure 9.1 depicts a stylized form of the 'production function' $H(T)$. The figure depicts the case where, for an initial interval following planting, the tree grows at an accelerated rate, and where this is followed by a fall in the rate of growth until an age $\hat{T}$ at which age the tree's rate of growth is nil. For an interval of time beyond $\hat{T}$ there is decline until the tree attains the age $\bar{T}$ at which point the tree begins to decay and the timber is worthless. I am ignoring chance factors here. Their introduction complicates the analysis considerably. But as an approximation, figure 9.1

[7] We are simplifying of course. Among other things, the density of trees affects their rates of growth. And 'exogenous' influences, such as average rainfall, the quality of the soil etc. are treated as parameters of the H function.

would appear to be a good one.[8] In what follows I shall suppose that $H(T)$ satisfies the characteristics depicted in figure 9.1. What I wish to do now is to determine the manner in which planting and felling of trees ought to be undertaken in this forest so as to maximize the present value of social benefits.

9.4 The optimal forest: the synchronized stationary case

A major analytical difficulty that such an exercise poses is the fact that trees in a forest are of different vintages, and that in general the age distribution of trees in a forest will change over the initial years along an optimal policy. I shall therefore take a simplifying route and assume that the forest is in a synchronized stationary state so that it provides a constant flow of timber.[9] In a synchronized stationary state the age distribution of trees is constant over time. At each instant the oldest trees – of age T, say – are felled, and the felled area is immediately replanted, so that stands of all ages below T are represented in equal degrees. Each tree, we take it, requires a fixed area of land. Given the area covered by the forest suppose N is the total number of trees that can be grown. Then along this synchronized stationary state there are precisely N/T trees of each vintage at each date.[10] It follows that at any date the total stock of timber in the forest, S, is simply N/T times the area under the curve in figure 9.1 between 0 and T; T being the age at which trees are felled. That is,

$$S = (N/T) \int_0^T H(\tau)\, \mathrm{d}\tau. \qquad (9.2)$$

I shall suppose that the area covered by the forest is given, so that N is given. Along a stationary state the forest is divided into T

[8] See, for example, UNESCO (1978, chapters 8–11). A good collection of essays on forestry is Svendsrud (1969).

[9] In the next section we shall consider a rotating forest and shall note that the optimum age of trees is the same as in the synchronized forest.

[10] We suppose N to be large, so that if we regard time as a continuous variable, N/T ought to be thought of as a density function.

plots, each sustaining N/T trees of a distinct vintage. What I wish to do is to calculate the socially optimal value of T – the age at which trees ought to be felled – if a synchronized forest is an optimal one.[11]

Let r (>0) be the social rate of discount. My aim is to choose T so as to maximize the present discounted value of the flow of social profits. Since we are postulating a synchronized forest, the planning problem is a restricted one, and it is this. Suppose we write by $f(\tau, t)$ the density function of trees of age τ that are felled at date t, so that $Nf(\tau, t)$ is the number of trees of age τ that are felled at date t. It follows that the value of timber obtained at t is

$$\int_0^{\bar{T}} pH(\tau)\, Nf(\tau, t)\, \mathrm{d}\tau,$$

and the present discounted value of this is

$$e^{-rt}\left[\int_0^{\bar{T}} pH(\tau)\, Nf(\tau, t)\, \mathrm{d}\tau\right]. \tag{9.3}$$

From expression (9.3) we conclude that the sum of the present discounted values of such a policy is:

$$\int_0^{\infty} e^{-rt}\left[\int_0^{\bar{T}} pH(\tau)\, Nf(\tau, t)\, \mathrm{d}\tau\right] \mathrm{d}t. \tag{9.4}$$

Our restricted planning problem is to find a synchronized forest comprising T vintages (i.e. $f(T, t) = 1/T$, and $f(\tau, t) = 0$ for $\tau \neq T$ for all $t \geqslant 0$), such that expression (9.4) is maximized at $f(T, t) = 1/T$ and $f(\tau, t) = 0$ for all $\tau \neq T$ for all $t \geqslant 0$, when choice is restricted to *all feasible* forests *if we were to start* from a synchronized forest of T vintages as the initial state.

It has been shown by Mitra and Wan (1981) that the solution of this problem (i.e. the optimal T in the synchronized forest) is the same as the optimal cropping pattern of an area of land that

[11] Whether a synchronized forest is the optimum long run target starting from an arbitrary distribution of vintages or whether a rotating forest (to be discussed in section 9.5) should be aimed at is not something that we attempt to solve here. The problem has been solved by Mitra and Wan (1981). See section 9.5.

sustains precisely *one* tree; i.e. a unit plot of forest land. I therefore proceed to obtain the optimum cropping pattern on a unit plot of land.

If a seed is planted today, and if the resulting tree is harvested at date T, the present discounted value of social profit from this activity is $pH(T)\,e^{-rT}$. But if this is followed immediately by replanting and the resulting tree is felled T years thence, and if the pattern is repeated indefinitely, the sum of the present discounted values of this recurrent activity is:

$$pH(T)\,e^{-rT}(1 + e^{-rT} + e^{-2rT} + \ldots) = pH(T)\,e^{-rT}/(1-e^{-rT}). \tag{9.5}$$

Let us denote this present-value expression by $R(T)/N$. Thus,

$$R(T)/N = [pH(T)\,e^{-rT}]/(1-e^{-rT}). \tag{9.6}$$

The planning problem is to choose T so as to maximize $R(T)$.

Thus, differentiating $R(T)$ with respect to T and equating the derivative to zero yields the necessary condition for the optimum maintenance rule

$$\mathrm{d}R(T)/\mathrm{d}T = 0$$

or, from equation (9.6)

$$p[H'(T) - rH(T)] = r[pH(T)\,e^{-rT}]/(1-e^{-rT}). \tag{9.7}$$

Let T^* denote the optimum period of rotation of each forest plot; that is, the optimum harvesting age of trees. Then T^* must be a solution of equation (9.7).[12]

The social cost–benefit rule (equation (9.7)) describes the fundamental principle in the economics of forestry. It was obtained by Faustmann (1849) and in what follows I shall call it the Faustmann Rule.[13] To see the intuitive meaning behind this rule, I use equation (9.6) to re-express equation (9.7) as

$$Np[H'(T) - rH(T)] = rR(T). \tag{9.8}$$

[12] It will be noticed that the function $R(T)$ in equation (9.6) is in general not concave. Therefore equation (9.7) typically possesses multiple solutions.

[13] Samuelson (1976) and Hartwick (1980) provide excellent analyses of the Faustmann Rule and contain historical accounts of the theoretical literature in the economics of forestry.

The explanation behind the Faustmann Rule should now be clear. From equation (9.6) we know that $R(T)/N$ represents the free-hold shadow price that can be extracted from this unit plot if T is the age at which a tree is felled. Thus $rR(T)/N$ is the flow of shadow forest rent per period that can be extracted from the unit plot. Multiply both sides of equation (9.8) by e^{-rT} to obtain

$$Np\,[H'(T) - rH(T)]\,e^{-rT} = rR(T)\,e^{-rT}. \tag{9.9}$$

But

$$p\,[H'(T) - rH(T)]\,e^{-rT} = \mathrm{d}[pH(T)\,e^{-rT}]/\mathrm{d}T.$$

Therefore, the Faustmann Rule, as expressed in equation (9.9), can be written as

$$(r/N)\,R(T)\,e^{-rT} = \mathrm{d}[pH(T)\,e^{-rT}]/\mathrm{d}T. \tag{9.10}$$

From the vantage point of the present (i.e. $t = 0$), the left-hand side of equation (9.10) is the present value of the shadow rental, paid at T, of the area of land occupied by a single tree. At the optimum value of T this should clearly equal the increase in discounted social profits from felling a tree if the age at which the tree is felled is increased marginally. Equation (9.10) represents this equality.

I now proceed to analyse some of the properties of the Faustmann Rule. From equation (9.9) it may be concluded that $H'(T^*) > rH(T^*) > 0$, and therefore that $T^* < \hat{T}$. That is, along the optimum synchronized state trees ought to be felled before they reach their maximum timber content (see figure 9.1). What of maximum sustainable timber yield? If T is the age at which trees are felled along the synchronized stationary state, N/T trees are felled at each moment, and so the flow of harvested timber is $NH(T)/T$. This is maximized at $\tilde{T}$ (see figure 9.1), where $\tilde{T}$ is the unique solution of the equation

$$H'(T)/H(T) = 1/T. \tag{9.11}$$

Thus, the maximum sustainable timber yield is obtained when trees are felled at the age at which their percentage rate of growth equals the inverse of the turnover period; that is, when a tree's marginal growth equals its lifetime average growth. A glance at the

Faustmann Rule (equation (9.7)) and equation (9.11) confirms that the maximum sustainable timber yield is also not optimal. We noted an analogue of this for the case of fisheries in chapters 6 and 7. To economists these observations are obvious. To environmentalists they obviously are not: 'In a sense, many forests have been treated as "terrestrial whales" – harvested with no consideration for maximum sustainable yield but rather with an eye on maximum return on capital' (Ehrlich *et al.*, 1977, p. 275). This obsession with maximum sustainable yield, pervasive in the ecology literature, is not easily understandable. The arguments offered in chapters 6 and 7, and the reasoning underlying the optimality condition (equation (5.5)) in chapter 5 should have made it transparent why neither the maximum sustainable timber yield, nor the maximum sustainable yield per tree is in general a desirable target. Any policy which is independent of shadow prices – and in particular social rates of discount – should immediately be suspect, and one expects in advance that it is only under special circumstances that the maximum sustainable timber yield is approximately optimal; i.e. that $T^* \simeq \tilde{T}$. Let us look into this.

From equation (9.7) we obtain the social cost–benefit rule,

$$H'(T) = rH(T)/(1 - e^{-rT}). \tag{9.12}$$

From this we may conclude that

$$H'(T)/H(T) = r/(1 - e^{-rT}) > r \tag{9.13}$$

and therefore, that the optimum age of harvesting trees, T^*, is even less than the age at which a tree's percentage rate of growth $(H'(T)/H(T))$ equals the social rate of discount. Now suppose that the social rate of discount is small. To be precise, suppose that r is sufficiently small to enable us to neglect second and higher powers of r in comparison with r itself. In this case we may approximate and write $e^{-rT} \simeq 1 - rT$. Using this approximation in equation (9.12) yields the approximate social cost–benefit rule.

$$H'(T) \simeq rH(T)/rT = H(T)/T. \tag{9.14}$$

We have proved that if r is sufficiently small, the optimum felling age is approximately equal to the felling age associated with maximum sustainable timber yield, that is, $T^* \simeq \tilde{T}$.

9.5 The optimal rotating forest

Although I have referred to the optimality condition, equation (9.7), for the synchronized forest as the Faustmann Rule, Faustmann (1849) did not actually analyse a synchronized forest. He was concerned with a rotating forest. In a rotating forest *all* trees are of the same vintage. The entire forest is cropped when trees attain the age T, say. The forest is replanted immediately, all trees are then felled when they attain the age T, and the process is continued. The rotating forest is the polar opposite of the synchronized forest. Timber is obtained from the latter at a steady rate at each moment; from the former it is obtained every T years. In between these two polar forms is a continuum of cases where the forest is divided into unequal plots and where the management of each plot follows a regular rotating pattern of T years. Such forests are *partially* synchronized. Since the growth of trees in any part of the forest has been assumed to be independent of the mode of management in the remaining part it is clear that the optimum period of rotation in a partially synchronized and rotating forest satisfies the Faustmann Rule. I confirm this for the case of a rotating forest. The reader can readily confirm it for the partially synchronized case.

If an area of virgin land, capable of nurturing N trees at any instant is seeded at date $t = 0$, and if these N trees are felled at date T, the present value of social profits from this rotation is $N[pH(T)\,e^{-rt}]$. Now this is clearly equal, in present value terms, to a constant flow of social profit per tree, $K(T)$, over the period $[0, T]$, if $K(T)$ satisfies the condition:

$$N[pH(T)\,e^{-rT}] = NK(T)\int_0^T e^{-rt}\,dt. \qquad (9.15)$$

Solving equation (9.15) we note that

$$K(T) = r[pH(T)\,e^{-rT}]/(1 - e^{-rT}). \qquad (9.16)$$

But by hypothesis the rotation pattern continues indefinitely. It follows that the present value of social profits obtained from the (rotating) forest equals $NK(T)\int_0^\infty e^{-rt}\,dt$. This we write as $R(T)$. Thus

$$R(T) = NK(T) \int_0^\infty e^{-rt}\, dt = NK(T)/r. \tag{9.17}$$

Using equations (9.16) and (9.17) we conclude that

$$R(T) = [pH(T)\, e^{-rT}]\, N/(1 - e^{-rT}), \tag{9.18}$$

which is N times the expression (9.6).

The analysis following equation (9.6) can now be repeated. I summarize: given the social objective function I have assumed in this and the previous section, the optimum age for felling trees, T^*, does not depend on whether the forest is a synchronized or a rotating one. It is readily checked that this is so for a partially synchronized forest as well.

At the date the planning problem is analysed a planner will typically have inherited a forest comprising trees of different vintages in plots of unequal sizes. Indeed, some plots may well have trees older than the Faustmann optimum T^*. Given such an arbitrary distribution of vintages what ought the cropping pattern to be? It has been shown by Mitra and Wan (1981) that the optimal cropping policy is this: at $t = 0$ harvest all stands of age not less than T^* and replant immediately; and at all $t > 0$, harvest stands of age T^* and replant immediately. Thus, the land occupied by each tree ought to follow the Faustmann rotation rule; but the distribution of vintages along the optimal stationary forest is heavily dependent on the initial distribution of vintages. The Mitra–Wan result, therefore, provides the formal justification of the analyses presented in this and the preceding section.

9.6 Commentary and extensions

The foregoing social cost–benefit analysis provides a framework for evaluating the value of forests. In the language of cost–benefit analysis each value of T represents a *project variant*, and the aim has been to locate the best project variant, T^*. A key point to observe is that the present value of social profits from the optimum forest, say $\bar{R}(T)$, is in general not a concave function of T (see equation (9.6)). If follows that marginal cost–benefit analysis as a means of locating the optimal project variant will not do. In general, global cost–benefit analysis is required. Our discussion in chapter 3 is relevant here. However, as usual, the optimum project variant, T^*, must satisfy the marginal social cost–benefit rule. This is the Faustmann Rule (equation (9.7)). Net social benefit from the forest land in some alternative use must be at least as large as $\bar{R}(T^*)$ before the idea of deforestation can legitimately be entertained. If in fact $\bar{R}(T^*)$ is in excess of net social benefits from *all* alternative uses, then it is a clear signal that, if ecologically suitable, yet more land ought to be under forest cover. But I emphasize once again that the foregoing analysis identifies a lower bound on the social profitability of a forest. As we have noted on several occasions, the social value of a forest typically exceeds the value of the timber it provides. If such external benefits are approximately taken into account, as they would be if an integrated project were evaluated, then deforestation would be justified only if the value of the forest land in some alternative use were to exceed $\bar{R}(T^*)$ by some margin.[14]

The Mitra–Wan result, it is clear, depends sensitively on the social objective function that has been assumed so far. For a 'small' forest the objective function may appear reasonable. It would not be a reasonable one to use for developing a national forest policy. The point is that the *flow* of net social benefits depends on whether the forest is synchronized or not; and this will typically matter from the social point of view. For one thing, seeding typically requires labour. In the optimum rotating forest this labour input is required every T^* years and none at other times; while the optimum synchronized forest requires $1/N$th of this labour input continuously. The welfare criterion adopted so far has been insensitive to this employment issue, and so the pattern of employment was of no concern. For another, the *marginal* social value of the flow of timber, p, has been assumed independent of the flow of timber and so it is not surprising that

[14] In chapter 2, section 2.4, we described such an integrated ecological system. *Analytical* results of even a two-'species' system such as in section 2.4 are very difficult to come by, and so we have avoided discussing them here. A good case study of a watershed development project is in Gil (1979).

the pattern of timber output from the forest as a whole emerged as being of no concern. Typically, one supposes that a nation would prefer a regular flow of timber to an intermittent one. Such a preference would be caught by an objective function which reflects diminishing marginal social value of timber yield. We have so far supposed that if Z_t is the output of timber at date t the social value is pZ_t. Suppose instead that it is $B(Z_t)$, where $B(Z)$ is an increasing function of Z but where $dB(Z)/dZ$ is a declining function of Z.

The assumption that the marginal social value of yield is a declining function of yield (i.e. that $dB(Z)/dZ$ is a decreasing function) implies that other things being the same a constant yield is more desirable than a fluctuating one. This suggests that the (optimal) synchronized forest is the target a social planner ought to aim at in the long run. However, 'other things' are not the same. In particular, the initial distribution of vintages in the forest can be quite arbitrary and, since I have assumed the social rate of discount, r, to be positive, the 'costs of adjustment' in moving to a synchronized forest may well be high. To date, no general results are known about the characteristics of an optimal forest management policy given an arbitrary distribution of vintages. The problem is an unusually difficult one. Mitra and Wan (1981) have shown that if $r = 0$, and if planting is costless, then maximum sustainable yield (see equation (9.11)) is the optimal long run policy, which means of course that in the long run the optimal forest is a perfectly synchronized one. This is so no matter what is the initial distribution of vintages. In particular this means that even if the forest land is initially virgin, the planner should aim in the long run for a synchronized forest yielding the maximum sustainable flow of timber. This, as I suggested earlier, is what intuition would seem to dictate. But if $r > 0$ nothing positive is known in general about the characteristics of optimal plans starting from an arbitrary initial distribution of vintages. One knows of course that optimal planting within a unit plot does *not* satisfy the Faustmann Rule (9.7), even in the long run. This should be contrasted with optimal policies described at the end of section 9.5 for the case where the benefit function is linear in yield. There we noted that in the long run the optimal forest depends sensitively on the initial forest – the initial forest determining the extent to which the forest is synchronized in the long run. But the optimal rotation in each plot was seen to satisfy the Faustmann Rule no matter what the initial forest. This is the central unifying feature of optimal forests when the benefit function is linear. Small wonder that it is the 'linear' case that has most often been discussed in the literature.

10 Uncertainty, Irreversibility and Option Values

> Our understanding of the dynamics and capacities of many ecosystems, particularly tropical ones, is often insufficient to assume rational use allocation or high quality management. Scientific knowledge of the production capacities of most tropical ecosystems, as well as their ability to absorb pollution and other impacts, is generally inadequate. Land and water use, therefore, should be located and managed so that as many options as possible are retained.
>
> (Allen, 1980, p. 122)

Economists as a general rule encourage planners to maximize expected social benefits, whereas environmentalists continually urge them to keep future options open. As a prescription the latter will clearly not do. Injunctions, such as, 'choose programmes so as to maximize the number of future options', are patently silly: they disregard the social costs that would be associated with such plans. On the other hand, if such a prescription is softened somewhat, it rather readily deteriorates to a non-operational sentiment, such as the end of the passage quoted above. Nevertheless, there is a sound intuitive basis for the environmentalists' concern with future options. The concern is founded on the recognition that the use of environmental resources may well have irreversible effects – so that decisions today will constrain the choices that are feasible later – and that it is desirable to insure against adverse states of nature. If everything that can be done can also be undone one cannot but help keep one's options open. At the same time, if the future is known with certainty, there is no cost involved in foreclosing one's future options. It is the twin presence of uncertainty and irreversibility that makes *flexibility* such an attractive feature of a planned course of action. In this chapter I shall study the *worth* of flexibility measured in terms of expected social benefits, and thereby relate the environmentalist's concern to the economist's prescription.[1]

In chapter 4 I conducted a lengthy discussion of schemes for sustaining the optimal use of environmental resources under uncertainty. Throughout it was assumed that the criterion of social choice is the maximization of expected net social benefits. Among the conclusions that were emphasized was the one which suggested strongly that in the presence of threshold effects governments ought to rely on incentive schemes resembling quota restrictions on the use of environmental resources. A restrictive quota can almost guarantee that resource use will not go beyond an uncertain threshold level. This is what makes quotas attractive in extreme cases.

Identifying the use of quotas with maintaining flexibility may seem paradoxical; in fact it is not. To be sure, the imposition of quota restrictions implies that the immediate production options of resource users are constrained. On the other hand, protecting the environmental resource from total destruction is a means of keeping future options open. Indeed, the value of future options can be computed, as was implicitly done in the analysis in chapter 4, in terms of expected social benefits. But the valuation was conducted only implicitly, through a social damage function, because the discussion was conducted for simplicity, in a timeless setting. It should be clear though that the analyses of chapter 4 are perfectly relevant for intertemporal stochastic problems. Nevertheless there are issues that can only be captured in a construction that explicitly recognizes the passage of time. An explicit computation of option values is one such item.

We have noted on several occasions that in managing environmetal resources a feature that must be kept in mind is the fact that

[1] The criterion of expected net benefits (or utility) does not explicitly address itself to the question of flexibility, but as we shall see, the value of keeping options open can be assessed from the 'expected utility' criterion. The important work of Kreps (1979) presents a representation theorem for preference relations defined directly on feasible sets of actions. In this work preference for flexibility is a primitive ingredient in the analysis. Koopmans (1964) contains an illuminating discussion of these matters.

decisions that pertain to their use often have an element of irreversibility about them so that future options are curtailed. The concept of threshold effects is of course geared precisely to capture the notion of irreversibility. However, even if a resource is not entirely exhausted its rate of rejuvenation may be very slow. Deforested land takes time to be brought back to its original state.

In chapters 6 and 7, while developing the economics of renewable natural resources, I emphasized threshold effects. The constructions were devoid of uncertainty, though. This was a perfectly defendable research strategy. Deterministic optimization problems are much easier to analyse than stochastic ones and it is for this reason that an overwhelming majority of environmental case studies are conducted in a deterministic framework. At any event, we have throughout this book been interested in obtaining broad qualitative results, and in developing intertemporal arguments it was best to ignore uncertainty. However, the most natural way to interpret the intertemporal models developed in the last four chapters is to regard all future values of parameters occurring in them as representing some sort of *average* values of the corresponding random variables. On many occasions one would be justified in using their *expected* (or *mean*) values as proxies. Now, such a treatment of stochastic problems – namely to convert it into a non-stochastic one by replacing random variables by expected values – is a most common practice. It also leads naturally to errors.[2] The question is whether the error is likely to be large and also whether there is reason for supposing that it results in a *bias* in resource utilization. Whenever the latter occurs one can make a correction in the appropriate direction to remedy the defective analysis approximately. This is the advantage of locating biases and I shall illustrate it in this chapter by means of an example. More striking, perhaps, is the fact that for many forms of future uncertainty the error in question is likely to be small (see Mirrlees, 1974). Not so for managing environmental resources.

[2] The term 'certainty equivalence' is used to characterize results which identify models in which no error in fact occurs. As would be expected models permitting certainty equivalence results are highly restrictive (see Theil, 1968).

Where threshold effects are of importance, the error may well be considerable.

I began by noting that if the environmental effects of investment programmes are both irreversible and uncertain the chosen plan ought to be flexible – i.e. future options ought not to be overly circumscribed – to cope with the fact that as time passes one will obtain better information about the social benefits and costs associated with environmental resource use. Nowhere has the desirability of future options been advanced as vociferously as in the environmentalists' discussion of the need for the on-site preservation of *genetic diversity* of crops and plants (see for example Allen, 1980, chapter 5). The tropical forests, in this context, are particularly noted for providing a habitat for a rich genetic pool, most of which is so far untapped for direct use in our consumption, but some of which are an ingredient in a substantial fraction of pharmaceutical products (see for example Farnsworth and Morris, 1976). Much attention has also been drawn to the continued decay of the genetic variability of crops resulting from the increased reliance on a few high-yielding varieties throughout large parts of the globe (see Frankel and Hawkes, 1975). The point here is that as new varieties of crop pests and diseases appear, the chance of locating crop varieties that are resistant to them will be that much lower if genetic reserves are small. Here, a genetic pool is a public (or collective) good whose value becomes more and more sharply etched with the passage of time. I present a simple example to illustrate the idea of option values; that is, the value of keeping options open.[3]

Before presenting the example formally it is as well to draw attention to its salient features. Since I am concerned with the

[3] The example is based on the important analysis presented in Arrow and Fisher (1974) and Henry (1974). Mäler (1977) provides further extensions. Greenley *et al.* (1980) is an interesting case study, estimating the option value for recreation and water quality that are degraded irreversibly due to mining activity in the South Platte River Basin, Colorado, USA. The formal model they use for conducting their estimation is similar to the one presented in this chapter. Using a 6 per cent discount rate per annum and an infinite time horizon they estimate that the present value of annual benefits from water quality improvement in the River Basin is about 1 billion US dollars, of which 169 million US dollars can be attributed to option value.

question of flexibility, the example is concerned with the possibility of a sequence of decisions over time. To capture the problem in a sharp form I suppose as well that today's decision is irrevocable; that is today's action cannot be undone tomorrow. Finally, I suppose that the social planner is risk-neutral. I do this for good reason. Since a risk-neutral decision-maker under normal circumstances can replace random variables by their expected values. I shall easily be able to compute the value to him of keeping his options open.

Imagine two instants of time, $t = 0, 1$. There is a forest region, of a given size, which sustains a genetic pool. I assume that off-site preservation of this genetic material is prohibitively costly, but suppose that the forest land has an alternative use (e.g. urban development) which necessitates deforestation, and therefore destruction of the genetic material. For simplicity of exposition we identify genetic diversity with the extent of forest cover. The net social benefit from developing a marginal unit of forest land at $t = 0$ is b_0 and this is assumed to be independent of the area which is developed at $t = 0$. There are two possible states of nature θ_s $(s = 1, 2)$. The state of nature is revealed at $t = 1$. If θ_1 prevails (the probability of this is π), the net social benefit flowing from a unit of developed land is b_1 (assumed independent of the amount developed). If θ_2 prevails (the probability of this is, by definition, $(1-\pi)$), the net social benefit flowing from a unit of developed land is b_2 (also assumed independent of the amount developed). We shall take it that if at $t = 0$ the entire region is not deforested, then at $t = 1$, when the state of nature is revealed there is further choice about how much further land is to be developed. Thus development decisions can be made at both instants. It is only if at the initial date the entire region is developed that future options are closed.

Without loss of generality let the initial forest be of unit area. I denote by D_0 the area that is developed at $t = 0$ (with $0 \leqslant D_0 \leqslant 1$) and we let D_1 and D_2 denote the area of developed land at $t = 1$ under the two states of nature, θ_1 and θ_2. Finally, let r (>0) denote the social rate of discount. It follows that the expected present value of net social benefit from a proposed development policy (D_0, D_1, D_2) is

$$b_0 D_0 + [\pi b_1 D_1 + (1-\pi) b_2 D_2]/(1+r). \qquad (10.1)$$

Notice that since the expected present value of net social benefits is linear in D_0, D_1 and D_2, I am hypothesizing risk-neutrality. To have an interesting problem assume $b_1 < 0$, $b_2 > 0$ and $\pi b_1 + (1-\pi) b_2 > 0$. Thus, in state θ_1 the net social benefit from developed land is *negative*, but the *expected* net social benefit from developed land at $t = 1$ is positive. The way to interpret this for the example at hand would be as follows: either there will be a need for the diverse genetic material at $t = 1$ or there will not. In the former case (θ_1) the loss in genetic material from deforestation exceeds the gain from urban development. In the latter case (θ_2) urban development is socially beneficial. Furthermore, it is expected that urban development is beneficial.

To see the role that irreversibility plays in optimal decision imagine first that land can be *un*developed costlessly and thereby the diverse genetic material retrieved *in toto*; that is, imagine that the decision to deforest at $t = 0$ is a fully revocable one. In this case the present and the future are completly disconnected, and one would maximize expression (10.1) by choosing D_0, D_1, D_2 subject to three independent constraints $0 \leqslant D_0 \leqslant 1$, $0 \leqslant D_1 \leqslant 1$ and $0 \leqslant D_2 \leqslant 1$. The optimal policy is clear enough. One chooses $D_1 = 0$ and $D_2 = 1$. The optimal value of D_0 depends solely on the value of b_0. If $b_0 < 0$ then one sets $D_0 = 0$. Likewise, if $b_0 > 0$ then one should set $D_0 = 1$. If $b_0 = 0$, there is no unique optimal choice of D_0: any amount of land developed is acceptable.

Let us continue to suppose that the loss of genetic diversity is fully reversible, but now let the stochastic problem be replaced by a deterministic one as a customary simplification. Thus suppose that the present value of net social benefit from a unit of developed land is assumed to be known with certainty to be $(\pi b_1 + (1-\pi) b_2)/(1+r)$. For vividness one might think that a commitment is made at date $t = 0$ regarding the area of developed land at $t = 1$ irrespective of what the true state of nature is. The problem then is to choose D_0 and $\tilde{D}$ (the area of developed land at $t = 1$) with a view to maximizing

$$b_0 D_0 + [\pi b_1 + (1-\pi) b_2]\, \tilde{D}/(1+r). \qquad (10.2)$$

Since by hypothesis $(\pi b_1 + (1-\pi) b_2) > 0$, it is clear from expression (10.2) that in order to maximize the present value of net social benefits of this deterministic problem one must set $\tilde{D} = 1$;

that is, complete deforestation ought to be planned for the future. Therefore the optimal initial level of land development, D_0, depends solely on the sign of b_0. In other words, no bias results in *current* decision as a result of replacing the random variable by its expected value in the social objective function.

We now come to the issue of irreversibility and suppose that the destruction of genetic diversity is irrevocable. If we continue to pretend that the net social benefit from developed land at $t = 1$ is known at $t = 0$ with certainty to be $\pi b_1 + (1 - \pi) b_2$, then the argument in the previous paragraph goes through. Admittedly, irreversibility implies that $D_0 \leqslant \tilde{D}$. But from expression (10.2) we know that the optimal commitment for $\tilde{D}$ is unity. Therefore, the optimal value of D_0 depends once again on the sign of b_0. But while this formulation of the problem has incorporated irreversibility, it has eschewed uncertainty. For recall that the *true* stochastic problem consists in choosing D_0, D_1, D_2 so as to maximize the social objective function (10.1). Irreversibility means that $0 \leqslant D_0 \leqslant D_1,\ D_2 \leqslant 1$. We now compute the true optimum policy. The way to do this is to work backwards from a state of greater knowledge. If D_0 is the initial extent of deforestation we shall obviously wish to set $D_1 = D_0$, since further development will certainly not be desirable at $t = 1$ if it transpires that θ_1 is the true state of nature. Plainly also, one knows in advance that one will wish to set $D_2 = 1$, since if θ_2 is the true state of nature the need for genetic diversity will not be great. This backward argument involving optimal decision in the future implies that in deciding what to do today we ought to consider a reduced form of the social objective function (10.1), which is $b_0 D_0 + (\pi b_1 D_0 + \pi b_2)/(1 + r)$; or

$$[b_0 + \pi b_1/(1 + r)]\, D_0 + \pi b_2/(1 + r). \qquad (10.3)$$

It follows that today's decision, D_0, should be based *not* on the sign of b_0 as earlier, but rather on the sign of the term $b_0 + \pi b_1/(1 + r)$. Since by hypothesis $b_1 < 0$, it is clear that the criterion for positive initial development is stiffer, it being that $b_0 + \pi b_1/(1 + r) \geqslant 0$. In other words, if $0 < b_0 < -\pi b_1/(1 + r)$, then one ought to set $D_0 = 0$; that is, one ought to preserve the entire genetic diversity, even though in the earlier analysis such a circumstance would signal the desirability of deforestation. I conclude then that if the degradation of an environmental resource is judged irrevocable, there may well be a tendency toward excessive degradation currently if uncertain future benefits from the resource are replaced by their expected values in the calculation of the optimal rate of current use. That is, replacing future random variables by their expected values is an incorrect move even for the risk-neutral decision-maker if current decisions are irrevocable.

This conclusion is important to bear in mind. For the example we have just studied even a risk-neutral planner will require a rate of current net social benefits from land development of at least $-\pi b_1/(1+r)$ (which is greater than zero) in order to foreclose his options. Which is why $-\pi b_1/(1+r)$ would be called the *option value* for deforestation. But the general moral emerging from the example is clear enough. When future costs and benefits are uncertain *and* when current investment decisions are irrevocable, such as that which often happens when environental resources are exploited, *current* resource usage ought to be more 'conservative' than when decisions are not irrevocable. This is due to the fact that a more 'conservative' resource-exploitation policy enables the planner to maintain greater flexibility. In the field of resource exploitation there is a very good reason for not doing today something that can be postponed until tomorrow: for tomorrow we shall know more.

11 Envoi

The class of phenomena embraced by any theoretical construct can usually be partitioned in a variety of ways. Consequently all classification schemes are up to a point arbitrary. But only up to a point. For classifications can be judged by their fruitfulness, and this to a certain extent depends on the purpose at hand. Much of what I have discussed in this book (most especially chapter 5 onwards) consists of special problems in what is known as capital theory. Our reason for restricting attention to regenerative natural resources has been based on the belief that when one talks of 'environmental' resources it is this class that one has in mind. The environmentalists' literature suggests this strongly (see for example Ehrlich *et al.*, 1977). In a very real sense, the conceptual apparatus that is needed to study the economics of pollution control is the same as the one required for fisheries, groundwater basins, forestry, and so on. They are all examples of renewable natural resources (see chapters 1, 6, 8 and 9). At the theoretical level there is therefore no reason for keeping them separate as subjects of inquiry, and every reason for bringing them together. Insights obtained in the study of one can then readily be used in the study of another.

Most economists would agreed with this.[1] Nevertheless, for the most part books and monographs on environmental pollution – even those that have a strong theoretical core – have gone their separate ways from those dealing with replenishable resources such as fisheries.[2] In part this must be due to the fact that each such

[1] The preoccupations of a leading quarterly, *The Journal of Environmental Economics and Management* suggests that this is so.

[2] Even the excellent theoretical work by Baumol and Oates (1975) is for the most part concerned with developing the theory of externalities in rich details and then using it on pollution issues. Applications to other renewable resources are somewhat tangential.

resource has its own special characteristics and a detailed analysis must take such features into account. Any attempt at integrating all such resources in one body of theory, as has been done here, inevitably requires one to ignore these special characteristics. Here too, selection of which features to ignore is dictated to a large extent by the kinds of issues one wants to highlight. Thus, for example, in my simple account of the economics of forestry issues connected with the need for 'thinning' – something that forestry experts, rightly, place a great emphasis on – were eschewed; but the question of vintages, central to the theory, was not. On the other hand, in the discussions on fisheries no distinction was drawn between cohorts in a population. A species' biomass was regarded as the state variable. It is clear of course that the pattern of harvesting a species will alter the age distribution of the population and indeed, that harvesting may introduce a bias in biological selection, in the sense that if animals of only a certain size are taken, then slow growth will have survival value. In fact, even the empirical economics literature most often ignores these features (as in the Henderson–Tugwell case study mentioned in chapter 6) because the data do not usually permit their inclusion. Short cuts are thus inevitable and a concentration on biomass is the result. Then too, we have presented no analysis of the exploitation of interacting species, a subject which is patently of importance. The detailed analytics of such a problem are really rather complicated, and to the best of my knowledge no simple general prescription has so far been forthcoming.[3]

The central aim in this book has been to highlight what would appear to be the unifying characteristics of environmental resources, and then to see what general prescriptions can be offered for their exploitation. This is precisely what a substantial fraction of research by environmentalists and economists over the past two decades has attempted to do. One central common characteristic of these resources is their regenerative power. From this observation it is but a short step to consider steady states in their use (see Daly, 1973, 1979).[4] One of the things I have tried

[3] The recent work of Clemhout and Wan (1981) is an exception.

[4] In contrast, non-regenerative resources, such as fossil fuels cannot be harvested at a steady rate indefinitely. That does not mean of course that

to do in this book is to identify circumstances under which a steady state in the use of any particular resource is a desirable long-term policy. Now it needs hardly to be emphasized that steady states are not meant to be taken literally. Scientists assure us that the world will not last forever. An infinite time horizon is merely a long-hand for a long time horizon – a useful surrogate because one does not have to specify a last moment. Moreover, I have concentrated my attention on the use of some particular natural resource, keeping the workings of the rest of the economy in the background. A steady state in the use of a particular regenerative resource, at a particular location, does not by any means imply that the rest of the economy is at a stationary state. One reason why environmentalists' writings frequently appear quaint to the hard-nosed economist is the draconian measures they often advocate for curbing aggregate activities. It is one thing to claim that short-term gains from an increased growth in output can often be at the expense of output in the long run (e.g. via the degradation of soil). It is quite another to demand that economic growth ought to be curbed forthwith. One finds it difficult to believe that environmental problems have in recent years grown as rapidly as the concern that environmentalists have shown about them. Nevertheless, this growth in concern has had one important salutary effect: it has forced such issues to be included on the agenda of public debate.

---

substitute sources of supply may not be discovered which will allow for growth in their consumption, at least for a long while. On this see Dasgupta and Heal (1979).

References

Alchian, A. and Demsetz, H. (1973), The property rights paradigm, *Journal of Economic History*, **33**, 16–27.

Allen, R. (1980), *How to Save the World: Strategy for World Conservation*, Kogan Page Limited, London.

Anderson, L. G. (ed.) (1977), *Economic Impacts of Extended Fisheries Jurisdiction*, Science Publishers, Ann Arbor, Michigan.

d'Arge, R. C. and Kogiku, K. C. (1973), Economic growth and the natural environment, *Review of Economic Studies*, **40**, 61–78.

Arrow, K. J. (1971a), Political and economic estimation of social effects of externalities, in M. Intriligator (ed.), *Frontiers of Quantitative Economics*, vol. I, North Holland, Amsterdam.

Arrow, K. J. (1971b), *Essays in the Theory of Risk-Bearing*, Markham Publishing Company, Chicago.

Arrow, K. J. and Fisher, A. (1974), Preservation, uncertainty and irreversibility, *Quarterly Journal of Economics*, **87**, 312–19.

Arrow, K. J. and Hurwicz, L. (1977), *Studies in Resource Allocation Processes*, Cambridge University Press, Cambridge.

Arrow, K. J. and Kurz, M. (1970), *Public Investment, the Rate of Return and Optimal Fiscal Policy*, Johns Hopkins University Press, Baltimore.

Atkinson, A. B. and Stiglitz, J. E. (1980), *Lectures on Public Economics*, McGraw-Hill, New York.

Aumann, R. J. (1976), Agreeing to disagree, *The Annals of Statistics*, **4**(6), 1236–9.

Bali, Y. P. and Kanwar, J. S. (1977), Soil degradation in India, *FAO Soils Bulletin* (Rome), **34**.

Barnett, A. H. and Yandle, B. (1973), Allocating environmental resources, *Public Finance*, **28**, 11–19.

Barraclough, S. (1977), Agricultural production prospects in Latin America, *World Development*, **5**, 459–76.

Baumol, W. J. (1968), On the social rate of discount, *American Economic Review*, **57**, 788–802.

Baumol, W. J. and Oates, W. E. (1975), *The Theory of Environmental Policy*, Prentice Hall, Englewood Cliffs, New Jersey.

Bell, F. W. (1978), *Food from the Sea: The Economics and Politics of Ocean Fisheries*, Westview Press, Boulder, Colorado.

Beverton, R. J. H. and Holt, S. V. (1957), On the dynamics of exploited fish populations, *Fisheries Investigations*, vol. 29, ser. 2, Ministry of Agriculture, Fisheries and Food, London.

Black, S. C. and Niehaus, F. (1980), Comparison of risk and benefits among different energy systems, in W. Bach, J. Pankrath and J. Williams (eds), *Interactions of Energy and Climate*, D. Reidel Publishing Company, Amsterdam.

Blackorby, C. and Donaldson, D. (1980), Moral criteria for evaluating population change, Department of Economics, University of British Columbia, Vancouver (mimeo).

Blitzer, C., Clark, P. and Taylor, L. (eds) (1975), *Economy-Wide Development and Planning Models*, Oxford University Press, Oxford.

Blitzer, C., Dasgupta, P. and Stiglitz, J. (1981), Project appraisal and foreign exchange constraints, *Economic Journal*, **91**, 58–74.

Bohm, P. (1972), Estimating demand for public goods: an experiment, *European Economics Review*, **3**, 111–30.

Broome, J. (1981), On valuing life in economics, Department of Economics, University of Bristol (mimeo).

Brown, G. (1974), An optimal program for managing common property resources, *Journal of Political Economy*, **82**, 163–74.

Brown, G. and McGuire, C. B. (1967), A socially optimum pricing policy for a public water agency, *Water Resources Research*, **3**, 33–44.

Buchanon, J. and Karfoglis, M. (1963), A note on public goods supply, *American Economic Review*, **53**, 403–14.

Burt, O. (1964), Optimal resource use over time with an application to groundwater, *Management Science*, **11**, 80–93.

Burt, O. (1966), Economic control of groundwater resources, *Journal of Farm Economics*, **48**, 632–47.

Burt, O. (1967a), Temporal allocation of groundwater, *Water Resources Research*, **3**, 45–56.

Burt, O. (1967b), Groundwater management under quadratic criteria function, *Water Resources Research*, **3**, 673–82.

Calabresi, G. and Bobbitt, P. (1978), *Tragic Choices*, W. W. Norton, New York.

Cassen, R. (1978), *India: Population, Economy, Society*, Macmillan, London.

Chenery, H. *et al.* (1974), *Redistribution with Growth*, Oxford University Press, Oxford.

Chervel, M. and Le Gall, M. (1978), *Manual of Economic Evaluation of Projects: The Effects Method*, Ministre de la Cooperation France, Paris.

Chopra, K. (1981), Alternative sources of irrigation and land use patterns, Institute of Economic Growth, Delhi (mimeo).

Christy, F. T. (1977), Limited access systems under the Fishery Conservation and Management Act of 1976, in L. G. Anderson (ed.), *Economic Impacts of Extended Fisheries Jurisdiction*, Science Publishers, Ann Arbor, Michigan.

Clark, C. W. (1973), Profit maximization and the extinction of animal species, *Journal of Political Economy*, **81**(4), 950–61.

Clark, C. W. (1976), *Mathematical Bioeconomics: The Optimal Management of Renewable Resources*, John Wiley, New York.

Clemhout, S. and Wan, H. (1981), A dynamic analysis of common property problems – resource exploitation and environmental degradation, Working Paper no. 195, Department of Economics, Cornell University.

Coase, R. (1960), The problem of social cost, *Journal of Law and Economics*, **3**, 1–44; reprinted in R. Dorfman and N. S. Dorfman (eds) (1972), *Economics of the Environment: Selected Readings*, W. W. Norton, New York.

Cooper, R. (1975), An economist's view of the oceans, *Journal of World Trade Law*, **9**(1), 347–77.

Cooper, R. (1977), The oceans as a source of revenue, in J. N. Bhagwati (ed.), *The New International Economic Order*, MIT Press, Cambridge, Massachusetts.

Crutchfield, J. and Pontecorvo, G. (1969), *The Pacific Salmon Fisheries: A Study of Irrational Conservation*, Johns Hopkins University Press, Baltimore.

Dales, J. H. (1968), *Pollution, Property and Prices*, University of Toronto Press, Toronto.

Daly, H. (1971), Toward a stationary economy, in J. Harte and R. Socolow (eds), *The Patient Earth*, Holt, Reinhart, Winston, New York.

Daly, H. (ed.) (1973), *Toward a Steady-State Economy*, W. H. Freeman, San Francisco.

Daly, H. (1979), Entropy, growth and the political economy of scarcity, in V. Kerry Smith (ed.), *Scarcity and Growth Reconsidered*, Johns Hopkins University Press, Baltimore.

Das, D. C. (1977), Soil conservation practices and erosion control in India: a case study, in *FAO Soils Bulletin* (Rome), **33**.

Dasgupta, P. (1969), On the concept of optimum population, *Review of Economic Studies*, **36**, 295–318.

Dasgupta, P. (1974), On optimum population size, in A. Mitra (ed.), *Economic Theory and Planning: Essays in Honour of A. K. Dasgupta*, Oxford University Press, Calcutta.

Dasgupta, P. (1978), Project appraisal, foreign exchange constraints and shadow exchange rates, in R. Stone and W. Peterson (eds), *Econometric Contributions to Public Policy*, Macmillan, London.

Dasgupta, P. (1980), Decentralization and rights, *Economica*, **47**, 107–24.

Dasgupta, P., Hammond, P. and Maskin, E. (1979), The implementation of social choice rules: some general results in incentive compatibility, *Review of Economic Studies*, **46**, 185–216.

Dasgupta, P., Hammond, P. and Maskin, E. (1980), On imperfect information and optimal pollution control, *Review of Economic Studies*, **47**, 857–60.

Dasgupta, P. and Heal, G. (1979), *Economic Theory and Exhaustible Resources*, James Nisbet and Cambridge University Press, Cambridge.

Dasgupta, P., Marglin, S. and Sen, A. (1972), *Guidelines for Project Evaluation*, sales no. E.78.II.B.3, United Nations, New York.

Dasgupta, P. and Stiglitz, J. (1980a), Industrial structure and the nature of innovative activity, *Economic Journal*, **90**, 266–93.

Dasgupta, P. and Stiglitz, J. (1980b), Uncertainty, industrial structure and the speed of R&D, *Bell Journal of Economics*, Spring, **11**, 1–28.

Davies, J. C. (1973), Standard-setting, in A. C. Enthoven and A. M. Freeman (eds), *Pollution, Resources and the Environment*, W. W. Norton, New York.

Demsetz, H. (1967), Toward a theory of property rights, *American Economic Review*, Papers and Proceedings, **57**, 347–59.

Domenico, P. A. (1972), *Concepts and Models in Groundwater Hydrology*, McGraw-Hill, New York.

Dorfman, R. and Dorfman, N. S. (eds) (1972), *Economics of the Environment: Selected Readings*, W. W. Norton, New York.

Dreze, J. P. (1981), Public investment criteria in a rationed economy, Indian Statistical Institute, Delhi (mimeo).

Eckert, R. D. (1979), *The Enclosure of Ocean Resources*, Hoover Institution Press, Stanford.

Ehrlich, P., Ehrlich, A. and Holdren, J. (1977), *Ecoscience: Population, Resources, Environment*, W. H. Freeman and Co., San Francisco.

Enke, S. (1966), The economic aspects of slowing population growth, *Economic Journal*, **76**, 44–56.

Enthoven, A. C. and Freeman, A. M. (eds) (1973), *Pollution, Resources and the Environment*, W. W. Norton, New York.

Farnsworth, N. R. and Morris, R. W. (1976), Higher plants: the sleeping giant of drug development, *American Journal of Pharmacy*, **146**, 45–52.

Faustmann, G. (1849), On the determination of the value which forest land and immature stands possess for forestry, reprinted in English in *Oxford Institute Papers* (1968), **42**.

Feder, E. (1977), Agribusiness and the elimination of Latin America's rural proletariat, *World Development*, **5**, 559–71.

Feder, E. (1979), Agricultural resources in underdeveloped countries: competition between man and animal, *Economic and Political Weekly*, **14** (30–2) (special number, August), 1345–66.

Food and Agriculture Organization (1969), *Report of the FAO Committee on Fisheries*, 4th Session, FAO, Rome.

Food and Agriculture Organization (1973), *Yearbook of Fishery Statistics*, vols. 36–7, FAO, Rome.

Food and Agriculture Organization (1978), *The State of Food and Agriculture, 1977*, FAO, Rome.

Food and Agriculture Organization (1979), *Yearbook of Fishery Statistics*, FAO, Rome.

Frankel, O. H. and Hawkes, J. G. (eds) (1975), *Crop Genetic Resources for Today and Tomorrow*, Cambridge University Press, Cambridge.

Freeman, A. M. (1979), *The Benefits of Environmental Improvement: Theory and Practice*, Johns Hopkins University Press, Baltimore.

Freeman, A. M., Haveman, R. H. and Kneese, A. V. (1973), *The Economics of Environmental Policy*, John Wiley, New York.

Furubotn, E. G. and Pejovich, S. (1972), Property rights and economic theory: a survey of recent literature, *Journal of Economic Literature*, **10**, 1137–62.

Galbraith, J. K. (1974), *Economics and the Public Purpose*, Andre Deutsche, London.

Georgescu-Roegen, N. (1970), The economics of production, *American Economic Review, Papers and Proceedings*, **60**, 1–9.

Georgescu-Roegen, N. (1971), *The Entropy Law and Economic Processes*, Harvard University Press, Cambridge, Massachusetts.

Georgescu-Roegen, N. (1979), Comment, in V. Kerry Smith (ed.), *Scarcity and Growth Reconsidered*, Johns Hopkins University Press, Baltimore.

Gil, N. (1979), *Watershed Development: with Special Reference to Soil and Water Conservation*, FAO Soils Bulletin No 44, FAO, Rome.

Gordon, H. S. (1954), Economic theory of common property resources, *Journal of Political Economy*, **62**, 124–42.

Gottlieb, M. (1945), The theory of optimum population for a closed economy, *Journal of Political Economy*, **53**, 289–316.

Green, J. and Laffont, J.-J. (1977), Characterization of satisfactory mechanisms for the revelation of preferences for public goods, *Econometrica*, **45**, 427–38.

Greenley, D. A., Walsh, R. G. and Young, R. A. (1980), Option value: empirical evidence from a case study of recreation and water quality, mimeo, and forthcoming, *Quarterly Journal of Economics.*

Groves, T. (1973), Incentives in teams, *Econometrica*, **41**, 617–31.

Groves, T. and Ledyard, J. (1977), Optimal allocation of public goods: a solution to the 'free rider' problem, *Econometrica*, **45**, 783–810.

Hahn, F. H. (1971), Equilibrium with transaction costs, *Econometrica*, **39**, 417–40.

Hammond, P. J. (1980), Cost-benefit analysis as a planning procedure, in D. A. Currie and W. Peters (eds), *Contemporary Economic Analysis*, vol. 2, Croom Helm, London.

Hammond, P. J. (1981a), Ex-ante and ex-post welfare economics under uncertainty, *Economica*, **48**, 235–50.

Hammond, P. J. (1981b), On welfare economics with incomplete information and the social value of public information, IMSSS Technical Report no. 332, Encina Hall, Stanford University.

Hardin, G. (1968), The tragedy of the commons, *Science*, **162**, 1243–8.

Hare, R. M. (1973), Rawls' theory of justice, parts I, II, *Philosophical Quarterly*, **23**, 144–55, 241–52.

Hartwick, J. M. (1980), The intertemporal externality in a dynamic common property renewable resource problem, Department of Economics, Queens University, Ontario (mimeo).

Hartwick, J. (1980), *Principles of Natural Resource Use*, Department of Economics, Queens University, Ontario (mimeo).

Heal, G. M. (1973), *The Theory of Economic Planning*, North Holland, Amsterdam.

Heal, G. M. (1982), Equivalence of saddle points and optima for non-concave programmes, *Advances in Applied Mathematics* (forthcoming).

Helmers, F. L. C. H. (1979), *Project Planning and Income Distribution*, Martinus Nijhoff, London.

Henderson, J. V. and Tugwell, M. (1979), Exploitation of the lobster fishery: some empirical results, *Journal of Environmental Economics and Management*, **6**, 287–96.

Henry, C. (1974), Investment decisions under uncertainty: the irreversibility effect, *American Economic Review*, **64**, 1006–12.

Holt, S. V. (1975), Marine fisheries and world food supplies, in A. Bourne (ed.), *Man/Food Equation*, Academic Press, New York.

Hotelling, H. (1931), The economics of exhaustible resources, *Journal of Political Economy*, **39**, 137–75.

Jodha, N. S. (1980), The process of desertification and the choice of interventions, *Economic and Political Weekly*, **15**(32), August, 1351–6.

Keeler, E., Spence, A. M. and Zeckhauser, R. (1972), The optimal control of pollution, *Journal of Economic Theory*, **4**(1), 19–34.

Khalatbari, F. (1977), Market imperfections and optimal rate of depletion of an exhaustible resource, *Economica*, **44**, 409–14.

Kneese, A. V., Ayres, R. U. and d'Arge, R. C. (1972), *Economics and the Environment: A Materials Balance Approach*, Johns Hopkins University Press, Baltimore.

Kneese, A. V. and Bower, B. T. (1968), *Managing Water Quality: Economics, Technology and Institutions*, Johns Hopkins University Press, Baltimore.

Kneese, A. V. and Schultze, C. L. (1975), *Pollution, Prices and Public Policy*, Brookings Institution, Washington, D.C.

Kohn, R. (1975), Input–output analysis and air pollution control, in E. Mills (ed.), *Economic Analysis of Environmental Problems*, National Bureau of Economic Research, New York.

Koopmans, T. C. (1964), On the flexibility of future preferences, in M. W. Shelly and G. L. Bryan (eds), *Human Judgments and Optimality*, John Wiley, New York.

Kreps, D. (1979), A representation theorem for 'preference for flexibility', *Econometrica*, **47**(3), 565–78.

Kurien, J. (1978), Entry of big business into fishing: its impact on fish economy, *Economic and Political Weekly*, **13**(36), 1557–64.

Kwerel, E. (1977), To tell the truth: imperfect information and optimal pollution control, *Review of Economic Studies*, **44**, 595–601.

Laffont, J.-J. (ed.) (1979), *Aggregation and Revelation of Preferences*, North Holland, Amsterdam.

Lane, J. (1977), *On Optimum Population Paths*, Springer-Verlag, Berlin.

Leone, R. A. (ed.) (1976), *Environmental Controls*, Lexington Books, Lexington, Massachusetts.

Leontief, W. *et al.* (1977), *The Future of the World Economy: A United Nations Study*, Oxford University Press, Oxford.

Lewis, T. and Neher, P. (1980), Consistent and revised plans for natural resource use, Resources Paper no. 50, Department of Economics, University of British Columbia, Vancouver.

Lind, R. (ed.) (1982), *Discounting for Time and Risk in Energy Policy*, Johns Hopkins University Press, Baltimore.

Lindblom, C. (1977), *Politics and Markets*, Basic Books, New York.

Little, I. M. D. and Mirrlees, J. A. (1969), *Manual of Industrial Project Analysis in Developing Countries*, Vol. II, *Social Cost–Benefit Analysis*, OECD, Paris.

Little, I. M. D. and Mirrlees, J. A. (1974), *Project Appraisal and Planning for Developing Countries*, Heinemann, London.

Little, I. M. D. and Scott, M. F. G. (eds) (1976), *Using Shadow Prices*, Heinemann Educational Books, London.

Lotka, A. J. (1956), *Elements of Mathematical Biology*, Dover, New York.

Luce, D. and Raiffa, H. (1957), *Games and Decisions*, John Wiley, New York.

Mäler, K.-G. (1974), *Environmental Economics: A Theoretical Enquiry*, Johns Hopkins University Press, Baltimore.

Mäler, K.-G. (1977), Optimal land use: some theoretical aspects, Stockholm School of Economics (mimeo).

Mäler, K.-G. and Wyzga, R. E. (1976), *Economic Measurement of Environmental Damage*, OECD, Paris.

Malinvaud, E. (1972), *Lectures in Microeconomic Theory*, North Holland, Amsterdam.

Manabe, S. (1971), Estimates of future change of climate due to an increase of carbon dioxide concentration in the air, in W. Mathews, W. Kellogs and G. Robinson (eds), *Man's Impact on Climate*, MIT Press, Cambridge, Massachusetts.

Manabe, S. and Wetherald, R. T. (1975), The effect of doubling CO_2 concentration on the climate of a general circulation model, *Journal of Atmospheric Sciences*, **32**, 3–15.

Marschak, J. and Radner, R. (1972), *An Economic Theory of Teams*, Cowles Foundation Monograph, Yale University Press, New Haven.

Marx, K. (1961), *Capital*, vol. I, Foreign Languages Publishing House, Moscow.

Maskin, E. (1978), A theorem on utilitarianism, *Review of Economic Studies*, **45**, 93–6.

May, D. A. and Heer, D. M. (1968), Son survivorship motivation and family size in India: a computer simulation, *Population Studies*, **22**, 199–210.

McHugh, J. L. (1972), Population dynamics and fisheries management, in R. Thompson (ed.), *Marine Fishery Dynamics*, Oregon State University Press.

Meade, J. E. (1955), *Trade and Welfare*, Oxford University Press, Oxford.

Meade, J. E. (1973), *The Theory of Externalities*, International Economics Series, 2, Institute Universitaire de Hautes Etudes Internationales, Geneva.

Mirrlees, J. A. (1974), Optimum accumulation under uncertainty: the case of stationary returns to investment, in J. Dreze (ed.), *Allocation under Uncertainty: Equilibrium and Optimality*, Macmillan, London.

Mishra, S. N. and Beyer, J. (1976), *Cost-Benefit Analysis: A Case Study of the Ratnagiri Fisheries Project*, Hindustan Publishing Corporation, Delhi.

Mitra, T. and Wan, H. (1981), On the Faustman solution to the forest management problem, Department of Economics, Cornell University (mimeo).

Musgrave, R. (1959), *The Theory of Public Finance*, McGraw-Hill, New York.

Narveson, J. (1967), Utilitarianism and new generations, *Mind*, **76**, 62–72.

Narveson, J. (1973), Moral problems of population, *Monist*, **57**.

Neher, P. (1976), Democratic exploitation of a replenishable resource, *Journal of Public Economics*, **5**, 361–71.

Niehaus, F. (1980), Developing criteria to compare the safety of energy systems, *Angewandte Systemanalyse Band*, **1**, 4, 149–57.

Nijkamp, P. (1980), *Environmental Policy Analysis: Operational Methods and Models*, John Wiley, New York.

Nordhaus, W. (1977). Economic growth and climate: the carbon dioxide problem, *American Economic Review*, Papers and Proceedings, **67**(1), 341–6.

Nordhaus, W. (1980), Thinking about carbon dioxide: theoretical and empirical aspects of optimal control strategies, Cowles Foundation Discussion Paper no. 565, Yale University.

Nordhaus, W. and Tobin, J. (1972), *Is Growth Obsolete?*, National Bureau of Economic Research, 50th Anniversary Colloquium, Columbia University Press, New York.

Nozick, R. (1974), *Anarchy, State and Utopia*, Basic Books, New York.

OECD (1974), *Problems in Transnational Pollution*, OECD, Paris.

Ohlin, G. (1967), *Population Control and Economic Development*, OECD, Paris.

Parfit, D. (1976), On doing the best for our children, in M. Bayles (ed.), *Ethics and Population*, Schenkman, Cambridge, Massachusetts.

Pearce, P. H. *et al.* (1979), Symposium on managing fishing effort, *Journal of the Fisheries Research Board of Canada*, **36**(7).

Pella, J. J. and Tomlinson, P. K. (1969), A generalized stock production model, *Inter-American Tropical Tuna Commission Bulletin*, **13**, 421–58.

Persson, R. (1974), *World Forest Resources*, Royal College of Forestry, Stockholm.

Pitchford, J. D. (1974), *Population in Economic Growth*, North Holland, Amsterdam.

Plato (1970), *Laws*, translated by T. J. Saunders, Penguin, Harmondsworth.

Portes, R. (1971), Decentralized planning procedures and centrally planned economies, *American Economic Review*, Papers and Proceedings, **61**, 422–9.

Radner, R. and Stiglitz, J. (1975), Fundamental non-concavities in the value of information, Department of Economics, Stanford University (mimeo).

Raiffa, H. (1968), *Decision Analysis*, Addison-Wesley, Massachusetts.

Ramsey, F. (1928), A mathematical theory of savings, *Economic Journal*, **38**, 543–59.

Randall, A. *et al.* (1974), Bidding games for valuation of aesthetic environmental improvements, *Journal of Environmental Economics and Management*, **1**, 132–49.

Rawls, J. (1972), *A Theory of Justice*, Oxford University Press, Oxford.

Roberts, M. and Spence, A. M. (1976), Effluent charges and licenses under uncertainty, *Journal of Public Economics*, **5**, 193–208.

Roedel, P. M. (ed.) (1975), *Optimum Sustainable Yield as a Concept in Fisheries Management*, American Fisheries Society, Special Publication no. 9, Washington, D.C.

Rousseau, J.-J. (1946), *The Social Contract*, translated by Sir E. Barker, Oxford University Press, Oxford.

Rudra, A. (1973), The use of shadow prices in project evaluation, *Indian Economic Review*.

Ryther, J. H. (1969), Photosynthesis and fish production in the sea, *Science*, **166**, 72–6.

Samuelson, P. A. (1954), The pure theory of public expenditure, *Review of Economics and Statistics*, **36**, 387–9.

Samuelson, P. A. (1958), Aspects of public expenditure theories, *Review of Economics and Statistics*, **40**, 332–8.

Samuelson, P. A. (1976), Economics of forestry in an evolving society, *Economic Inquiry*, **14**, 466–92.

Samuelson, P. A. (1979), *Economics: An Introductory Analysis* (eleventh edition), McGraw-Hill, New York.

Scherr, B. A. and Babb, E. M. (1975), Pricing of public goods: An experiment with two proposed pricing systems, *Public Choice*, **23**, 35–48.

Schmorak, S. (1967), Salt water encroachment in the coastal plain of Israel, *International Association Science Hydrology, Symposium*, Haifa, Publication 72, 305–18.

Schumacher, E. F. (1973), *Small is Beautiful: A Study of Economics as if People Mattered*, Bonds and Briggs, London.

Scitovsky, T. (1951), *Welfare and Competition*, Richard Irwin, Chicago, Illinois.

Scott, A. D. (1955), The fishery: the objectives of sole ownership, *Journal of Political Economy*, **63**, 116–24.

Scott, A. D. (1973), Transfrontier pollution: are new institutions necessary?, Document AEU/ENV/73.10 (10 August), OECD Environment Committee, Paris.

Scott, M. F. G., MacArthur, J. D. and Newbery, D. M. G. (1976), *Project Appraisal in Practice: the Little–Mirrlees Method Applied in Kenya*, Heinemann Educational Books, London.

Sen, A. (1970), *Collective Choice and Social Welfare*, Holden Day, San Francisco.

Sen, A. (1979), Welfare basis of real income comparison, *Journal of Economic Literature*, **17**, 1–45.

Sen, A. (1982), Approaches to the choice of discount rates for social cost-benefit analysis, in R. Lind (ed.), *Discounting for Time and Risk in Energy Policy*, Johns Hopkins University Press, Baltimore.

Shaefer, M. B. (1954), Some aspects of the dynamics of populations important to the management of commercial marine fisheries, *Inter-American Tropical Tuna Bulletin*, **1**, 27–56.

Sidgwick, H. (1907), *The Methods of Ethics* (seventh edition), Macmillan, London.

Smith, V. Kerry (ed.) (1979), *Scarcity and Growth Reconsidered*, Johns Hopkins University Press, Baltimore.

Smith, V. L. (1968), Economics of production from natural resources, *American Economic Review*, **58**(3), 409–31.

Solow, R. M. (1971), *Growth Theory: An Exposition*, Clarendon Press, Oxford.

Sommer, A. (1976), Attempt at an assessment of the world's tropical forests, *Unasylva*, **28**, 5–24.

Spence, A. M. (1974), Blue whales and optimal control theory, in H. Gottinger (ed.), *Systems Approaches and Environmental Problems*, Vandenhoek and Ruprecht, Gottingen.

Spence, A. M. and Starrett, D. A. (1975), Most rapid approach paths in accumulation problems, *International Economic Review*, **16**, 388–403.

Spofford, W. D., Russell, C. S. and Kelley, R. A. (1976), *Environmental Quality Management: An Application to the Lower Delaware Valley*, Resources for the Future, Washington, D.C.

Squire, L. and Van der Tak, H. (1975), *Economic Analysis of Projects*, Johns Hopkins University Press, Baltimore.

Starrett, D. (1972), Fundamental non-convexities in the theory of externalities, *Journal of Economic Theory*, **4**, 180–99.

Starrett, D. and Zeckhauser, R. (1971), Treating externalities: markets or taxes, Kennedy School of Government, Discussion Paper no. 3, Harvard University.

Streeter, H. W. and Phelps, E. B. (1925), *A Study of the Pollution and Natural Purification of the Ohio River – III: Factors Concerned in the Phenomena of Oxidation and Aeration*, Public Health Bulletin no. 146 (February).

Svendsrud, A. (ed.) (1969), *Forest Economics*, Universitetsforlaget, Oslo.

Theil, H. (1968), *Optimal Decision Rules for Government and Industry*, North Holland, Amsterdam.

Tietenberg, T. H. (1980), Transferable discharge permits and the control of stationary source air pollution: a survey and synthesis, *Land Economics*, **56**, 391–416.

Tulkens, H. (1974), An economic model of international negotiations on maritime transfrontier pollution based on 'math. modelsea', CORE Discussion Paper, Heverlee, Belgium.

United Nations (1978), *Round-up Plan of Action and Resolutions*, Conference on Desertification, New York.

UNESCO (1978), *Tropical Forest Ecosystems*, ISBN 92 3 101507 9, UNESCO, Paris.

UNIDO (1972), *Guidelines for Project Evaluation*, by P. Dasgupta, S. Marglin and A. Sen, sales no. E.72.II.B.11, United Nations, New York.

UNIDO (1978), *Guide to Practical Project Appraisal*, by J. Hansen, sales no. E.78.II.B.3, United Nations, New York.

Walter, I. (1975), *International Economics of Pollution*, Macmillan, London.

Wan, H. (1971), *Economic Growth*, Harcourt Brace Jovanovich, New York.

Weitzman, M. L. (1970), Optimal growth with scale economies in the creation of overhead capital, *Review of Economic Studies*, **37**, 555–70.

Weitzman, M. L. (1974), Prices vs. quantities, *Review of Economic Studies*, **41**, 477-91.

Weitzman, M. L. (1976), Free access vs. private ownership as alternative systems for managing common property, *Journal of Economic Theory*, **8**, 225-34.

Weitzman, M. L. (1978), Optimal rewards for economic regulation, *American Economic Review*, **68**, 683-91.

Wilson, R. (1975), Informational economies of scale, *Bell Journal of Economics*, **6** (Spring), 184-95.

Author Index

Subject Index